TRAINING GOD'S ARMY

TRAINING GOD'S ARMY

The American Bible School,
1880–1940

VIRGINIA LIESON BRERETON

INDIANA UNIVERSITY PRESS

Bloomington and Indianapolis

The paper used in this publication meets the minimum requirements of
American National Standard for Information Sciences—Permanence of
Paper for Printed Library Materials, ANSI Z39.48-1984.

∞™

Manufactured in the United States of America

Library of Congress Cataloging-in-Publication Data

Brereton, Virginia Lieson.
Training God's army : The American Bible school, 1880–1940 / Virginia
Lieson Brereton.
p. cm.
Includes bibliographical references.
ISBN 0-253-31266-3 (alk. paper)
1. Bible colleges—United States—History. I. Title.
BV4030.B74   1990
207'.73—dc20   89-46007
CIP

1 2 3 4 5   94 93 92 91 90

CONTENTS

PREFACE

Given a general dearth of attention to Bible schools, many readers will have only the vaguest idea of what this kind of school is (or was). This whole study is, of course, an attempt to define the nature and purposes of these institutions, but a more immediate introduction might be in order. First a brief definition: As it had evolved by 1920, a Bible school was an institution—sometimes denominational, sometimes nondenominational— operating at roughly a high school level and training men and women as evangelists, missionaries, religious teachers, musicians, pastors, and other workers for the conservative Protestant evangelical churches. To this end the schools sent their students out to supplement their classroom experience with actual religious work and offered subjects such as the history of missions, Sunday school pedagogy, methods of evangelism, and, above all, Bible study. For a sense of what a Bible school looked like we can scarcely do better than take a brief look at Moody Bible Institute in Chicago during the twenties.

The self-styled "West Point of Fundamentalism" was located in downtown Chicago, less than a mile north of the Loop. It had started out in a three-story building in 1889; in the first three decades the Institute's constantly expanding evangelistic program encouraged its leaders to buy up a considerable portion of the real estate surrounding the original property, converting some of the existing buildings to Institute uses and constructing others. By late 1927 the school held title to thirty-four buildings and several city blocks, and the value of its property amounted to about four and a half million dollars.

The school was not difficult to spot; its name was painted in billboard-size letters high on an outside wall. A visitor to the vestibule of one of the main Institute buildings was likely to notice one of the displays celebrating the school's evangelistic purposes: perhaps an exhibit of the religious educational work done at the Institute, a "Missionary Museum" containing mementoes and curios from missionary lands, a large honor roll of the numerous "Former Students of the Moody Bible Institute Who Have Gone to Foreign Mission Fields," photographs of Bible and missionary lands, or an "electrically illuminated relief map of Palestine."[1] Another sign of the Institute's evangelical outreach, if one could find a high enough vantage point, was the transmitter for the Institute's radio station, WMBI, located to the west in Addison, Illinois.

The streets and buildings in the area buzzed with students all day and evening, all year. By the late twenties the student body usually exceeded 1,000 in each of the Day and Evening Schools; the faculty numbered between thirty and forty. The curriculum had assumed the essential shape and content it would retain for the next few decades. At its heart was study of the Scriptures. The objective was to familiarize the students with the entire Bible by the end of their two-year stay. Students could elect any of several programs, all heavily biblically oriented: the General, Missionary, Pastors, Religious Education, Jewish Missions, and Swedish-English Courses, with by far the largest number of students choosing the General Course.

The evangelical arms of the Institute reached far and wide. By the late 1920s the Institute mailed its magazine, the *Moody Monthly,* to between 20,000 and 30,000 subscribers. The *Monthly,* no mere house organ, contained Bible study lessons, hints for pastors, and stories on missions, in addition to news of the school and its graduates. Radio station WMBI carried worship services, Bible exposition, religious music, reports of "Little Trips in Holy Lands," the International Sunday School Lesson, and programs directed at special groups such as women, shut-ins, and Yiddish speakers. By 1928, the Correspondence School, which had started with only two offerings in 1901, provided twenty-eight courses, most of them on the Bible or methods of Christian work, and enrolled more than 11,000 students. In 1928 the most popular correspondence courses were "Great Epochs of Sacred History," the "Introductory Bible Course," and the "Practical Christian Work Course." Another Institute agency, the "Bible Institute Colportage Association," peddled inexpensive devotional paperbacks aimed at a popular audience, and also distributed free religious books to groups as diverse as prisoners and lumberjacks. The Extension Department of the Institute employed eleven full-time "Bible Teachers and Evangelists," who ranged all over the United States conducting Bible conferences, evangelistic services, and Bible classes. In the summer of 1928, eleven Bible conferences were conducted under Extension Department auspices, in resort areas of Colorado, Illinois, Michigan, Pennsylvania, and North Carolina. The Institute's extension activities also included a yearly Founder's Week Conference at the Institute which featured prominent Bible teachers and evangelists. In 1924, the Extension Department added money-raising to its list of duties, fielding a staff of full-time fundraisers who covered most of the United States.

Almost daily, students went out, two-by-two and in groups, to their "practical work" assignments in city missions, churches, jails, hospitals, old people's homes (as they were called), young people's clubs, and Sunday schools. They also knocked on tenement doors or held services on street corners. From the earliest years the students had done practical work of this sort, for Dwight Moody, the school's founder, had concurred in the thinking popular at the time, that classroom instruction should be accompanied by experience ("Study and work go hand in hand," read the first prospectus).[2] By the 1920s students were spending nine to ten hours a week at practical work, and were required to recount their experiences in a monthly "report hour," when they received comments and suggestions from their mentors.

Moody Bible Institute was merely the largest and richest of a growing number of Bible schools whose leaders tried to promote study of the Bible and vigorous evangelization. These schools played a critical role in the development of twentieth century evangelicalism, a role that has been little studied and thus little understood. This book attempts to explore the nature of that role. It examines the beginnings of the oldest schools in the 1880s and their development in subsequent decades. And it tries to give as vivid a sense as possible of what actually happened in the lives of Bible school students, both inside and outside the classrooms.

To my knowledge this is the first published history of American Bible schools by an outsider. Others have chronicled the development of the movement and of individual Bible schools, to be sure, but they have done so as partisans of these institutions. Particularly in the last three or four decades, the existence of a Bible school accrediting association has spurred Bible school educators to publish books and articles examining the past and present of their schools; however, they have addressed their peers rather than a general audience.

That I am an outsider is I think indisputable: I have not attended a Bible school or taught in one. Not so long ago, in fact, I would not have been able to say what a Bible school was. My interest in these institutions began a decade ago while I was working with several other historians on a Lilly Endowment–funded study of Protestant theological education in America. From the beginning we had determined we could not limit our purview of theological education to seminaries, and so it became my particular assignment to research the late nineteenth century missionary training schools and the twentieth century Bible schools. To my dismay I soon discovered that almost nothing had been written on the Bible school. But if the subject yielded few ready sources, it presented some irresistible challenges. I dug in. This study is a beginning in what I hope will be a continuing effort to understand this important institution of conservative American Protestantism.

My status as an outsider poses certain dangers, of course. It is possible that I have misinterpreted facts or situations whose meaning would be obvious to those who have experienced Bible school education firsthand. On the other hand, I write from the vantage point of being relatively free of strong positive or negative convictions (except that the subject deserves more attention). Objectivity, generally considered an important value in historical studies, has been in short supply when writers have turned to subjects connected with twentieth century Protestant evangelicalism.

Those who are skeptical about the kind of education offered by Bible schools and wary of the religious groups they represent might wish this study were more critical. But, aware as I am that historians and educators have dealt harshly with Bible schools—on the rare occasions when they have noticed them at all—I have tried hard to bring empathy and even appreciation to the purposes and viewpoints of Bible school educators. I have largely postponed consideration of the question of whether Bible schools have educated for well or ill, whether they have in fact educated or miseducated. The first task, it seemed to me, was simply to understand what was happening on a descriptive level, and to tease out some basic themes in the history of Bible school education. After these tasks are completed, we will be in a better position to examine certain themes in more detail and with more discrimination; and we can study the impact of Bible school educational practices on students and on Protestant movements—once we understand what those practices were.

Careful readers will notice that I have paid particular attention to the histories of certain Bible schools, namely the Missionary Training Institute (now Nyack College), Moody Bible Institute, Gordon College (begun as the Boston Missionary Training School), the Boston Bible School (Berkshire Christian College until its recent demise), and the Bible Institute of Los Angeles (Biola). The original study on which this book is based, a Columbia University dissertation, contained separate chapters on all these schools except Biola. Though these institutional portraits have dropped out of the present study, the institutions themselves remain as focal points. And the reasons for my original concentration on these particular schools still hold true. First, they were all founded early, and so represent important elements of the formative stage of Bible school history. Then too, for reasons of balance it was important to include a Midwestern and a Western school (Southern Bible schools were a later development). Boston Bible School, with its Advent Christian ties, helps shed light on the character of a thoroughly denominational institution. Finally, Moody Bible Institute is not only the Midwestern representative but, as what one informant called the "bell cow" of the Bible school movement, it must command a starring role in any study of these schools.

Some readers may wonder why, except for some brief forays into the postwar period, this study concludes with 1940. Part of the reason was practical; I simply wanted to make my research task—quite staggering, since I was starting almost from scratch—more manageable. But it also seems to me as if the decade of the forties represents a significant watershed in Bible school history; after about 1940, leaders of the oldest schools become much more concerned about the academic status of their schools. They begin to worry about how their schools might qualify for accreditation, and to institute the kinds of changes that would eventually make accreditation possible. When a Bible school accrediting association came into being in the late forties, its requirements were obviously modeled in part on those of the accrediting associations for liberal arts colleges.

The result of this accelerating concern for academic respectability was that the oldest Bible schools moved much closer to the educational mainstream and gave up part of their former distinctiveness. The story of the accreditation of Bible schools is an important one and needs to be told at some length; among other things, it nicely illustrates the power of the forces making for educational standardization in the twentieth century. However, the post-1940 history must await another volume; it is not a major focus of this study.

In an even fuller sense than usual, this study represents a collegial effort. It arose out of my participation in the Auburn Seminary history of Protestant theological education in America. Because many questions about fundamentalism and the history and function of Bible schools remained unanswered even after a chapter on Bible schools had been drafted, I decided to adopt the subject as the topic of my doctoral dissertation at Columbia University. At the core of this study are the insights and shrewd questionings of my colleagues: James Fraser, Christa Ressmeyer Klein, Robert W. Lynn, and Glenn T. Miller. From the start Robert Lynn has encouraged my interest in the education and religion of Americans of the past and has lent countless kinds of aid. Most recently, through the Lilly Endowment, he provided the funds to allow me to revise the original dissertation manuscript.

Lawrence A. Cremin, as my dissertation director, supported an intellectual endeavor that was not very "fashionable," read my drafts with care, and generally cheered on my efforts every step of the way. I, like many others, have greatly benefited from the breadth of his vision of American education; under his tutelage the field of educational history has taken on an excitement it would not otherwise have had. I would also like to thank Douglas Sloan, who seconded my interest in the impact of faith and doubt upon late nineteenth and twentieth century Americans, and Walter Metzger, who posed some of the questions and themes that are reflected in these pages. Finally, I would like to acknowledge Robert T. Handy and Diane Ravitch, who contributed suggestions and generous encouragement.

During the research phase of this study the superb Union Theological Seminary library was my second home. I would like to acknowledge the help there of Barbara Griffis and Seth Kasten, who repeatedly addressed themselves to my sometimes out-of-the-way requests. Librarians at Biola College, Gordon College, Berkshire, Christian College, Nyack College, and Moody Bible Institute frequently put themselves at my disposal. I would like to express particular appreciation to Ruth Bailey at Nyack, Edna Amnott at Berkshire, and John Beauregard at Gordon. James O. Henry generously allowed me to peruse his history of Biola in draft form.

Treading new intellectual territory can be lonesome at times. Joel Carpenter and William Trollinger, laboring in areas very closely related to my own, have provided a sense of companionship on many occasions. I will always be grateful for Joel's warmth and encouragement.

Finally, I owe a great deal to my husband Jack, who encouraged, supported, discussed, and exhorted. He patiently read every word I wrote on a subject far removed from his usual area of concern, and offered innumerable suggestions, both stylistic and substantive. Not least important, he has acted as troubleshooter in the technical phase of shepherding this manuscript through computer and printer.

INTRODUCTION

By now it has become commonplace to invoke the "resurgence" of Protestant fundamentalist—or evangelical (the preferred term of many present-day adherents)—influence in any discussion of contemporary American politics.[1] The nation has passed through several national elections and numerous state and local campaigns in which the Christian right has demonstrated an impressive ability to publicize its causes, pressure politicians, register and mobilize voters, and raise large sums of money.

What is less often noticed is that the political achievements of groups such as the Moral Majority have depended to a great extent upon a whole array of interconnected educational efforts. Most obvious, of course, is evangelical schooling. Some of the largest theological seminaries today—for example, Fuller Theological Seminary in Pasadena, California, and Gordon-Conwell Divinity School in Wenham, Massachusetts—come out of the conservative evangelical tradition. Also among the largest seminaries are those of the Southern Baptist Convention, which partakes of the fundamentalist heritage. The roster of Christian private schools at the elementary and secondary level increases yearly. Many Christian liberal arts colleges flourish, benefiting from a clear sense of goals, while numerous other small colleges fall on hard times.[2] New Bible schools appear every year, some offering classes in churches, others providing full-time programs for day students.[3]

Another part of the educational endeavor has been carried on through the mass media. In 1980 evangelical radio and television programs attracted an audience of about 129 million weekly. Evangelicals have showed no less proficiency in handling film. Technically impressive and widely distributed movies produced by the Moody Institute of Science celebrate the power of the creator as manifested in the "wonders" of nature. The film department of fundamentalist Bob Jones University is admired by evangelicals and non-evangelicals alike.

The print media carry a sizeable part of the educative burden too. Evangelical writers and publishers enjoy huge sales. Hal Lindsay's *The Late Great Planet Earth,* a popular version of the fundamentalist doctrine of dispensationalism, has sold some ten million copies. Other recent best sellers have included evangelical efforts such as Marabel Morgan's *Total Woman,* Billy Graham's *Angels,* and *The Living Bible,* a condensed translation intended particularly for a popular audience.

And finally, evangelicalism has conducted its educational campaign through less orthodox instructional practices: ubiquitous bumper stickers that advertise "I Found It," anticipate "the Rapture," and promote the PTL ("Praise the Lord") Club; crooked pens—handed out gratis—that bear the message, "Let Jesus Straighten Out Your Life"; prominent signs on church lawns admonishing that the last days are at hand and that troubled humanity would do well to turn to the Lord for salvation. Evangelicalism persuades by means of catchy slogans no less persistently than Madison Avenue.

And yet very little in the traditional historical records appears to explain the current political and educational power of evangelicalism. After perhaps a quick glance at the teens, most popular and some scholarly accounts describe fundamentalism as emerging during the twenties, a colorful but ultimately inconsequential chapter in American history. In 1925 fundamentalists led by William Jennings Bryan make a brief but theatrical appearance in the Scopes "Monkey Trial" in Dayton, Tennessee. The "Great Commoner," it is said, chose a fight he was ill-equipped to wage, with the result that he and his followers became butts of ridicule for the national press. Though the anti-evolutionists won the Scopes verdict, they gained a pyrrhic victory at best and the decision was finally overturned (on a technicality) in a higher court. Ultimately anti-evolutionary legislation introduced during the twenties failed everywhere. In another strand of the story, fundamentalists in alliance with other prohibitionists manage to push through the 1919 Volstead Amendment, only to discover that it is unenforceable and must be repealed in little more than a decade. In yet another strand, fundamentalists participate in one of the periodic waves of hatred for immigrants and "alien" political philosophies. After World War I, right-wing fundamentalists are prominent in vituperative attacks upon bolsheviks, anarchists, communists, and foreigners. This period is ugly and distasteful, but it is short-lived: exeunt fundamentalists once more. Again, fundamentalists during the twenties emerge in the Ku Klux Klan movement; however, the common assumption confines the white-hooded Klanners with their fundamentalist sentiments mostly to remote and backward areas of the South; the rest of the nation is too progressive for such racist nonsense.

What all these themes have in common is the assumption that fundamentalists lost most of their political, cultural, and religious struggles, or, alternatively, that their efforts to enforce their views proved futile in the end. Thus they suffered the usual fate of religious fanatics and obscurantists in the skeptical and science-minded twentieth century: they faded from view.

Not that this assumption totally falsifies the past. Fundamentalists did indeed fare badly in many of the public political and ecclesiastical battles for power that took place in the twenties. But if the rout was as thorough as most accounts suggest, then how can we account for the political and educational strength of the present heirs of the movement?[4] One possible answer is that fundamentalists did not lose on other less visible fronts after all. Could it be that through a quiet work of education conducted over several decades, they may have succeeded in winning more of the hearts and minds of Americans than has hitherto been supposed? But such speculation has been difficult to confirm, because fundamentalist educational efforts have been so totally ignored.

Those who wish to understand the educational work of fundamentalism must begin by going back to the nineteenth century. In the years soon after the Civil War, a discernible but loosely knit group of like-minded Protestants had begun a variety of educative efforts, intended both for their own edification and that of others. At this time the instigation was not primarily doctrine or evolution or other threats to traditional under-standings of the Bible but rather discontent with the Protestant churches; much like other reformers before them, they complained that congrega-tions were lukewarm and that ministers were bent on their personal success rather than the salvation of souls. In the view of reformers, pastors and communicants alike had lost any sense of closeness with God or his son; they had ceased to take seriously the second advent of Christ; and they exhibited a contentious and narrow-minded denominationalism. When they picked up their Bibles at all, they read isolated passages, too often using them merely as proof texts to attack the positions of other Protes-tants. They concentrated more on sumptuous church buildings, profes-sional musicians, and impressive trappings than upon the state of their souls or the plight of the unconverted. Congregations were made up of complacent people who gave mere lip service to foreign missionary work and manifested little concern for the working classes. The result of their indifference on the foreign front was that millions were dying without hearing the name of Christ; on the domestic front, that the "masses" were shunning the Protestant churches. In short, they suggested the by-then familiar diagnosis: American Protestantism was suffering from one of its periodic declensions.

Many of these complaints are familiar to students of the Social Gospel movement, that liberal and socially activist group of Protestant ministers and lay people who turned to "social Christianity" in the late nineteenth and early twentieth centuries, and who later allied themselves with secular Progressivism and, in some cases, the socialist movement. The response of these Social Gospelers to cultural and religious malaise has received much attention, but it has seldom been recognized that other Protestants of a generally more conservative cast of mind were also troubled by the problems faced by the churches and the nation in the post-Civil War pe-riod.

To the ills of the church and society this conservative group of Protes-tants responded not with social, political, or economic involvement but with cries for spiritual renewal. Like the leaders of earlier American reli-gious revivals, they began with education, and the educational effort took many different forms. One of their first measures was the interdenomina-tional Bible conference, starting in 1868 in Boston. The best known series of annual Bible conferences were the "Niagara Conferences," which met between 1875 and 1900, but there were many other similar series of conferences. Some of these gatherings focused particularly on the prophetic portions of scripture—"prophetic conferences"—and were attended by premillennialists who believed that Christ would return to earth very soon to reign over an earthly kingdom in Jerusalem.[5]

Conferences followed a standard pattern. Held at resorts in summer, or at large urban churches in other seasons, they went on for several days and offered opportunity for prayer and for extended study of scripture, usually with the aid of a prominent Bible teacher. The goal of the meetings was a personal appropriation of God's word through close study and meditation. Inseparable from devout Bible study was another aim, the cultivation of deeper and more meaningful spiritual experiences, and renewed dedication to active evangelism.

Among evangelical reformers connected to the Wesleyan tradition particularly, the renewed popularity of camp meetings constituted another sign of renewal. Less formal and sometimes less dignifed than Bible conferences, they often resembled them in intention. One of the most famous series of camp meetings had a special purpose, the cultivation of a religious experience known as "holiness," which functioned as a sort of second conversion or spiritual rededication.

The educational impetus of this conservative renewal manifested itself also in the appearance of several widely read books. W. E. Blackstone's *Jesus Is Coming* (1878) argued the imminence of Christ's second advent. In *Rightly Dividing the Word of Truth* (1888), C. I. Scofield offered one of the first formulations by an American of dispensationalism, a form of premillennialism which had originated earlier in the century in Great Britain. Later, through copious notes appended to the King James Version of scripture, he adumbrated dispensationalism at greater length. This *Scofield Reference Bible,* published by Oxford University Press in 1909, served as a valued study aid for many a conservative Bible student.[6] In the following year came the first of twelve volumes of *The Fundamentals,* a collection of essays designed to establish for all time the verities of Christian doctrine and experience in the face of widespread attempts at reinterpretation. The production of *The Fundamentals* was financed by the oil fortune of the Stewart family in California and most of the 300,000 copies were sent out free of charge to ministers and lay persons.[7]

A number of journals, most of them with small circulations, focused on such subjects as premillennialism, Bible study, and foreign missions. Probably the best known of the early journals was the *Sunday School Times,* which dated from an 1857 revival. Its voice, conservatively evangelical from the start, took on recognizably "fundamentalist" tones after the turn of the century. A few conservative publishing companies dated from this era, for instance, Fleming H. Revell, Gospel Union Publishing Company, and the Bible Institute Colportage Association.

Another educational vehicle of the spiritual renewal was the revival, that series of daily religious meetings intended to issue in a large number of conversions. The revival was by then a time-honored instrument of American Protestantism. Beginning with his tour of the British Isles in 1872, evangelist Dwight Moody employed revival meetings with great success. Others emulated his efforts in the closing decades of the nineteenth century: D. W. Whittle, J. Wilbur Chapman, Sam Jones, Reuben A. Torrey, and George Pentecost.

Many of the educational activities were conducted by ministers or evangelists who sought to reach beyond comfortable congregations to appeal to the unconverted masses of the metropolis. In the effort to communicate more widely they employed sermon and writing styles that were plainer, less literary, and more biblically oriented than prevailing ones.[8] They attempted to make the churches hospitable to immigrants and other urban populations by removing pew rentals, assessments, highly formal worship procedures, and other impediments to a larger attendance. Like their more liberal counterparts, they widened the scope of services available at their churches, sometimes transforming them into virtual city missions. As part of their effort to evangelize, they often taught English and other skills needed by immigrants and other urban residents.

Finally, spiritual renewal resulted in the development of the Bible school. What appears to be the first such institution was founded in New York City in 1882, the result of the efforts of Albert B. Simpson, a minister who had left the Presbyterian church and had begun an independent ministry. The early schools that followed his were not always called "Bible schools" or "Bible institutes"—as was usually the case later on—but often had the words "training" and "missionary" in their names. Simpson's school, for instance, was called the "New York Missionary Training College," though it was hardly a college in the usual sense. The schools taught the Bible, evangelistic methods, and other practical skills useful to students who planned to become missionaries, evangelists, pastors, Sunday school teachers, and Christian workers of other kinds.

All these educational efforts continued without much fanfare for several decades. In about 1920, however, the situation changed. By then the informal grouping of Protestant conservatives had emerged to public attention as an identifiable movement dubbed "fundamentalism." Their diagnosis of America's ills had grown more radical; no longer was the nation threatened with another in the series of periodic spiritual declensions; rather it was marching toward outright, defiant apostasy from which there might be no return. As the twentieth century advanced these fundamentalists had a sense of being on the outside of the cultural and religious establishment, and they developed a sharp, often defensive sense of "enemies," among whom they counted biblical critics, teachers of evolution, "permissive" and "atheistic" college faculties, and persons of "lax" morals. Furthermore, some in the movement had adopted an aggressive rhetoric with which to castigate their opponents.

Though they often conveyed to observers a sense of desperation and beleaguerment before the advancing "tides of apostasy," fundamentalists of the twenties embraced education as enthusiastically and optimistically as had their conservative predecessors. Many of the same activities continued and in fact multiplied: Bible and prophetic conferences, books, and Bible schools. Conservative periodicals and publishing companies, many of them run by Bible school personnel, assumed a more important role than heretofore. Fundamentalists learned that the new medium of radio could serve as a powerful educational tool; so also could film. A number of large metropolitan pulpits occupied by articulate and outspoken fundamentalists became powerful sources of instruction and centers of fundamentalist activity.[9] Missionary societies educated and evangelized the unconverted at home and abroad; they also directed large and successful campaigns for contributions.

It is a fairly straightforward task to talk generally about a fundamentalist movement that had its roots in the post-Civil War years and emerged to public view in the twenties; however, it is very difficult to define the fundamentalist movement precisely: exactly what groups and individuals ought to be considered fundamentalist—and during what period of their histories? For example, were members of the Church of the Nazarene fundamentalists? If so are they still? What about Southern Baptists? The attempt to answer such questions can easily grow into protracted, complicated, and acrimonious debate, particularly given the negative connotations clinging to the label "fundamentalist."

Whatever it was or was not, the fundamentalist movement was decidedly an educational movement and most fundamentalists were educators; education was implicit in their overriding objective, which was the evangelization of America and the world. To understand fundamentalists, then, it is absolutely necessary to examine their educational efforts. And among those efforts, none assumed more importance than the Bible schools. They were in fact inseparable from most of the other educational activities of the movement. Many a Bible school grew out of a Bible conference or a church Bible class; and not a few Bible schools sponsored their own Christian publishing company, or radio program, or annual Bible conference.

Still, anyone who judged the significance of Bible schools by looking at total enrollments might overlook their importance. The schools have recently reached their peaks in regularly enrolled students—30,308 in all schools acredited by the Accrediting Association of Bible Colleges.[10] This is an unimpressive figure when one considers that there were at the same time some 11.4 million college and university students in the United States. However, the numbers are deceptive in two respects: first, Bible schools have reached and influenced many more learners, through correspondence, extension courses and the like, than tallies of regularly matriculated students would suggest. Second, large numbers of Bible school graduates have gone into religious work, often in leadership positions, and traditionally they have been staunchly, unequivocally evangelical. Because of their strong activism they have shaped and guided conservative evangelicalism—and through that, American culture in general—more effectively than the figures on Bible school enrollments would ever lead us to expect. In fact, the late Ernest R. Sandeen perceived the Bible school as a "headquarters" of fundamentalism and asserted—correctly I think—that the movement "owed its survival to the Bible institutes."[11]

But Sandeen—though recently joined in his judgment of the Bible schools' importance by a small group of scholars—has represented a minority among historians. By and large accounts of the history of education have ignored their very existence. Carnegie Commission on Higher Education studies, which have surveyed diverse institutions of higher education, including theological seminaries, failed to include more than brief reference to them.[12] When they have received any notice at all, Bible schools have been dismissed as standing beyond the pale. On the contrary, however, they are fully comprehensible within the major themes of American educational history, as I have attempted to show in the following pages.

TRAINING GOD'S ARMY

I

ENTHUSIASMS

Whatever their theological and cultural differences, those who founded, staffed, and attended Bible schools shared a definite spiritual kinship. Bible school people revered and studied and interpreted the Bible in similar ways, usually with careful attention to prophecy; almost all believed in the necessity of conversion and other central religious-emotional crises; most were premillennialists; they held similar opinions on questions of education, morality, and culture; and most looked back to common heroes—Dwight Moody, Charles Spurgeon, J. Hudson Taylor, George Muller, for example—and shared the memory of certain significant events—for instance, the pioneering Bible and prophetic conferences immediately after the Civil War. Indeed, these common attitudes and memories originally gave rise to the Bible schools, and the schools in turn played a crucial role in preserving and fostering them.

Those who sought out and supported Bible schools had usually undergone certain spiritual events—conversion, sanctification, sometimes divine healing, and, in the case of pentecostals, speaking in tongues. Though these experiences were central in the lives of fundamentalists, they have received little attention from historians, perhaps because those who were writing from within took them for granted and those who were writing from without could not or would not comprehend or sympathize. As a result, doctrine, which yields relatively easily to the formulaic phrase, has been overemphasized in accounts of the movement. Furthermore, fundamentalists themselves have tended to stress doctrine because they were engaged in polemics against opponents who, they felt, gave too much prominence to subjective experience. Nevertheless, in quieter, less contentious moments they have admitted that experience and not dogmatic statement is the starting place of their faith and even, in the last analysis, of their apologetics. The New York Baptist fundamentalist, John Roach Straton, conceded that "Sceptics and infidels can answer argument with argument, they can pit philosophy against philosophy; but there is one thing that they cannot answer and that is a personal experience of the redeeming grace and power of Jesus Christ as the Son of God."[1] And it was often their accounts of their own experience that fundamentalists depended upon when they were trying to convert others.

Conversion

From the time of Luther to the beginning of the twentieth century, the primary event in the life of most Protestants had been conversion. The experience occurred at different ages and under varied circumstances, but some form of emotional and spiritual crisis was necessary in order for Protestants to believe that they had been saved. It was often initiated by a period of feeling worthless, a "conviction of sinfulness" as it was frequently called, which could be long and painful. Finally, often through the agency of Scripture, a close relative or a friend, or a particularly compelling preacher, the individual would become convinced that he or she was rescued from the consequences of sin by the simple act of faith in the saving power of Christ's death on the cross. This was usually a glorious experience, the zenith of the Christian's life.

However, during the late nineteenth century, conversion gradually came to be seen as a less necessary ingredient of Christian life; fewer and fewer American Protestants regarded this radical experience as part of their very definition of themselves as believers. Horace Bushnell's *Christian Nurture* (1847) contained one of the first arguments that individuals should gradually grow and be nourished into faith and never need suffer through a spiritual emergency. Although Bushnell did not belittle the experience of conversion, he hardly saw it as a requirement for an exemplary Christian life. For many Protestants his ideas were in advance of their time, but as the century went on more and more came to agree with him, at least tacitly. Conservative evangelicals, to the contrary, dissented strongly from this trend, and continued to stress conversion as the sine qua non of Christian life.

One of the theaters for the gradual change in attitudes toward conversion was higher education. Not the least important function of the antebellum colleges and theological seminaries had been to foster this spiritual crisis, and to encourage the cultivation of its fruits in Christian service.[2] This continued to be the case after the Civil War, although with diminishing universality. Gradually student conversion ceased to be a major concern of professors and college presidents and devolved instead upon outside agencies, such as the Young Men's Christian Association and its sister organization, the YWCA, both of which operated on college campuses. To be sure, piety did not desert even the most "advanced" universities in abrupt fashion, but it gradually yielded to other concerns. The increasing secularization of higher education did not go unnoticed. The perennial books and articles accusing colleges and universities of abandoning their religious function began to increase in frequency after 1890, and reached a crescendo in the 1920s.

But an alternative existed for those who continued to regard the conversion experience as central: the Bible schools. They provided a safe environment where conversion could take place (if it had not already) and where the fragile convictions of the newly converted could be fostered, confirmed, and deepened by the presence of like-minded peers and elders. While most college and university professors came increasingly to serve their students as models of scholars and critical thinkers, Bible school teachers became primarily exemplars of the consecrated life.

The Bible

Nearly equal in importance to conversion was an intense and reverent approach to Scripture that characterized fundamentalists and their predecessors. This Bible-centeredness was of course not limited to religious conservatives; American Protestants of many theological descriptions shared it, at least until the 1920s. But fundamentalists exhibited the attitude with particular intensity, and they continued to exhibit it even after other Protestants began to turn to Scripture with a more critical eye, or at least with a different understanding.

At the first level, this biblicism meant simply an extraordinary and unquestioning reverence for the sacred book as the very word of God, which extended even to the existence of the Bible as a physical object. Members of the Open Bible League, organized about 1910 in the United States, followed a common practice when they promised to obey three rules: "1. Keep your Bible always open; 2. Turn over a page every day; 3. Never allow the book to be covered up." The same reverence is reflected in the popularity of books such as *Beams of Light on Scripture Texts*, a "volume of passages and brief texts selected from the Bible, illuminated by striking illustrations and apt comments gathered from a large number of devotional and other writers."[3] Another mark of this biblicism was the value placed on memorizing vast portions of Scripture. And the common practice of filling the margins of one's Bible with notes signified an act of devotion as much as an aid to study.[4]

Biblicism also displayed itself in an endless fascination with the intricacies of scripture, particularly the prophetic passages. In one sense, interpretation could be seen as a source of pious entertainment for those who, out of a stern moralism, had severely limited the scope of their possible leisure time activities. In *Father and Son*, Edmund Gosse, son of English Plymouth Brethren (the ultra-Protestants who originated the dispensationalist system of interpreting biblical prophecy), recalled,

> My father was in the habit of saying, in later years, that no small element
> in his wedded happiness was the fact that my Mother and he were of one
> mind in the interpretation of Sacred Prophecy. Looking back, it appears
> to me that this unusual mental exercise was almost their only relaxation,
> and that in their economy it took the place which is taken, in profaner

families, by cards or the piano. It was a distraction; it took them completely out of themselves. During those melancholy weeks at Pimlico [when his mother was dying], I read aloud . . . the "Horae Apocalypticae" of a Mr. Elliott. . . . My recollection distinctly is that when my Mother could endure nothing else, the argument of this book took her thoughts away from her pain and lifted her spirits.[5]

And another manifestation of biblicism was an intense interest in every physical detail of the Holy Land and often a lifelong wish to make a pilgrimage to the land of Jesus' birth and ministry.

Holiness

In the late nineteenth century, large numbers of Protestants came to expect and anticipate the experience of holiness or sanctification. In fact, the experience ranked as an emotional crisis so important that evangelicals commonly compared it to conversion, sometimes calling it the "second blessing," or even a "second conversion." Like conversion the experience could happen in a crowd or in solitude; it could be associated with a high degree of excitement or with an intense but quiet sense of "assurance," but it had a radical effect on the believer.

The doctrine of sanctification was not new in the nineteenth century; it simply underwent a revival at this time. Walter Marshall's *Gospel Mystery of Sanctification,* written in 1690, had run through many editions and was still frequently cited by holiness advocates in the nineteenth and early twentieth centuries. One tradition of holiness dated from John Wesley, who had written *A Plain Account of Christian Perfection and Brief Thoughts on Christian Perfection.* In America, Wesley's holiness writings had disappeared after 1812 from the Methodist manual of faith and practice, the *Discipline,* but the ideas were revived during the 1830s, when two Methodist sisters in New York City, Phoebe Palmer and Sarah Lankford, organized a "Tuesday Meeting for the Promotion of Holiness." Camp meetings for the purpose of "learning about and entering the experience of holiness" took place during the 1850s.

Holiness teachings were not limited to Methodists; one of the most popular manuals of the holiness movement, *The Higher Christian Life* (1859), was written by a Presbyterian layman, William E. Boardman. In the latter part of the nineteenth century, interdenominational holiness associations were formed, beginning with the National Association for the Promotion of Holiness (1867). About the time the fervor of the American holiness movement was beginning to abate, three Americans traveling in Great Britain, Robert Pearsall Smith, his wife Hannah Whitall Smith, and W. E. Boardman, helped ignite the British movement. The first of the famous annual Keswick holiness meetings, called "Conventions for the Promotion of Practical Holiness," took place in 1875 in England's Lake District. (Unlike the American movement, the Keswick gathering was composed chiefly of upper class Anglicans and Calvinists.) The example of Keswick in turn renewed the holiness movement in the United States. Not only did Americans attend the Keswick conventions, but also Keswick leaders frequently spoke in the United States. Many of them addressed the Northfield (Massachusetts) conferences begun by Dwight Moody; in fact, Moody reportedly hoped Northfield would become the "American Keswick." However, an official American Keswick movement, the "Victorious Life Movement," was formed only in 1913, and a site in New Jersey, "Keswick Grove," became its permanent home in 1923.[6]

In the United States the Wesleyan and Keswick traditions of holiness generally mingled. The most obvious difference between the two lay in their nomenclature: Wesleyans preferred the term "holiness," while Calvinists favored "sanctification." Beyond distinctions in terminology, Wesleyan holiness tended in the direction of "sinless perfection," the total eradication of human sin made possible by the experience of holiness. The extreme of this position was exemplified in the Salvation Army, whose founders came from Wesleyan backgrounds. The Keswick adherents, on the other hand, remained Calvinists in orientation and took pains to stress that depraved humanity could never be truly free of sin in this life. But they went far beyond what traditional Calvinists would have allowed in arguing that those who managed constantly to experience the "indwelling Christ" in their lives could achieve "victory" over at least their conscious sins.[7]

Though sanctification, or the achievement of holiness, was generally described as an instantaneous experience, it required preparation, usually in the form of Bible study, prayer, or the example of someone else who had undergone the same experience. Once holiness was "entered upon," the sense of consecration had to be carefully and continually cultivated. Indeed, when earnestly espoused, the experience made an enormous difference in the way Christians conducted their lives. Often the behavior of the sanctified exhibited a moral perfectionism. A. T. Pierson, an American Bible teacher and missionary leader who was sanctified in 1895, declared that Keswick followers avoided as sinful those things which were "done primarily to please one's self," which gave "undue prominence to self."[8] In this case, Pierson was referring to such "sins" as tobacco, alcohol, dancing, fiction, and the theater. But deliverance from sin did not mean only a narrow moralism. Adherents often testified to having conquered (although they cautioned that it was really God who conquered) bad tempers and habitual impatience with others. The highest praise their biographers could bestow was to report that their "sanctified" subjects had never lost their sweetness of disposition even under the most trying human or natural provocations.

The effort to "shun all things" that did not enhance the Christian's relationship with God led to attempts to "separate" from the world as much as possible. A. B. Simpson, founder of the Christian and Missionary Alliance and of the earliest Bible school, preached separation from the text "be ye separate" (2 Cor. 6:17):

> So, beloved, before we an enter the Land of Promise we must get out of the other land. What is the land God calls us to leave? It is the world. We cannot enter upon the fulness of Christ's salvation and have the pleasures of the world at the same time. The two things cannot go together. The command is as imperative as it was to Abraham, "Get thee out of thy country."[9]

For Simpson, the drive to separate issued out of a fear of contamination from participation in "worldly" activities, especially those that came under the category of "amusements." (Even "innocent" fiction was off-limits.) As an object lesson, for example, Simpson related the story of a woman, a "consecrated Christian," who unwisely ventured to attend a horseshow and became physically ill: "God made her understand that the very atmosphere of the place was worldly, that the spirit of the prince of the power of the air saturated both the place and the crowd, and that it was no safe place for a child of God. There are places and there are places."[10]

Other times separation meant avoiding acquisition of the material goods of life for their own sakes; at the very least it involved zealous tithing for missions and other worthy Christian causes. Certainly it meant trying to curb one's desire for the admiration of others and for the signs of worldly success. In a typical gesture, Simpson turned down a proffered honorary degree because he feared it would elevate him undeservedly above his fellows.[11] At its most rigorous, separation could mean battling against even the intensity of one's affections for family and friends if these emotions conflicted with missionary imperatives.

It seems likely that Simpson's commitment to separation helps explain a central event in the history of his school—the first Bible school—the Missionary Training Institute. In 1897 he moved the Institute from New York City some thirty miles up the Hudson River to the small town of Nyack. From one perspective it made no sense for Simpson, who spoke so convincingly of the need for students to obtain practical experience, to shift the school from the major laboratory of experience, New York City. To be sure, cost was a factor. The school had outgrown its quarters and it would cost much less to build in Nyack. But perhaps of greater importance, Simpson thought Nyack would provide a more protected educational environment for his students. As he said of the hillside upon which the school was located, "There is about the place an air of delightful quiet and retirement. You feel utterly separated from the great, uneasy world, yet there it lies at your feet."[12]

For Simpson and others of like mind, entering upon the holiness experience usually was interpreted as a surrender of the individual will to God's. And how was the divine will to be known? It was to be ascertained through constant prayer and diligent study of Scripture. The annals of fundamentalism are rife with stories of people who, facing decisions both trivial and monumental, searched the divine book for just the right passage which would indicate God's will for them. Iva Vennard, for example, founder of the Evangelistic Training Institute of Chicago, adopted a new scriptural passage every January to serve as her guide for the coming year.[13]

Holiness also entailed learning to "rely on God's promises," or, "trusting the Lord" enough to "step out upon his promises." In the largest sense, "promises" referred to biblical declarations about the return of the Lord, a glorious future for the true church, and rewards in the afterlife for the saints. But in more mundane and more personal usage, when believers referred to "promise" they meant the assurance that the Lord would provide for their daily needs. He would answer all their requests that grew out of faith, whether the prayer was for the discovery of a lost article or provisions for a thousand missionary volunteers.

One celebrated model for this attitude was George Muller (1805–1898), who had established a large orphanage in Bristol, England, simply by praying for what he needed when he needed it. One of Muller's great operating texts was John 24:13–14: "Whatsoever ye shall ask in my name, that will I do." Trusting completely in God, he purportedly spurned all endowments, solicitations for money, salaries, or budgets.[14] The other great exemplar of faith of this kind was J. Hudson Taylor (1832–1905), founder of the much admired China Inland Mission. He was convinced that foreign missionaries could find their own support in the field by relying upon God. His idea worked; whatever hardships missionaries of the CIM had to suffer, they apparently did so gladly; and Taylor was able to send out thousands of missionaries to the most difficult assignments in the interior of China for a small fraction of what it cost regular missionary boards. Hudson's enterprise became the model for any number of "faith" missions which bore the names "inland" or "interior" and were founded or led or staffed by Bible school personnel.[15]

The ideal of the sanctified person was to achieve a conviction of constant communion with God, a perpetual sense that "God lives in us." Few completely attained this ideal, but many came to know such a sense of peace and assurance that they sometimes referred to the experience of holiness as "entering into rest." An Alliance missionary, for example, testified to the total serenity and refreshment that came of letting God "take care of the consequences." He described a hot day of work in the slums:

> Today the sun shone with the same fierce intensity that it did yesterday and the day before, but I was under the Shadow of the Rock and felt no faintness, no fear, no repugnance to the unsightly objects that met my

eyes in the tenement houses or on the sidewalks. Though I have walked up and down as many stairways as usual, I am not even *tired* tonight. It has been "Jesus all the way long."[16]

The notion of holiness, or sanctification, spread among American evangelicals through books, periodicals, conferences and conventions, camp meetings, and through the founding of such holiness denominations as the Church of the Nazarene (1908). Bible schools also played an important role in its dissemination. One of Iva Durham Vennard's major reasons for opening the (Methodist) Epworth Evangelistic Institute in St. Louis in 1902 was to ensure that future Christian workers would receive instruction in holiness, from teachers who had themselves been sanctified.[17] The cultivation of holiness was also a major objective in the 1899 founding of the Training School for Christian Workers in the Los Angeles area by a group of California Quakers. An early schedule for the school included "many prayer meetings including one on Monday evening especially devoted to giving the students the opportunity to 'seek the blessing.'"[18] One of the school's first students, William Abel, an American Indian from a California reservation who had had little formal education, "was gloriously sanctified and gave his life to Christ at the first meeting of the Training School in March, 1900. . . ."[19] And holiness was a central concern at Moody Bible Institute. An account from the autobiography of Charles Stelzle, who attended the Institute in the 1890s, reveals how intensely the experience was promoted and sought at that time:

> Much was said about the "second blessing." I was anxious to get this added gift. When it was announced that an all-night prayer-meeting of the four hundred students would be held to pray for this blessing, I eagerly attended. There was a great deal of singing and much exhortation until midnight, and then they all fell upon their knees and audible prayer began. In about an hour student after student after student joyously rose and shouted that he "claimed the promise," that he had "received the blessing." I couldn't see it. I remained on my knees until after about four o'clock in the morning. Meanwhile, the leader stood over me—I had taken a seat up front, so that I could see and hear everything, for I certainly wanted that gift if it was for me—and he berated me for my lack of faith. I was made a subject of special prayer. I honestly felt that I needed it.[20]

Stelzle never did receive the blessing (he went on to become a theological liberal), but he may have been an exception in the highly charged atmosphere of schools such as Moody.

Divine Healing

An experience often linked in conservative evangelicalism to that of holiness was the belief in divine healing. Ultimately for some, relying on

God meant letting him—rather than doctors—take care of one's sick body also. Interest in healing by extramedical means was not limited to the forerunners of the fundamentalists; it pervaded late nineteenth and early twentieth century culture generally. This was the era in which Mary Baker Eddy attracted a large following of "Christian Scientists." (She first published her major work, *Science and Health,* in 1875.) "Mind cure" groups flourished and multiplied. Even popular novels dealt with the subject, for instance, Edward Eggleston's *The Faith Doctor: A Story of New York* (1891).

As explanation for this widespread interest in healing, Donald Meyer has pointed out in *The Positive Thinkers* that the medical profession was then just starting to anticipate "wonders" it could not yet deliver.[21] Meanwhile, as Meyer indicates, nervous diseases had begun noticeably to afflict large numbers of Americans, though physicians had only started to grope toward a recognition of the relation between the health of the mind and that of the body. The word "neurasthenia," meaning physical disturbances attributable to neurotic anxiety, came into fashion in the 1880s and 90s. A New York neurologist, George Beard, wrote a book called *Nervous Exhaustion* in the late 1870s, and another called *American Nervousness* (1881). Among the symptoms of nervous exhaustion listed by Beard were insomnia, "flushing," drowsiness, eyestrain, atonic voice, nervous dyspepsia, "sweating hands and feet," fear of lightning, fear of responsibility, indecisiveness even in trivial matters, back pains, and "a feeling of profound exhaustion." Protestants had traditionally shown scant concern for the prevention and cure of illness, particularly nervous disorders; for the orthodox sickness was often seen as a sign of humanity's general sinfulness, or, more positively, as a lesson in resigning one's will to God. For Protestants of more liberal tendencies illness could seem to indicate a weakness of character, best treated by stiffening one's will, or could simply be downplayed as a temporary hiatus in advancing medical knowledge.

Nevertheless, many American Protestants who were ill wanted immediate cures. Mary Baker Eddy and Christian Science heard their demands; as Stephen Gottschalk has shown, many of the converts to her church were former orthodox Christians. Apparently in response to Mrs. Eddy's challenge, Boston's Emmanuel Episcopal Church started a healing movement in 1905, an innovation that was soon emulated by Episcopalian churches in Chicago and San Francisco. (Unlike Christian Scientists, these Episcopalians combined the use of doctors with extramedical means.) Fundamentalists and their progenitors showed much interest in divine healing. In the *Ministry of Healing* (1882), A. J. Gordon, the founder of Gordon College, an early Bible school, argued for the sort of healing practiced in apostolic times. A. B. Simpson himself claimed to have been miraculously cured and later won many of his followers through his healing ministry. The early decades of the journal he edited abound with testimonies to the efficacy of divine healing.[22]

Those who testified to being healed by "the Great Physician" under the ministrations of men like A. B. Simpson usually manifested great amounts of hitherto undiscovered energy, as invalids turned into strenuous missionary organizers and evangelists. Annie McFedries, who immigrated to the United States from Scotland in 1886 at the age of twenty-eight, had reportedly suffered from "chronic synivitis of both knee joints," a condition so serious that the doctors had suggested amputation. On Staten Island, however, she was introduced to the idea of divine healing and "experienced a miraculous touch from God." As McFedries recounted it,

> God met me. I straightened myself, dropped the crutch and the blind girl's arm, stepped out boldly and walked. He held me up and gave supernatural strength to my limbs. . . . I immediately proceeded to throw away all my medicines, drugs, and appliances, and to strip off the plaster of Paris casing from my limb, and put a gulf between me and my invalidism. I was made whole and free from every ache and pain. . . . He called me, soon after healing me, to give my life to others in the slums of our large cities, and I gladly obeyed.[23]

What Stephen Gottshalk said about Mary Baker Eddy's followers rings true when applied to Simpson's as well: to the serious Christian Scientist, he wrote, "a healing was important more as the occasion of a conversion experience than as a physical recovery. Indeed, Christian Science made its deepest appeal not so much to sick bodies as to troubled souls. And the ranks of the movement were recruited from those who had come to despair quite as much of orthodox religion as of *materia medica*."[24] Thus, the experience of divine healing, like that of sanctification, could be a powerful occasion for conversion—or rededication—to God. Because many of the founders and principal teachers of the early Bible schools subscribed to the concept and practice of divine healing, the idea played a significant role in shaping the ethos of these institutions. The chief teacher at the Boston Missionary Training School (later Gordon College) during the 1890s, F. L. Chapell, resisted accepting any drugs to combat his last illness in 1900 because "he feared that by resorting to medicine he might miss some opportunity of glorifying God who had kept him in health for many years."[25] Most likely, his behavior in this personal crisis served as a model for his students. Divine healing was probably even a concern in the classroom, for instance in a class at Simpson's Missionary Training Institute entitled "Christian Experience," which was taught "with special reference to the Enduement of Power."[26]

Premillennialism

For many Protestants of the late nineteenth century, premillennialism, the tenet that Jesus Christ would return before the thousand years of a peaceful kingdom he would inaugurate on earth, amounted to virtually a way of life. Most American premillennialists of that era expected the coming of their Lord "at any time." Though they refrained from predicting an actual date, they assumed "his appearing" would occur very soon and excitedly read the "signs of the times"—earthquakes, wars, and other disasters—for confirmation of this belief. The most sanguine even dared hope they would not die but would be "caught up" to meet the Lord in the sky before his actual return to earth as ruler of his millennial kingdom.[27] The excitement of this hope is captured in a reminiscence from the early days of A. B. Simpson and the Christian and Missionary Alliance:

> We were a hilarious company in those first days of the flush of conquest, when with whole-souled enthusiasm, we were certified we should never have to adopt glasses, lose our teeth, behold falling or grey hair, nor suffer any impairment of physical faculties. . . . The cherished hope of passing from [ordinary] sleep into the presence of the Lord, should we be called ere His descent from heaven, was the ideal of expectation.[28]

Premillennialism in one form or another had had a long history in the Christian church and had often, as in the nineteenth century, been associated with periods of intense religious activity.[29] The early Christians lived in expectation of Jesus Christ's swift bodily return. Though since the time of St. Augustine, the majority of the church has not been premillennialist, every age has given rise to groups which preached the imminent second coming and self-consciously patterned themselves after the expectant Christians of the apostolic age.[30] The United States had a flourishing premillennialist tradition in the early nineteenth century. The belief fell into disrepute, however, after a leading millenarian, William Miller, inaccurately predicted a date in 1843 (and then 1844) for the Lord's return. Because Miller had attracted a large following and wide publicity, his failure at prediction was particularly devastating to the premillennialist movement. After a hiatus of about twenty-five years, the idea began to revive in America, though most of its adherents—except those who called themselves "Adventists"—denied any historical ties with the Millerites.

"That blessed hope," as the second coming was often called, transformed the way believers lived their lives. Thus, like sanctification, it was at its most intense a "practical" experience. Above all, the belief lent urgency to the cause of missions. Believers who were convinced that only a little time remained before the Lord's coming understood it as their duty to prepare his way by proclaiming the gospel around the world. Many found exhortations such as those of Bible teacher William E. Blackstone irresistible: "O! that the Church would work a hundredfold more earnestly for the conversion of souls and the edifying of the body of Christ, that the bride [i.e., the Church] might be complete, and thus hasten the coming of her Lord, ever listening to the midnight cry: 'Behold the Bridegroom

cometh!' and 'so be ready to go out to meet him.' Matt. 25:6."[31] Answering
that missionary call meant that many an aimless humdrum life became
fixed on a single consuming purpose.

Those who earnestly expected an imminent second coming lived almost
constantly in a state of religious excitement. Though no longer a premillennialist, Cornelius Woelfkin, a New York pastor, could recall the "religious appeal" of the doctrine: "Love craves to see the object of its affection
and longs to see him that is altogether lovely. When any loved one is
expected home, the passing hours are fraught with interest and preparation."[32]

But premillennialists also experienced a nether side; they often felt intense anxiety lest they be found unprepared—without their "lights burning," as they might have said. They avoided borrowing money, but when
they did they experienced dread that the Lord's coming would catch them
in debt. They suffered torments if members of their families or their
close friends remained unconverted, for they vividly envisioned being
"caught up" to be with their Lord, while their loved ones stayed behind
on earth, perhaps to undergo the horrors of the "Great Tribulation" that
would precede the millennium.

As long as premillennialism was believed intensely it completely altered
the way education took place. Who, for example, was concerned to build
schools for the ages if this decade might be the last? What place did
college endowments have in this scheme, or extensive record keeping?
If a certain kind of preparation was the goal—training missionaries, preparing saints to meet their savior in the sky—what use had premillennialists
for academic subjects which did not immediately contribute to this purpose? Since time was short, schooling must be brief and intense. A 1928
graduate of Central Bible Institute in Springfield, Missouri, captured the
sense of urgency when he recalled his education: "Everyone was going
into the ministry. The coming of the Lord would be very soon. We had
to get some training."[33] Bible schools like Central Bible Institute admirably
met the criteria of brevity and training that fervent premillennialists demanded.

Pentecostalism

Central Bible Institute was one of the first of many Bible schools founded
by pentecostals in the teens, twenties, and after. The pentecostal movement
had grown out of a revival at Bethel Bible College in Topeka, Kansas,
in 1901. There, students of Charles Parham had been studying anew the
Book of Acts, with particular attention to Acts 2:4: "And they were all
filled with the Holy Ghost, and began to speak with other tongues, as
the Spirit gave them utterance." The students began to speak in other
languages than English (sometimes the language was recognizable, some-

times not), understanding the phenomenon as a sign of the "baptism of the Spirit." In 1906 one of these students, W. J. Seymour, went on to preach this new experience in the Azusa Street Mission in Los Angeles. So strong was the "showering of the Spirit" which he precipitated that it led to the formation of pentecostal groups, and eventually pentecostal denominations, all over the United States.[34]

Pentecostalism intruded as one of the issues that most divided conservative evangelicals. First, it tended to attract the poorest and least educated groups of people, including large numbers of blacks. Poor people—especially black poor people—often elicited hostility from other, better off Protestant conservatives. More important, it was the religious experience that was least amenable to organization and education, since pentecostals especially distrusted anything which they thought haltered the Holy Spirit. Fundamentalist leaders who valued order (and there were many) customarily looked askance at these sometimes unruly outpourings of the Spirit. A. B. Simpson for one felt compelled to discourage pentecostals in the Christian and Missionary Alliance, even though his severity meant a temporary decline in the group's membership. At nonpentecostal schools, which generally discouraged the enthusiasm for speaking in tongues, pentecostalism among the students (and even among the faculty) was a problem that frequently plagued administrators.

Despite its strong anti-institutional proclivities, however, pentecostalism was eventually responsible for a large number of Bible schools, perhaps because of all educational institutions they were believed to least fetter the free operation of the Holy Spirit. Pentecostal Bible schools resembled Bible schools of other fundamentalist traditions in most respects, except that they tended to struggle under scarcer economic resources and lower academic levels. For example, the Central Bible Institute, the Assemblies of God school founded in 1922, was one of the earliest and most stable pentecostal schools. Yet its academic standards remained low until the 1940s when administrators started to press for accreditation. Students were not required to have a high school education until 1948, and the school offered no degrees until that year. The school's president between 1929 and 1931 and then again between 1939 and 1948, Ernest S. Williams, had only an eighth grade education. Pentecostal schools also suffered from a high mortality rate. As of 1959, for instance, only nine out of forty Bible schools started by the Assemblies of God had survived.[35]

II

SYSTEMS

If the enthusiasms that characterized fundamentalism were to be taught to the uninitiated in the present generation and handed down to the next, they had to be contained, preserved, and codified by means of systems and organizations. Among many fundamentalists the urge to codify and, further, the drive to introduce predictability, permanence, and stability into their thought and activity was pronounced. It was this propensity that gave fundamentalists their reputation for stating their theological positions in formulaic and dogmatic terms, the words and phrases apparently fixed and unchanging for all time. (This tendency also explains the ease with which fundamentalist positions could be parodied, and the frequency with which observers virtually identified fundamentalists with their theological formulations, overlooking the experiences that characterized the movement at least as much.)

The urge to systematize and codify may seem paradoxical when we consider how earnestly many fundamentalists sought after the Spirit-led life, how much they prized the break with their old selves in the experience of conversion, and how intensely they anticipated that Jesus Christ might come at any time and render all things utterly different. One might suppose that these experiences and anticipations would be resistant to codification and rationalization—indeed, even to the constraints of language itself. Yet, far from being mystics, many fundamentalists maintained a strong belief in human reason and in the ability of human beings to give a "reasonable" account of most events, even divine ones. Fundamentalism, in short, contained a strong stream of rationalism that was thoroughly hospitable to the work of systematization and codification.

Furthermore, many conservative Protestants saw no contradiction in preaching both far-reaching change on the individual level and absolute fixity on other levels of life. The fundamentalist Baptist, W. B. Riley, captured a pervasive yearning for permanence in the spiritual realm when he wrote: "Theology, instead of being under the necessity of adjusting itself to the ever changing experiences of men, is a fixed science, far more unchangeable than the science of astronomy. Sometimes a star wanders, but in the truth about God there is no possible variation."[1]

Fundamentalists also faced the real danger that religious enthusiasms might get out of control, particularly through the activities of unstable people who were inevitably attracted to exciting religious movements. Indeed, many evangelical critics claimed that this was precisely what had happened in the case of the pentecostal phenomenon. But other "excesses" in addition to pentecostalism threatened. Leaders of the Christian and Missionary Alliance, for example, found it necessary to discourage members who extravagantly claimed, counter to Alliance teaching, that individuals failed to be divinely healed only because they were harboring some hidden sin. To take another example, the teaching of sanctification sometimes bred those who arrogantly asserted that they were henceforth impervious to sin, and then went on to act in a most "unsanctified" manner. Or an exciting revivalistic atmosphere might disintegrate into mere noise and confusion. Against such developments as these, fundamentalists found it necessary to establish stable institutions and organizations and, by means of these, to promulgate "correct" teachings and set rules for acceptable belief and behavior in their ranks. Inevitably the Bible schools, by virtue of their role as educators, acted as allies and often as leaders in these systematizing efforts.

Some of the doctrines constituting the systems of conservative evangelicalism were derived from orthodox Protestantism; they were recognizable legacies from the Reformation and earlier. In the traditional manner of most Protestants, for instance, fundamentalists believed that Jesus Christ had been born of a virgin; they taught that his resurrection had been an actual physical event; they advanced the "substitutionary atonement"— that is, they argued that Christ had died *in the place* of human beings, to appease God's wrath—as against some liberal Christians who were beginning to interpret Christ's death on the cross primarily as a model of selflessness and sacrifice intended to inspire similar behavior in humanity. Conservatives held that miracles had happened precisely as related in the Bible (though they disagreed on the possibility or probability of the recurrence of comparable events in the present).

Much of fundamentalist doctrine, then, was essentially orthodox, just as its proponents claimed. But, as James Davison Hunter has pointed out, "orthodoxy" underwent a sea change simply by virtue of the fact that its cultural environment had changed; the presence and increasing influence of modernism altered conservatives' perception of what constituted orthodoxy, and they reacted by placing more emphasis on certain traditional doctrines and less on others. For example, they accentuated beliefs that most earlier Protestants had accepted but not found necessary to highlight or explicate, such as the divine authorship of Scripture. On the other hand, in reaction to the Social Gospel they associated with liberal Protestants, they tended to downplay many of the social concerns traditionally connected with Christianity.

Dispensationalism

Not all of fundamentalist thought was orthodox. The most elaborate theological formulation developed by fundamentalists, dispensationalism, was of recent origin; it dated from the early nineteenth century. A system that codified study and interpretation of the Bible, it was a sort of regularized form of premillennialism. Briefly, dispensationalism was a method of dividing the contents of the Bible into several time periods, each with its own characteristic themes. Since this periodization of time extended into future time, the system also served the important function of interpreting biblical prophecy.

The majority of Bible schools taught dispensationalism. In fact, omission of the doctrine at conventional religious schools was one reason for the establishment of the Gordon Missionary Training School; an early catalog announced, "considerable emphasis is given to the dispensationalist aspect of truth, because this line of study is so generally neglected."[2] Dispensationalism figured no less at pentecostal schools; for instance, the first curriculum of the Central Bible Institute provided a course in it.

The system emerged from the theology of John Darby, a Church of Ireland clergyman who became impatient with what he considered the failings of his church, and, beginning in the late 1820s, organized small groups of worshipers in Dublin, Plymouth, and Bristol. (The famed George Muller belonged to the Bristol group.) In time these loosely tied groups of congregations came to be known as "Plymouth Brethren." The Brethren decried what they saw as the false distinctions between clergy and laity, and therefore called no ministers from among their ranks. They also rejected formal church organization, designating their meeting place simply "the Room." Though many Brethren were prosperous and prominent people, they assumed plain dress and simple habits and practiced a degree of egalitarianism among their members. Except for the purpose of evangelization, they observed the doctrine of rigid separation from the world. So severely did Edmund Gosse's Plymouth Brethren parents isolate themselves and their son from the outside, for example, that he claimed never to have set eyes on another child until he was eight, and did not even know of the existence of fiction. The Brethren were to exert strong influence on American fundamentalist thinking about the nature of the church and the ministry.[3]

Darby and other Brethren wrote many volumes of Scripture exposition and disseminated their ideas during frequent post-Civil War trips to the United States. But it was primarily Americans themselves who, through periodicals, books, Bible conferences, and Bible schools, acquainted their countrymen with the system. Among American dispensationalists, W. E. Blackstone and Cyrus Ingersoll Scofield became the preeminent popularizers. Blackstone's impact was felt through his highly popular book, *Jesus*

Is Coming (1878), while Scofield wielded the bulk of his influence through his publication in 1909 of the heavily annotated *Scofield Reference Bible* and through his founding of the Philadelphia School of the Bible.

Through the use of the *Scofield Reference Bible* many a student of Scripture imbibed a dispensationalist viewpoint without even recognizing it. After its publication by Oxford University Press in 1909, the Bible went through many printings; and a new edition came out in 1917. Many factors explained its popularity: Oxford was a prestigious publisher; the translation was the traditional King James Version favored by most conservatives; and it furnished copious notes on the same page as the passages or words needing clarification. The notes supplied information about the dates of the events depicted, references to the Hebrew or Greek texts, and definitions of unclear terms. They also referred the student to other places in the Bible where the same topic, concept, or word was used. At the back of the Bible, students found a dictionary of proper names used in Scripture, a subject index, a concordance, and a set of maps of biblical lands. Those who read all the notes of the Scofield Bible felt assured that they were conducting a thorough and systematic study of Scripture.[4]

The name of dispensationalism came from one of its chief tenets, the belief that history as laid out in the Bible is divided into a number of ages or "dispensations." In the dispensationalist scheme, each age or dispensation has its motifs; each is opened by God's choice of a certain method with which to save human beings from the results of their sin, and each ends with human rejection of God's proffered instrument for salvation.[5]

Some of the details in the dispensationalist scheme remained open to discussion. Not all dispensationalists agreed with C. I. Scofield that "the rapture" (the event in which the living "saints" would be "caught up" into the air) would happen before the "tribulation," a time of trouble and persecution on earth, and so there came to be parties of "pre-tribulationists" and "post-tribulationists" according to opinion on this question.[6] Furthermore, though not everyone concurred with Scofield on the precise number of dispensations (he described seven), or on their beginning and closing points, almost all dispensationalists agreed on basic matters: first, that the true church, composed of the faithful saints, would be "caught up" from the earth to join Jesus Christ in heaven; second, that Christ would rule over a literal Jewish kingdom in Jerusalem lasting a thousand years, thereby fulfilling the biblical promises to the Jews; and third, in the end the wicked would be damned and the faithful would enjoy eternal blessedness. Finally, most dispensationalists expected that the next significant event in the sequence would happen very soon, though they refrained from assigning any dates.

Dispensationalism taught ecclesiological doctrines that reflected considerable hostility to the conventional church. Traditionally, orthodox Christians had assumed that their church was the successor to God's chosen people, Old Testament Israel, since the Jews had failed to recognize Jesus as their Messiah. Consequently, when they dealt with the unfulfilled promises made to the Jews, they interpreted them as now intended for the Christian church. Dispensationalists countered with the argument that God had in fact—as always—meant precisely what he said and still intended to fulfill his promises to the Jews. Though he had needed to delay his plans, he had done so only temporarily. The church, then, was often called a "parenthesis," or an "intercalation" in God's intentions. Actually, dispensationalists claimed, the true church belonged to heaven, not to earth, and was in the world only briefly. Thus, the true church did not at all correspond to the nominal church.

Such an ecclesiology affected American fundamentalism in important ways. It encouraged the interdenominational—or undenominational—outlook of many fundamentalists; it also reduced fundamentalist loyalty to any given denomination and abetted the tendency of fundamentalist churches frequently to splinter and break off, and the propensity of fundamentalists to desert a given congregation without serious misgivings to go in search of another one more congenial, sometimes several times in one lifetime. Most important for the Bible school story, the rather low estimate of the visible church increased the importance of the schools as organizing centers for fundamentalist groups and for the fundamentalist movement as a whole. Whether or not their leaders intended it, schools such as Moody Bible Institute functioned as headquarters of new groups that operated in a manner not unlike that of traditional denominations.

Another tenet relevant to Bible school education was the dispensationalist belief in the importance of proselytizing Jews. Dispensationalists held that the conversion of the Jews was necessary to the literal fulfillment of God's plans—the restoration of a Jewish state in Jerusalem—and therefore it was imperative to carry the Gospel to "the Jews first." If dispensationalists were to hope to have any success in converting Jews, they reasoned that evangelists had to have adequate knowledge of Jewish language and culture. During the early decades of this century, when immigrant Jews spoke Yiddish, Russian, or German, the typical Bible school provided "Jewish missions" classes or in some places a whole department of Jewish missions, which taught such subjects as Yiddish, Hebrew, Jewish customs and traditions, and Jewish sacred writings. At some Bible schools the level of sophistication about Jewish learning was remarkable considering that it was a Christian institution operating at only a modest academic level.

Any sign that the Jews were converting to Christianity en masse or that they were returning to Palestine in impressive numbers signaled to dispensationalists that the second coming might be at hand. Because of their desire to see the Jews restored to Jerusalem, dispensationalists—including Bible school leaders—were Zionists of an unusual sort.[7] As a result of excitement over the news that General Allenby and the British had marched into Jerusalem during World War I, A. B. Simpson, founder of the earliest Bible school, is said to have become so exercised that he suffered a heart attack. As a dispensationalist, he fully expected that Allenby's action would clear the way for the Jews to return to their traditional homeland, thus initiating the second advent.[8]

So vigorous and successful were efforts to propagate dispensationalism in America that for many, premillennialism became virtually synonymous with dispensationalism. (It was not exactly synonymous, of course; all dispensationalists were premillennialists, but not all premillennialists were dispensationalists.) No matter how effective the vehicles for its purveyance, however, it hardly seems likely that the system would have achieved such hegemony among fundamentalists had it not carried a deep and inherent appeal.

First, at the most elementary level, the system furnished the faithful with a way of reading the Bible that was at once reverent and methodical. It answered certain nagging questions about Scripture. "Rightly dividing the word of truth"—a Scripture-derived slogan constantly invoked by dispensationalists, including Bible school students—meant, among other things, the decision to assign some passages of the Bible to the Jews and some to the Christian church. Thus, when one part of the Bible advocated an "eye for an eye" as a response to injury, whereas another part taught turning the other cheek, it did not mean one part of the Bible had to be disregarded, or that God as the author of the whole Bible had contradicted himself. The solution of the apparent discrepancy was simple: the first command was meant for the Jews in a prior dispensation; the second command was intended for the "saints" in the present age.[9] It was this clarifying power of dispensationalism that elicited the encomium of a fundamentalist editor: "dispensational truth . . . without which the Bible would be a helpless enigma."[10]

Despite its apparent complexity, dispensationalism offered a simple view of the Bible, one in harmony with the elementary level of most Bible schools. To dispensationalists, the Bible was in reality one voice, the creation of a single mind. C. I. Scofield felt confident that in offering students of the Bible a dispensationalist reading he was helping them "to perceive the greater outlines of truth, something of the ordered beauty and symmetry of that Word of God which, to the natural mind, seems a mere confusion of inharmonious and conflicting ideas."[11] At one blow it could dispose of what seemed the higher critics' babble about various biblical speakers, different cultures with diverse world views, and confusing (and threatening) questions of authorship. It revealed the Scriptures as proof against relativism and change. Humanity was the same at all times, everywhere— always depraved and ever in danger of damnation. The only element that changed was God's manner of dealing with human sinfulness.

Moreover, in considering the Bible as a whole, many Protestants were struck with how large a portion of Scripture was devoted to prophecy.

Dispensationalism, its students argued, properly reflected the prominence of prophetic books and passages. And taking prophetic statements literally offered a satisfying consistency. To many, W. E. Blackstone seemed to have a point in *Jesus Is Coming* when he asked why tradition took the passages about Jesus being born of a virgin at face value, but not a statement like, "the Lord God shall give unto him the throne of his father David" (Luke 1:33).

Finally, dispensationalism aided in the understanding of history. The late nineteenth and early twentieth century, a historically conscious age, placed great emphasis on concepts such as "evolution," "growth," and "development." Any system that attempted to offer religious and philosophical explanation at any level needed to take history into account. Judged by the canons of twentieth century historical scholarship, dispensationalism was of course ahistorical. On the other hand, it *was* an interpretation of history, one which gave God the leading role. He was the "mover" and "doer," not humanity. Dispensationalism, then, offered turn-of-the-century evangelicals a welcome alternative to the emerging versions of history which assumed that human beings were the primary agents, and progress the dominant direction. While other histories then current envisioned a straight, upward line, whose terminus was a troubling question mark, dispensationalism posed a cyclical history culminating in what seemed to its practitioners a blessed end to history. (And later, after World War I, dispensationalism was able to offer its optimistic vision of history to counter the darker visions of Spengler and his troubled contemporaries.)

One way of summing up the appeal of dispensationalism was to say that it offered certainty and clarity to Protestants who otherwise would have faced the present and future with exceeding anxiety. One common human response to uncertainty has always been the creation of elaborate plans and lists. To go into unknown territory, one tries to acquire detailed maps. The dispensationalists were experts at drawing charts and defining words. There were those who could create minute descriptions of the earthly millennial kingdom, almost down to the last brick. To such people the apocalypse ahead held no terrors. One wonders whether they were people of little or suppressed imagination, as Edmund Gosse described his Plymouth Brethren parents, or whether they were people with particularly fertile imaginations and exceptional power to believe. Probably there were dispensationalists to fit both descriptions.[12]

Given this analysis, it becomes apparent why Bible schools have served as a primary vehicle for the dissemination of dispensationalism. The system, with its "facts," charts, and outlines, proved easy to teach large numbers of students possessing varied educational abilities and backgrounds. Though dispensationalism sounds complex to the outsider, it has made a lot of sense to those who have grown up regarding the Bible as the primary text for human history.

An example may help demonstrate how easily dispensationalism could be adapted to the Bible school environment. During the thirties a class in dispensational history was taught by Samuel Sutherland at the Bible Institute of Los Angeles. Four or five class days were devoted to each of the seven dispensations. The students were required to develop their own original charts for each dispensation; they could study already existing charts but not copy them. To fulfill her assignment on the flood, one student baked a large flat cake and decorated it with symbols of that dispensation: Noah's ark, the rainbow, Noah's altar after the flood, and, finally, the tower of Babel. The cake-dispensation became "the talk of the semester" and was put on display in the school lobby. Sutherland transferred some of the (non-cake) charts to slides, which he then used to illustrate church lectures. And students themselves reported using their charts repeatedly in their later teaching and missionary work.[13]

Methods and Manuals

Fundamentalists exhibited a special enthusiasm for methods of accomplishing tasks and achieving goals, and contributed more than their share of manuals to the genre of American self-improvement literature (as they continue to do today).[14] Most of the early manuals addressed a few essential tasks: gaining a thorough knowledge of the Bible, learning effective ways to evangelize individuals and groups, and achieving a fuller spiritual life. The words "how to" figured in any number of titles issued by conservative evangelical presses. Dwight Moody had contributed manuals bearing such titles as *Heaven and How to Get There* and *The Way to God and How to Find It.* In the *Pocket Treasury* offered by the Bible Institute Colportage Association were selections on "How to Become a Christian" and "How to Live the Christian Life."[15] In return for taking out a subscription to *The King's Business,* the periodical of the Bible Institute of Los Angeles, readers received books such as R. A. Torrey's *How to Bring Men to Christ* and *How to Study the Bible for Greatest Profit.*

The area of holiness also attracted the attentions of conservative evangelicals eager to distill the experience into a series of steps that almost anyone could follow. The official historian of the Keswick movement described with gentle irony the activities of A. T. Pierson, the well-known American spokesman for the cause of foreign missions, and R. A. Torrey, American evangelist and Bible school educator, at a Keswick convention around the turn of the century:

> With much that enhanced Kewswick's value Pierson and Torrey introduced one less valuable constituent. A journalist said Dr. Pierson's brain "seemed to be a set of pigeon holes, alphabetically arranged"; Torrey had trained his massive intellect to present doctrines in pithy, ordered snippets for easy

digestion by his Bible Institute [Moody Bible Institute and Bible Institute of Los Angeles] students. The two had been impressed by Keswick's consecutive unfolding of the theme of sanctification, each day's addresses building on the previous, and they promptly pressed this into a close knit system. Pierson even laid down a "Keswick Plan . . definite, complete and progressive," having "a definite Beginning, Course and Culmination," Six Successive Steps "to and in the blessed life." Somewhat oddly, "Aim a deadly blow at self (be dead to Ambition, Avarice, Appetite and the amusing and alluring Pleasures of the World)" was Second Step in Pierson's particular Plan, placed right back two steps before "the infilling of the Spirit"; thereby, though nobody seems to have noticed, sabotaging the entire ethos of "the blessed life." Such codifying encouraged lesser minds to narrow, for a period, Keswick's exposition.[16]

In 1938 another American, Donald Grey Barnhouse, also a Bible school educator and author of *God's Methods for Holy Living* (1936), conducted the Bible reading session at Keswick and outlined a device he used to incorporate holiness into his life:

> He told, simply and self-consciously, what "walking with God" meant to him in a twenty-four hour period of his ordinary life. . . . He described how he had discovered the way to go to sleep turning a Scripture verse into prayer, so that "soon He became more real than the inside of my eyelids," and the first waking moments of the new day were fresh with the sense of the last night's prayer and of Christ's presence.[17]

But probably no area of interest to fundamentalists gave rise to more preoccupation with methods than Bible study. Conservative presses turned out scores of inexpensive manuals on "how to study the Bible," and fundamentalist journals were crowded with columns offering helps in interpretation and hints on methods of Bible study. Bible dictionaries, Bible handbooks, Bible commentaries, and concordances to the Bible (particularly Cruden's *Concordance*) enjoyed brisk sales.

The subject of the best Bible study methods occupied many Bible school teachers, and some schools came to be known for the ways they taught the Bible. An attempted merger of two Philadelphia Bible schools foundered in 1952 over different ideas on how to approach Bible study: one school's teachers traditionally taught by means of single books and in the order of the English Bible, while leaders in the other school believed in proceeding by thematically unified groups of books and also argued that because of their special difficulty the Old Testament prophets should be introduced only in the last year.[18]

The enthusiasm for methods that pervaded Bible schools was not limited to classroom study of the Bible. Bible school authors and publishing outfits played a large role in the production of manuals and the dissemination of methods that helped evangelicals study their Bibles, proselytize others, and lead more meaningful spiritual lives. In fact, the preoccupation with methodology suggests a great deal about the kind of education conducted by the schools. Their pedagogy was highly practical, oriented to the achievement of specific goals; the methods—clearly laid out and uncomplex—could be taught to almost anybody by almost anybody. This practical, confident, and method-centered style of Bible school education was captured in an advertising slogan used by the Philadelphia School of the Bible during the twenties: "The School with a Message, and a Definite Programme with which to Put It Over."[19]

The Language of Fundamentalism

A part of the educative power of fundamentalism—as well as of its very identity—has resided in the distinctiveness and effectiveness of its characteristic speech. An outsider who has read or listened to fundamentalist utterances from the past or present knows that they possess a certain distinctive sound of their own and carry a decided appeal regardless of the sense of the words or the possible resistance of the reader or listener to their message. Many of the same phrases recur and invoke the pleasure of recognition; the rhythms are pronounced; the choice of words is often memorable and arresting. Bible school educators did their share to encourage and foster this valuable instrument of evangelism.

A thorough analysis of fundamentalist rhetoric must await a systematic survey of the speech and writing of several decades. And at the outset one must caution that the rhetoric has varied from group to group, depending on particular theological emphases and factors such as the social, educational, and economic standing of a group's membership. And the rhetoric, though distinctive, was of course not discontinuous from that of the rest of the culture; fundamentalist speech shared many elements with that of other Protestants and, indeed, with other English-speaking Christians, for instance, its penchant for military images. It also borrowed heavily from Protestant rhetorical traditions of the past; fundamentalists of the 1920s still used some of the same phrases to describe their conversions as had Puritans of 1630. Finally, one cannot talk about a phenomenon that was uniform over time; the rhetoric clearly changed between 1880 and 1940, though it is not entirely apparent what changes might be attributable to general shifts in American English and what might stem from currents within the movement itself.

Nevertheless, despite these caveats, it is possible to risk some generalizations. First, the rhetoric fulfilled at least two major purposes. Most obviously, it served as a missionary vehicle, an instrument for persuasion and exhortation. Second, it helped conservative evangelicals recognize each other. Anyone who spoke of "stepping out on the promises" or "being washed in the blood of the Lamb," for instance, located him or herself squarely in an identifiable theological and cultural camp (and outside other camps). The common language helped to forge a sense of unity long before disparate conservative groups could manage to achieve any formal organizational cohesion.

Whatever the variations among fundamentalist speakers, few were unaffected by the Bible, particularly the King James Version. Fundamentalists have constantly quoted, echoed, and alluded to Scripture. They have employed biblical constructions ("builded," "used of God," "cometh," "unto," "thy") and archaic or old fashioned words that retained a "biblical" ring ("tarry" and "quicken"—in the sense of come to life or bring to life). Though in recent decades other versions than the King James have come into use (e.g., *The Living Bible,* a popular and abbreviated translation), the seventeenth century prose of the earlier Bible still exerts considerable linguistic power.

Another characteristic of fundamentalist rhetoric, at least since the twenties, has been its folksy, colloquial quality.[20] This trait, perhaps inherited from early nineteenth century American Methodism, has increased in the movement as a whole as the twentieth century has gone on. Folksiness entails a number of elements: a penchant for anecdote, storytelling, slang, slogans, catchy epithets, nostalgia, sentimentality, and a simple brand of humor. (Folksiness sometimes conflicts with—or at least contrasts with—the King James influence.) As many others besides twentieth century evangelists have recognized (e.g., the operators on Madison Avenue), a folksy approach offers many advantages in the attempt to persuade. Good-natured sounding and democratic, it appeals to the largest possible number and therefore is ideally suited to evangelistic objectives.[21]

Finally, when like-minded people told and retold stories of similar experiences (as in their conversion narratives) or spoke of shared convictions, they were bound to repeat certain stock words and phrases (in fact, they *intended* to). The repeated phrases made the rhetoric easier to remember and disseminate. Thus, fundamentalists developed certain doctrinal formulations; for instance, they spoke repeatedly of the "personal and visible" coming of Christ, of "casting one's cares upon the Lord," or of "stepping out on His promises." Other phrases described the speaker's relation to the Lord: one "accepted Christ" as one's "personal savior," was "saved," and was "born again." A group of popular adjectives characterized good Christians (often Bible school students) as "wholesome," "winsome," "consecrated," "sanctified," "earnest," and "diligent." Some stock phrases described evangelists as "soul winners," as "burdened" or "on fire for souls," as having a "passion for souls," as "laboring in the Lord's vineyard." A faithful Christian who died was said to have been "mustered out," or to have "fallen asleep in Christ"; his or her death was often spoken of as a "home-going."

A wide variety of fundamentalist organizations—Bible conferences and classes, evangelistic services and revivals, conservative journals and books, and later radio and television—helped to standardize and disseminate the rhetoric to the widest possible audience. Bible schools, as they promoted popular Bible study, immersed large numbers of Americans in biblical phrases and usages. By means of textbooks and lectures on the Bible, doctrine, and missions, Bible school educators spread some of the characteristic formulations of the movement. Students and teachers listened to each other as they prayed, told the stories of their conversions, and spoke of their evangelistic activities, learning common ways to talk about their experiences and aspirations. And it seems fair to speculate that Bible school instructors and students, with their preference for quick, easy, and foolproof methods, for capsulated knowledge, and for outlines that rendered Scripture crystal clear and readily digestible, reinforced the rhetoric's propensity for slogans and formulaic phrases.

III

FUNDAMENTALISTS IN SOCIETY

The Society and the Economy

Historians have had difficulty describing the social and economic status of fundamentalists. In part this is because fundamentalists were (and are) more diverse than commonly recognized. In the matter of economic and social position, they stood out less from nonfundamentalists than might be imagined. In future research the question of their social and economic identity might be most fruitfully broken up into parts: who were the members, socially and economically speaking, of a particular independent Baptist fundamentalist congregation in 1930, for instance; or who read the Christian and Missionary Alliance publication; or who enrolled in a given Bible school? For the present, it is necessary to risk a generality. Most of the fundamentalists who figure in this study, and their immediate forerunners as well, came from the middle and lower middle classes. If they were poor, they were usually genteelly, as opposed to desperately, poor. Some broad distinctions could probably be predicted from knowing a person's denominational affiliation. Descendants of Calvinist groups tended to be better off, Methodists and other groups from Wesleyan traditions less so. Pentecostals constituted the major exception; to a greater extent than the others they tended to come from the urban and rural poor, or at least from the working classes.[1]

In general, fundamentalists and their conservative antecedents would have been considered neither ill nor well educated by the standards of the time. Here the exception lay with the leaders of the movement, many of whom had graduated from reputable colleges and often even from seminary. Most fundamentalists were readers of religious magazines and newspapers. They worked as small businessmen, tradesmen, ministers, teachers, skilled and semi-skilled craftsmen; a few were doctors, dentists, and lawyers. Relatively few manual workers swelled their ranks. They possessed enough substance to spare a portion for missions. Persons who came decidedly from the under classes—converted Catholic immigrants, reformed alcoholics, rescued women of the streets—were prized trophies of evangelistic efforts; they were not the normal constituency for fundamentalism. Occasionally a small businessman or manufacturer did well and became rich; men like Milton and Lyman Stewart (Union Oil Company, Los Angeles); Henry Parsons Crowell (Quaker Oats, Chicago); Robert G. LeTourneau (manufacturing and construction); John M. Studebaker; Charles L. Huston (Lukens Steel Company, Pittsburgh); and George F. Washburn (a realtor) contributed large sums to conservative missions, conferences, churches, publications, and schools.[2]

The essentially middle or lower middle class nature of these fundamentalists needs to be emphasized, because H. Richard Niebuhr's overly narrow picture of them as rural have-nots has persisted. The followers of A. B. Simpson in the Christian and Missionary Alliance, a conservative evangelical group which dates from the 1880s, clearly came from the middle or lower middle classes. They were people who had enough leisure to spend time in Bible study and Christian service, and they owned watches and jewelry that they could dramatically lay on the stage as contributions at missionary meetings. They read books and magazines. When Simpson took his first trip to the West Coast, he was pleased to discover how many of those he met there knew of his ideas through his books and articles.[3] Furthermore, to judge from the frequency of the references to investment and credit in the pages of the Alliance journal, its readers commanded enough substance to obtain or extend credit or to worry about how best to manage extra amounts of money. Finally, and perhaps most decisively, a substantial contingent of Alliance followers had enough money to winter or retire in Florida.[4]

Many of the fundamentalists from the lower middle class were apparently hardworking and upwardly mobile. It is possible, for instance, to speculate about the aspirations of the audience for the *Moody Bible Institute Monthly* from an advertisment which appeared repeatedly on its inside cover during 1926. The full-page ad, which featured the "Sherwin Cody School of English," promised "better business and social opportunity" for those who took advantage of Cody's offer and improved their grammar, pronunciation, and spelling.[5]

Like the readers of the *Monthly*, Bible school students were on the way up socially and economically. Most often they arrived at school with very little money and modest prospects. Their Bible school education helped them to get ahead, improve themselves, and develop basic academic skills, as well as to learn methods of Christian work. Probably the critical element which made upward mobility possible was the multiplication of opportunities for Bible school graduates to make use of their skills, as fundamentalist organizations expanded and prospered modestly during the twenties and even the thirties. Bible school graduates did not generally become the elite leaders in the movement (unless they went on to a four-year liberal arts college; those who attended schools such as conservative Wheaton

College in Illinois, and who had perhaps even gone on to seminary moved into the top leadership). But Bible school graduates nevertheless qualified as lesser leaders and valued workers in the movement.

The case of Christina Lang, a student at the New England School of Theology in the early 1920s, illustrates the opportunity that the Bible school held out to some students. After graduating from high school in rural Maine, she spent the summer working in a paper mill. "During that time," she recalled, "[I] felt that I wanted something more in my life than factory work. . . ." That desire propelled her to apply to the New England School of Theology. Clearly the Bible school offered the way to achieve "something more" than factory work. After graduation from the school, Lang went to India as a missionary, and in that role became a figure of some prominence in her denomination.[6]

Some concrete data do exist to indicate what regions of the United States fundamentalists and their spiritual forebears came from. Robert Wenger, after studying a number of sources dating from the teens and twenties, concluded that fundamentalist population centers lay not in the South but in the Middle Atlantic and East North Central States, with an additional contingent on the Pacific Coast. As time went on and the South, too, felt the effect of theological and cultural liberalism, larger and larger numbers of fundamentalists would come from that region, but not in the early twenties.

Wenger's findings are reinforced by the evidence available about the geographical distribution of Alliance adherents. They lived mostly in the Northeast, Middle West, and Far West. In the late 1880s groups of Simpson's followers had formed in New York, California, Chicago, Pittsburgh, Ohio, Florida, Boston, Maine, and New Jersey. Before about 1930 relatively few of them lived in the South (with the exception of Florida). In 1926 the leading states of residence, in descending order were New York, Pennsylvania, Ohio, Michigan, Florida, California, and Washington. Moreover, contrary to the usual assumption about conservative evangelicals, Alliance members were predominantly urban dwellers. Of the 22,737 members listed in the 1926 census, 18,988 lived in cities, and only 3,749 in rural areas.[7]

Unfortunately, no George Gallup polled the political opinions of conservative Christians between 1880 and 1940 (assuming he could have identified such a group of people). Wenger's list of "forty prominent fundamentalists," which includes the political party affiliations of some, gives the impression that most fundamentalist leaders identified themselves as Republicans, unless, of course, they were Southerners.[8] The likelihood that the leaders were Republicans, however, does not necessarily indicate the political leanings of ordinary fundamentalists, but they were probably also Republicans, again unless they lived in the South. Fundamentalists—in common with most Americans, it should be noted—opposed political ideologies that they perceived as "godless"; in 1878 W. E. Blackstone was already warning against "the atheistic and lawless trio of socialism, nihilism, and anarchy."[9] On the other hand, it is difficult to make any general statement about how fundamentalists regarded government activism. Most fundamentalists looked favorably upon governmental control in the form of legislation against liquor, Sunday business activity, and the teaching of evolution. A fundamentalist such as William Jennings Bryan worked all his life for progressive reforms that involved massive participation by the federal government in the affairs of its citizens. On the opposite end, J. Gresham Machen decried most forms of government activity as encroachments upon individual liberty, including even the Volstead Act of 1919 in this negative judgment.[10]

Many fundamentalists simply did not concern themselves with politics at all. This was particularly true of those with holiness leanings. Christian and Missionary Alliance members, for instance, were much more oriented toward strictly religious activity than toward political ideology or endeavor. Neither visions of systematic political reform, nor desire to preserve the status quo could much move Christians who fixed their attention upon the imminent coming of their Lord. Articles in the Alliance journal in 1893, during the thick of economic depression and labor troubles, admitted that the working man was not receiving his just portion and that his employer was unfairly benefiting from him, but rather than sanctioning such measures as unions or strikes, writers counseled the patience to wait for the second coming: "then the money which has been withheld from you will be paid by the Great Proprietor, with a compound interest that will astonish you."[11]

Fundamentalists in the Culture

For the most part fundamentalists were native white Americans who were dismayed by the conspicuous decline of Protestant hegemony in American culture, worried by the apparent weakening of religious faith, alarmed at the floods of (mostly Catholic) immigrants, uneasy about labor unrest (though not necessarily anti-labor), distrustful of cities (though they often lived in them), sentimental about the rural or small town life many of them had known as children, anxious about swift changes in morality and shifts in the scale of business and industry, and nostalgic for earlier and seemingly simpler times. In these fears they did not vary much from other native white Americans.

As the above ascriptions—and certainly their reputation in history—might suggest, fundamentalists were antimodernists in many senses. They continued to emphasize the centrality of religious faith at a time when increasing numbers of people were finding belief problematic or irrelevant, unless it was altered by substantial adjustments to modern culture. Set down amid those who hailed continuous material progress, they distrusted the mounting abundance of wealth except when it was hallowed by use in God's service. At a time when the prestige of science was at its height, they scoffed at the validity of scientific hypotheses, including, of course, the theory of evolution. They remained skeptical about technological advances and humanity's apparent growing ability to manipulate nature. Convinced that all creatures and particularly human beings depended upon God, they refused to accept the popular notion of human beings as the primary actors and agents in the world. They dissented from the nineteenth and twentieth century assumption that the dominant direction of life is change, adaptation, adjustment, and evolution. Truth, they believed, was the same always and everywhere, and institutions ought to remain unchanging to reflect this fact.

Fundamentalists, it is useful to remember, were hardly alone in their antimodernism. These attitudes were common in the late nineteenth century. Many other Americans—and Europeans as well—criticized "modern life" with varying degrees of acerbity. Searching for a style that was "realer," simpler, and more virtuous than that offered by what they considered a self-indulgent, over-civilized, over-industrialized culture, some dissenters joined the turn of the century revival of arts and crafts (and a cult of hard work with one's hands); others traveled back in imagination to medieval times, when human beings, they thought, were robust believers and also appreciators of beauty; still others turned to the nirvana of the mysterious Orient. After decades of anti-Catholicism, some Protestants at length came to appreciate the aestheticism and enduring qualities of the Roman faith.[12] And American Catholicism itself manifested a strong strain of antimodernism, between the world wars particularly. Dorothy Day and her Catholic Workers, for instance, harked back to earlier times with their voluntary poverty, their romantic experiments with agrarian communes, and their rejection of capitalism, industrialism, and bureaucratization.[13]

The fact that fundamentalists shared elements of antimodernism with many other Americans is important, for the well advertised fundamentalist aversion to modernity has often been interpreted as a major reason for their marginal historical status: while the rest of Americans were striding confidently forward, fundamentalists perversely looked backward. The truth is that many of their contemporaries were looking backward—though not always to exactly the same past—as a way of tolerating and coping with the present and the future.

Certain aspects of modernity have probably been overemphasized as objects of fundamentalist ire; ordinary fundamentalists thought less about Darwin's *Origin of Species* and the higher criticism than about developments in their own homes or communities: the irreligion of people they knew, sometimes including their own relatives; the suggestive way women dressed and fixed their hair; the rising number of divorces; the regrettable popularity of movies and jazz; the opening of nearby saloons; and the criminality of youngsters they knew. They probably perceived only dimly the actual content of higher critical teaching or evolutionary theory; at the most they simply *sensed* that these concepts posed a threat to all they held dear, particularly the Bible. In short, they were fairly safely isolated from intellectual trends that engaged university professors and other thoughtful students of history and society, less so from cultural currents that struck nearer home.

Some fundamentalists grew increasingly distressed about such cultural developments as the decades passed, and often their tones became increasingly strident. Nevertheless, despite a drift of events which often enraged or depressed them, true believers were able to maintain a certain detachment from their surroundings by keeping their eyes fixed upon the glories ahead. More than that, they sometimes sounded downright gleeful about the sad state of affairs, interpreting it as a sign that the time of Christ's coming was near and their deliverance at hand. In the meantime, as evangelicals, they were unable and unwilling to close themselves off and let the rest of the world go, quite literally, to hell. Far from being merely nay sayers and remaining defensively on the sidelines, they plunged into diverse evangelical tasks. The label of "pessimistic" they received from other Protestants is accurate in the sense that they expected little but evil to come from human affairs; it conveys a false impression, however, because it ignores the self-confidence and pleasure fundamentalists derived from contemplating the future God held out for his faithful.

Fundamentalists believed, in common with a majority of earlier Americans, that Christian belief was essential for a moral civilization. They explained the great moral "laxity" in American life by pointing to the decline of orthodox faith. In their sometimes strenuous attempts to uphold old standards of morality, they emphasized the importance of law and order. They revered the Old Testament decalogue and interpreted many biblical precepts as absolute commandments.

In common with many Americans, they held up the family as sacred, frowned upon divorce, and demanded that children show loyalty to their parents. Permissive sexual behavior provoked their unmitigated wrath and fear. They foreswore dancing, smoking, movies, theater, drinking, cursing, opera, and playing cards; they dressed conservatively (Machen and Bryan refused to change their dress with the fashion), and many women refrained from applying makeup or bobbing their hair when these practices came into fashion in the early twenties. They felt uneasy about owing money, and the failure to repay a loan when it came due was a source of distress. The discipline of the Bible schools naturally reflected these rigorous mores. Leaders at Johnson Bible School in Knoxville, Kentucky, were perhaps more severe in tone but not in goals than other Bible school educators when they admonished,

> We want young men of pure lives, and will not tolerate for a day any others. We are so strict that we are considered by some who do not want to do right, as dictatorial and extreme. We glory in the appellation. We put each student on his honor. If he is tempted to get off we may put him back on, but if he wilfully gets off we send him home. . . . If after we try a young man, he shows indifference to the work, we will dismiss him, even if he is not guilty of any great sin. The material on which we have to draw is so abundant that we cannot and will not give our time to young men whose morals make their future doubtful.[14]

Finally, fundamentalists distrusted the urge to build complex organizations so characteristic of the late nineteenth and the twentieth centuries. Here again they did not differ from other Americans and certainly from other Protestants, except in the outspoken nature of their protest. Hilyer Hawthorne Straton, the son of a well known fundamentalist, spoke for many of them when he remarked, "Organization is one of the curses of the liberals. They don't have anything else to do. Of course fundamentalists have the vice too, but not the same extent. They are too busy winning souls to bother with organization."[15] This distrust had several sources. Many conservatives had been disenchanted by their dealings with the machinery of their denominations. Others concluded that preoccupation with organization deadened piety and evangelical zeal; still others saw organization as a mark of the new and despised bureaucratic order. The irony of this view is that the achievement of fundamentalist evangelistic goals depended to a large extent upon the success of fundamentalists as organizers and institution builders.

In sum, fundamentalists dissented from what they perceived as the main directions in which American society was heading. The self-conscious sense they exhibited of standing over and against the major cultural developments in fact constitutes a salient characteristic of the movement. The degree of dissent varied, from mild to radical; it was expressed in diverse ways, from gentle remonstrance or quiescent piety to ugly vituperation; it led to differing actions, from educational efforts to the violence characteristic of the Klan. Sometimes the dissent seemed puzzling because it came from individuals who appeared quite skillful and competent working with the world as they found it, and who succeeded in that world by most of the conventional measures. A. B. Simpson despised worldly achievement, yet the more he rejected the world the more eagerly sympathetic humanity flocked to his leadership and helped him build up a complex of institutions and agencies to advance his unworldly beliefs. Worldly success seems to have dogged the footsteps of many another conservative evangelist as well (including Billy Graham in the present). If only by the rhetorical stance they have adopted, however, fundamentalists have attempted to put some distance between themselves and the dominant trends of the culture.[16]

The Fundamentalists and Education

In their losing battle for control of Protestant denominational agencies and institutions, fundamentalists claimed that the educational institutions of the denominations had fallen under the domination of liberal Protestants, and even of atheists. The denominational struggles had emerged to full public view in the 1920s, but they had started, often quietly, several decades before. In fact, the fundamentalists had all but lost the battle by the twenties.

Gradually in the decades following 1880, increasing intellectual and social prestige accrued to Protestant liberals and to the seminaries and universities where many of them them taught. In the 1890s conservatives successfully instigated some heresy trials to examine the orthodoxy of theology professors such as Charles A. Briggs of Union Theological Seminary in New York. Beginning in 1910 the Stewart brothers of Los Angeles launched the first of several volumes of *The Fundamentals*, designed to assert the "fundamentals" of Christian faith in opposition to the new intellectual climate. It was not until after World War I, however, that the conservatives in many denominations, particularly Presbyterians and Baptists, appeared to panic and triggered struggles that generally had two focuses: restoring orthodoxy to foreign missions enterprises, and purifying denominational colleges and seminaries of modernist influences. Almost without exception, the fundamentalists lost these battles. By the early 1920s, they had to face the fact that nearly every seminary had been given up to liberals and moderates, and that most denominational colleges had abandoned their religious affiliations or, though retaining them, had nevertheless patterned their curricula and styles after those of secular colleges.

In response to their defeats in the denominational struggles of the twenties, many conservatives broke from their old church bodies. Other conservative evangelicals had already left their denominations in the preceding decades of religious excitement and upheaval: pentecostals had "come out" from a number of groups, and holiness groups had departed from the Methodist and Presbyterian folds when they encountered opposition. (To be sure, not all conservatives forsook their former church homes, but the ones who stayed often tended to maintain a separate existence within the larger body.)

Despite the considerable differences among these groups, they found commonality in their dissent from the intellectual currents represented by the universities and university-influenced seminaries and agreed on the need to provide educational institutions for the instruction of the upcoming generation of "sound" religious leaders and Christian workers.

The contempt of conservative evangelicals for the American higher educational establishment should not too hastily be identified with hostility toward the intellect. Richard Hofstadter's description of fundamentalism as anti-intellectual derives from a particular understanding of the intellect, albeit one which prevails in the twentieth century. Many fundamentalists were eager, for instance, to disabuse potential detractors of the notion that they had arrived at their positions through ignorance or blind acceptance of what they had been taught.[17] Against the charge that they were obscurantists, they also strenuously protested their respect for science. Theirs, to be sure, was an older view of science as "classified and verified knowledge," a definition that quite pointedly excluded the theory of evolution on the basis that it had not been completely verified—and was indeed incapable of satisfactory verification.[18] The truth was that fundamentalists sincerely did not regard as "scientific" ideas which flew in the face of their understanding of God's word.[19]

Their conception of science as a body of "facts" was not unlike their understanding of knowledge in general. In contrast with many twentieth century thinkers, they were not interested in the process by which one sought knowledge, but in the end product. They disparaged the critical, inquiring, speculative, and restless scholar, who served as the model for most twentieth century intellectuals (including Hofstadter). In their view, knowledge worthy of the name did not constantly change and evolve, nor were its contents culturally determined. Rather, knowledge was a permanent treasure trove established once and for all by God, waiting to be rediscovered or merely acknowledged by those in every century who were serene and clear-eyed enough to discern it. This attitude is reflected in the contempt of one fundamentalist writer for "educators" who "announce to the world that the highest ambition of the student is, not to strive at certainty and finality, but to be a seeker after truth. The discovery of truth and the entering into rest of soul which accompanies a possession of it is a relatively unimportant matter compared to the continual seeking and perpetual failure to find."[20] In the realm of knowledge, as in others, "certainty and finality" were the great fundamentalist desires.

Fundamentalists also called the label "anti-intellectual" into doubt by virtue of their remarkable faith in the power of ideas *as ideas* to influence the human mind and shape human behavior; they held this attitude even toward teachings which they judged false. This striking confidence in the efficacy of ideas explains why they regarded education as critically important; it also suggests why they fought so vigorously and vocally for control of denominational schools and lamented so bitterly their losses.

In the teens and twenties, accordingly, the fundamentalists created new theological seminaries: Northern Baptist Theological Seminary (founded in Chicago, 1913); Eastern Baptist Theological Seminary (1925, in Philadelphia); Dallas Theological Seminary (1924—undenominational); Westminster Theological Seminary in Philadelphia (1929, out of the loss of control over Princeton Seminary to moderate Presbyterians); and, later, Faith Theological Seminary (after a split among the conservative Presbyterians at Westminster). They and their conservative allies also established a handful of new "Christian" colleges and maintained control over some old ones, including Wheaton College in Illinois, a school with a Congregational background which dated from 1853.[21]

But the creation of new colleges and seminaries was expensive, and some of the new institutions struggled along on scarce financial resources. Many fundamentalist groups which as a matter of principle devoted most of their funds to missionary and evangelistic activity were unable to afford colleges or seminaries at all. It is evident, however, that no fundamentalist groups, even those relatively well off, were equipped to establish an educational system equal in prestige and resources to the one they had seen swept away by the "tides of apostasy." As definitions of colleges, graduate schools, and theological seminaries sharpened and narrowed, some states made it more difficult for schools to achieve official recognition without comparatively lavish resources and without acquiescence to university norms. Given the growing hegemony of accreditation procedures, it became less possible to found an institution and call it a "college" or "seminary" regardless of its actual educational level or its intellectual outlook.

But for many decades educators seeking to define and delimit educational institutions did not take the Bible schools into their purview. These schools were protected by the fact that they diverged too greatly from emerging educational norms to be candidates for respectability among professional educators. Thus, in an evangelical world short of resources, the Bible school of necessity became the most pervasive form of "higher" education: the institutional form was already available in the precedent of the earlier missionary training school (see chapter 5); and the founding of a Bible school demanded only modest resources. Most of the early Bible school work was well below college level, and high school graduation was seldom a requirement for entrance. The early faculty, rarely professional educators, were often part-time employees or volunteers, and seldom boasted advanced (or even college) degrees.

Bible schools have been compared to the "log colleges" set up by eighteenth century revivalists. (They were sometimes referred to as "chicken coop colleges" by detractors.) Another possible analogy is the junior or community college of our time, which has allowed states and local communities to set up institutions less expensive, less ambitious, and less selective than four-year colleges or universities. Often community colleges have attracted lower middle class students, the first of their families to advance beyond high school; this also has been the case with most Bible schools. Furthermore, community colleges have typically been vocationally oriented; likewise, Bible schools have served as schools of practice, producing

Christian workers trained in methods of evangelism, Bible teaching, and missionary work.

With few exceptions, fundamentalists did not as a matter of preference substitute Bible schools for colleges and seminaries. They well knew where academic respectability resided. Had they been able to establish an entire system of regular colleges and seminaries and get them accredited without abandoning their educational and religious requirements, they might well have done so. (Indeed, they did so later.) In general, however, they did not possess the financial resources for an effort on this scale early in the century. The Bible school proved to be a satisfactory educational vehicle for those groups with limited budgets and an urgent desire to instruct the faithful in as brief a time as possible.

Fundamentalism and Other Protestants

A realization which eventually strikes the student of fundamentalism is how closely it resembles the rest of American Protestantism, and how remarkably continuous with earlier Protestantism it really was, at least compared to the received stereotypes. This revised view of the matter is important to the historian of Bible schools, because it helps explain why fundamentalist schooling, though unique, never strayed as far from prevailing educational norms as one might have expected.

Fundamentalists differed from other Protestants, of course; otherwise, there would be less point in telling their story. But they were not so set apart from other Americans by their ideas and experiences as historians and others have supposed. Fundamentalists and more moderate Protestants did, after all, share and respond to the same world, and they issued from the same evangelical ancestry.[22] Recognizing these circumstances, and correcting the popular misconception that fundamentalists have stood outside the pale of twentieth century history, might in fact constitute a first step in accounting for their current educational effectiveness.

Much has been made of the fact, for instance, that liberal Protestants at the turn of the century were seeking to make the divine immanent in human life; they felt that God's hand should be visible in social and economic life, even if his hand operated through human instruments. In their attempt to make Christianity "practical," they emphasized the human side of Jesus, and the application of his "ethics" to social and economic situations.[23] Fundamentalists likewise attempted to make God immanent. A. B. Simpson, founder of the Christian and Missionary Alliance, could have been speaking for all twentieth century American Protestants when he wrote of the quest for "a living God," "not merely on some far off throne but as a present and potent force in all human affairs."[24] In fact, one of the most prominent anxieties apparent in fundamentalist writing was the fear that a result of the higher criticism would be to put Jesus at a distance from human beings.

The desire for closeness to God and his son could be seen everywhere in the most valued fundamentalist experiences: Jesus was a "personal savior"; God was someone who made promises to his faithful, many of which were immediately redeemable. He could be taken at his word, the Bible. His guidance was available to the believer personally, and his followers could with sufficient faith know his will for their lives. The faithful could be in touch with him as with a father. Not only would he provide for their daily wants, but he even healed their bodies, just as he had done in apostolic days; as a benevolent father he had no wish to see his people suffering pain. His son was "indwelling" in Christians through the experience of sanctification, and could be expected to rescue the faithful from the world at any time through the vehicle of the "Rapture." No one could be truly lonesome who "knew" the Lord.

Traditionally, the difference between fundamentalist and liberal attitudes toward sin and evil has received emphasis. Liberal Protestants tended to see human evil as capable of cure or at least amelioration; in their view much evil resulted from ignorance, sickness, or social dislocation. Fundamentalists, who continued to take seriously the doctrine of original sin, considered evil to be more endemic to human nature; certainly the human race could not hope to approximate virtue or decency unless it depended upon God.

This said, it remains true that in analyzing the failings of American society, fundamentalists and liberals tacitly agreed; both groups attacked the mindless American pursuit of material goods. For the Social Gospel theologian Walter Rauschenbusch, sin was preeminently a matter of self-ishness. Likewise, many fundamentalists perceived sin as the cultivation of the things of the self without reference to God or his will for human beings. Contemplating a society that was rapidly accumulating more wealth than the world had ever known, earnest spokesmen in both conservative and liberal camps excoriated individual aggrandizement that was carried on for its own sake. In calling into question the American instinct for acquisitiveness, liberals and fundamentalists were in fact following a hallowed American practice. Emerson and his spiritual sons, William and Henry James, immediately come to mind.[25]

Fundamentalists have typically been viewed as doctrinaire, stubborn, and inflexible absolutists who divided the world into black and white, all or nothing, in violation of the "American" spirit of compromise and tolerance. Fundamentalist experience certainly did exhibit this side. Yet one who scans fundamentalist journals may be surprised to see how much tolerance for opposing views they contain. When it came to political, economic, and even religious questions, fundamentalists manifested a good deal of the American preference for the middle of the road. Furthermore, in addition to its doctrinaire spirit, fundamentalism contained a strong note of moderating pragmatism. Fundamentalists often argued for their visions of Christianity on the grounds that it upheld morality and civilization better than liberal religion. One of fundamentalism's champions, William Jennings Bryan, though often disposed to see matters absolutely, could argue against the theory of evolution not on the basis that it was wrong or evil or even untrue, but that its results would be disastrous: human beings who thought of themselves as descendants of monkeys would behave like animals. Similarly, premillenialists were likely to argue for their views on the basis that they inspired more earnest evangelists and a more intense spiritual life.

The difference between liberal and fundamentalist views of the city has also received much emphasis. Social Gospel exponents have been portrayed as the major group among late nineteenth century American Protestants who attempted to respond to the problems of the growing urban areas. Fundamentalists, on the other hand, have been counted among the ranks of those who hated and feared the city and therefore shunned its problems whenever possible. This judgment is only partially correct. While fundamentalists had their apprehensions (in common with Social Gospelers, it should be noted), they did not avoid urban life or even urban problems. A look at the list of Bible schools established before 1920, for instance, reveals that with only a few exceptions they were located in large or medium-sized cities. The city was, after all, the best arena for learning to do Christian work with all varieties of people. If one could acquire the skills for evangelizing immigrants in rough urban districts, then surely one could apply them anywhere, in China or in rural America. (The city also furnished the most abundant supply of potential students.)

True, the attention of fundamentalists tended to focus on the regeneration of individuals, to the exclusion of more comprehensive social and political solutions such as those sought by advocates of the Social Gospel. But they recognized that, for example, a converted drunkard who remained unemployed and out on the streets and without counsel would not stay a convert for long. Thus they realized the need for other measures besides direct evangelism, and established shelters, city missions, hospitals, rescue homes, orphanages, and even settlement houses. One of the best examples of a conservative evangelical religious organization which began with revivalism and personal evangelistic work but was forced to organize social agencies to further its urban evangelical efforts was the Salvation Army.[26]

During the twenties the two groups, liberal and conservative, would diverge more distinctly, if only because the intensification of hostilities forced each side to define its position more emphatically in opposition to the other. But the acrimonious rhetoric of the twenties should not blind us to the fact that fundamentalists and other Protestants still came from the same religious family and continued to share many of the same experiences and ideas and aspirations, even if they posed different answers and in contrasting styles.

IV

BEGINNINGS
SOME FOUNDERS

To observers in the twenties who noted the apparent informality and spontaneity with which Bible schools appeared, outside the supervision of educational officialdom, it might have seemed that the schools had sprung de novo from the needs of fundamentalists. To a great extent, the requirements of the fundamentalist movement did indeed shape the policies and practices of the schools. However, the Bible schools also inherited much of their character from nineteenth century religious training schools that had served a wide variety of Protestant groups. Except for their premillennialism, in fact, the earliest Bible schools were almost indistinguishable from this general group of religious training schools. The early Bible or religious training schools, products of the 1880s and 90s, were not even founded by fundamentalists as such—no such designation existed then—but rather by men and women who considered themselves simply earnest and mission-minded Protestants.

The Founders

Many of the early Bible schools emerged from the efforts of small groups; sometimes the groups were composed of denominational leaders who, worried about the future leadership of their church, sought to provide hitherto unavailable facilities for training. The Boston Bible School grew out of the activities of several prominent Advent Christians who had been lamenting the lack of denominational schools to turn out ministers and skilled lay people. In other instances the group members had originally organized a successful weekly class in the Bible or evangelistic techniques and wished to put the teaching on an expanded and more permanent basis. The Bible Institute of Los Angeles (1908) emerged from a "Fishermen's Club" for young men and a "Lyceum Club" for young women, both designed by their organizers to produce evangelistic workers well schooled in scripture. In other cases the founders' group consisted of Protestants who had been drawn together by a vivid spiritual experience

39

and wished to establish a school to nurture that experience in others. The Training School for Christian Workers (1900) in Los Angeles was started by a group of conservative Quaker missionary enthusiasts who had all been deeply stirred by a visiting holiness preacher and sought a vehicle for propagating his teachings.

Other times the major movers in the founding of the early Bible schools were individuals with magnetic personalities and powerful, driving religious visions. Whether they worked mostly alone or in close cooperation with others, however, Bible school founders often had similar backgrounds. Usually they shared certain formative spiritual experiences; they had undergone a definite conversion; as a result some had abandoned secular careers in order to carry on full-time evangelistic activities. Dwight Moody had once sold shoes; before adopting religious callings, C. I. Scofield, founder of the Philadelphia School of the Bible, and Ashley S. Johnson of the Johnson Bible College had trained as lawyers. Some time after their conversions, most founders had undergone deeper and fuller spiritual experiences such as sanctification or divine healing. And, of course, every founder was a fervent student of the Bible.

The early founders were also reformers, critics of the Protestant churches, whose members they accused of being lukewarm, nominal Christians, and whose ministers they attacked as unbiblical in their preaching and unevangelical in their approaches toward the unchurched. They condemned the practice of renting pews, hiring professional musicians, and encouraging elaborate devices such as church fairs for coaxing money out of congregations. Above all, they excoriated the churches' missionary efforts, both domestic and foreign, as feeble.

Their common perception of the weakness of the churches goaded these reformers to a number of restorative measures. Through a combination of Bible classes, foreign missions societies, periodicals, books, hymns, activist pulpits, city missions, and of course Bible schools, they sought to foster lay enthusiasm for missions, promote interest in Bible study, and encourage desire for more meaningful spiritual experiences. Very few confined themselves to a single activity or even a single region of the country. Before long, many Bible school founders came to oversee religious empires that demanded energy and organizing abilities worthy of a Rockefeller or a Carnegie.

It was not uncommon for Bible school founders to have departed from their original denominations and to have remained steadfastly unaffiliated or to have joined another denomination—often a new one—that better reflected their convictions. Those who retained some form of denominational affiliation nevertheless tended to downplay the importance of such loyalties. Rather, they recognized the value of larger alliances—union revivals, undenominational Bible conferences, the Salvation Army, the Young Men's Christian Association—in combating religious indifference. A striking number of Bible school founders had worked as YMCA agents or secretaries: Dwight L. Moody; C. I. Scofield; W. W. Rugh, founder of the Bible Institute of Pennsylvania; William LeRoy Pettingill, a founder of the Philadelphia School of the Bible; and T. C. Horton, a founder of the Bible Institute of Los Angeles, to name some of the most prominent.

Besides being joined by common interests and goals, early Bible school founders were often linked by personal ties. Almost all knew Dwight L. Moody personally, or at least had heard him preach. Most had sat at the feet of well known Bible teachers, such as James Brookes and A. T. Pierson. Often Bible school founders had received common inspiration from the biographies of George Muller and J. Hudson Taylor; Scofield had even met Taylor, and Simpson claimed friendship with Muller. Finally, Bible school founders maintained ties with each other. A. B. Simpson and A. J. Gordon were friends; in fact, Simpson preached Gordon's funeral sermon.

A. B. Simpson

The founder of what is usually recognized as the earliest Bible school, Albert B. Simpson (1843–1921), was typical of the first generation of Bible school founders. Like many of the others, he searched long and strenuously for ever deeper and more meaningful religious experiences, and his life was full of religious upheavals and discontinuities. As a youth, he suffered an extended crisis of faith. Later, after a series of successful Presbyterian pastorates, he abruptly abandoned the conventional churches to launch into a ministry of his own. Starting with a single independent congregation in New York City, he went on to establish a national organization. The network of institutions that came to be called the Christian and Missionary Alliance included a system of churches, a newspaper, a publishing house, annual conventions, and a number of Bible schools both in the United States and abroad in the mission fields. Because he was so typical of conservative evangelicals of the period (and because the materials on his life are unusually revealing), his biography invites extended scrutiny.

He was born on Prince Edward Island in Canada; his father, originally a shipbuilder, miller, merchant, and exporter, turned to farming on the frontier of western Ontario after a business failure in the late 1840s. Simpson's pioneer childhood amply demonstrated to him his need for more than human help and guidance. An early memory haunted him long after he had reached adulthood: "The first recollection of my childhood is the picture of my mother as I often heard her, in the dark and lonely night, weeping and wailing in her room, in her loneliness and sorrow, and I still remember how I used to get up and kneel beside my little bed even before I knew God for myself and pray for Him to comfort her.[1] Mrs. Simpson could not adjust to life on the frontier:

In that lonely cabin and that desolate wilderness, separated for the rest of her life from the friends she held so dear, and from the social conditions to which she had been accustomed, was it a wonder, with her intense and passionate nature, which had not learned to know God in all his fulness [sic] as her self-sufficient portion, that she should often spend her night in cruel lot, and that her little boy should find his first religious experience come to him in trying to grope his way to the heart of Him, who alone could help her.[2]

The boy had early decided he wanted to be a minister, but his parents had already dedicated his older brother to the ministry and lacked money to prepare them both. Nevertheless, Simpson educated himself as well as he could on his own resources. He studied Greek, Latin, and mathematics with a neighborhood pastor and earned a certificate to teach common school. By age fifteen he was in charge of forty students, many of them adults. In his spare time he was preparing himself to enter college.[3]

Shortly after embarking on this strenuous regimen, Simpson suffered a nervous breakdown.

One night there came a fearful crash, in which it seemed to me the very heavens were falling. After retiring to my bed I suddenly seemed to see a strange light blazing before my eyes and then my nerves gave way and I sprang from bed, trembling and almost fainting, and immediately fell into a congestive chill of great violence that almost took my life.[4]

When he returned home his doctor ordered him not to open a book for a year: "Then began a period of mental and physical agony which no language can describe. I seemed possessed with the idea that at three o'clock on some day I was to die, and every day as that hour drew near, I became awfully distracted and watched in agonized suspense till it passed, wondering that I was still alive."[5] Simpson hoped desperately for conversion before what he was sure was his imminent demise. Very much a Calvinist in upbringing, he struggled to attain assurance that he was saved, but no amount of effort seemed to bring it. Nevertheless, the troubled youth had religious resources in his background to draw upon in this emergency. His father, a church elder, was a "good Presbyterian of the old school and the belief in the Shorter Catechism and the doctrine of foreordination and all the conventional rules of a well ordered Presbyterian household." The elder Simpson arose before dawn to read his Bible and to "tarry long at his morning devotions." His son recalled that "the picture filled my soul with a kind of sacred awe."[6]

On Sundays the family had traveled miles by cart to church, or had "sat for hours while father, mother, or one of the children read in turn from some good old book, that was beyond our understanding." Though he recalled feeling a "chill" long afterwards whenever he saw one of these books, he turned to them after he was converted to help guide his spiritual life.[7]

Thus, it seems the basis for Simpson's conversion was set long before he reached his crisis, but first he had to shed some of the determinism of his father's stern Calvinism. By chance he came upon Marshall's *The Gospel Mystery of Salvation,* which instructed him to "believe in the Lord Jesus Christ . . . in spite of your doubts and fears, and you will immediately pass into eternal life, will be justified from all your sins and receive a new heart and all the gracious operations of the Holy Spirit."[8] At long last Simpson could stop struggling. "How often since then has it been my delight to tell poor sinners that they do not need as the old lines say, 'To knock and weep, and watch and wait,' For God is waiting and wondering why we do not open the gate and enter in."[9] On January 19, 1861, at age eighteen, Simpson signed a covenant with God "in which I gave myself wholly to God and took Him for every promised blessing, and especially for the grace and power to use my life for his service and glory."[10] The idea for the covenant came from one of the "chilling" books of his boyhood, Philip Doddridge's classic conversion manual, *Rise and Progress of Religion in the Soul.*

Despite the toll exacted by his emotional and spiritual life, Simpson passed the examination to enter Knox College, Toronto, where he took a ministerial course. At Knox he encountered the first challenge to his strict upbringing. Not that the obvious vices of city life presented any problems; he credited the discipline of his childhood with making him impervious to them. His upbringing, he explained, "threw over my youthful spirit a natural horror to evil things which often afterward safeguarded me when thrown amid the temptations of the world." It was more innocent but nevertheless worldly pleasures, such as oyster suppers with his fellow students, that gave him trouble. As a result, he said, he lost "the sweetness and preciousness of my early piety,"[11] and did not regain them until he had been a minister ten years. His "religious life was chiefly that of duty, with little joy of fellowship, and my motives were intensely ambitious and worldly."[12] He never forgot the deleterious effect of the college environment on his devotional life; in his future school he would strive to protect his students from this kind of worldliness.

During summers Simpson preached in mission churches and stations, and the trials of these early preaching occasions turned him against a highly formal style of sermon delivery. He recalled the terror of the first time he was scheduled to preach in his home church, before his mother and father:

In those days preaching was an awful business, for we knew nothing of trusting the Lord for utterance. The manuscript was written in full and the preacher committed it to memory and recited it verbatim. On this occasion I walked the woods for days before hand, repeating to the trees and squirrels the periods and paragraphs which I had so carefully composed.

> The misfortune sometimes was that the forgetting of a word would blot
> out from the frightened brain of the poor preacher all the matter that
> followed.[13]

Because this method of preaching was not suitable for the evangelist he
would become, it eventually yielded to more extemporaneous styles.

Others must have been impressed by the young man's preaching, however, even if he himself was not, because upon graduation from college
he was called to Knox Church in Hamilton, Ontario, a plum among Cana-
dian churches. There he showed he was not content to lead a quiet and
secure life as pastor of a well-to-do congregation, but rather added 750
members to the rolls, started activities such as prayer meetings and a
women's auxiliary, and, it is said, "sparked his people on to such fervent
missionary-giving as they had not thought possible."[14]

About the time of his first ministerial charge, Simpson married Margaret
Henry. But neither a new wife nor a flourishing pastorate brought peace
of mind; Simpson later recalled his early years in the ministry:

> When I entered ... upon my regular ministry, I knew but little of the
> Holy Ghost and the life of faith and holiness, and while conscientious and
> orthodox in my pastoral work and preaching, and really earnest in my
> spirit, yet I fear, I was seeking to build up a successful church, very much
> in the same spirit as my people were trying to build a successful business.[15]

Apparently his first trip abroad, in summer 1871, while he was at Knox
church, was an attempt to recover from severe depression. He wrote his
wife from Cologne on June 8: "The best thing I find is that my mind
has resumed its old buoyancy and vigour. I can think and talk now and
have got over that mental numbness which made me almost an imbecile
the last two months I was at home, and which I felt like a weight of
lead upon my spirit. I am feeling a returning confidence in my powers
under God."[16] Other letters to his wife during this journey reveal a man
much preoccupied with his physical and emotional health, a man in quest
of more fulfilling—and healing—religious experiences.

In 1873 he moved on to Chestnut Street Church, the largest Presbyterian
church in Louisville, Kentucky. Because of his Old School background,
he had thus far resisted revivalistic methods, but Louisville in the early
1870s bore the scars of Civil War divisions and needed extreme measures.
Simpson initiated a city-wide revival, engaging the well-known evangelist,
D. W. Whittle, to lead it. After that successful effort, Simpson himself
held weekly Sunday night revival meetings in his church. So popular was
he in this role that his congregation built him a two thousand-seat tabernacle in the center of the city. Simpson probably turned to premillennialism
as well as revivalism during his Louisville years. One of his old associates

was of the opinion that he came to know James Brookes, the prominent dispensationalist and Bible teacher, during this period.[17]

In 1879 Simpson accepted a call from the Thirteenth Street Church in New York City. A diary which survives from the first weeks in New York reveals much about Simpson's spiritual state of mind at this time. First, it suggests that he tried to keep himself disengaged from ordinary life, including his family, as much as possible. His wife adamantly opposed the move to New York. Shortly after the family had arrived there, her husband wrote, "Alternate feelings of compassion, tenderness and dreadful pain and even fear about Maggie who is so set in her seeming hatred to me that I can hardly speak to her, and have shut myself up in my Saviour leaving her simply and fully with Him, and praying to be kept perfectly in his way and temper toward her in all things."[18] As his family troubles continued, he exhorted God, "Help me to leave all these cares on Thee—be independent of all natural feelings and filled with God."[19] Three weeks later he prayed, "Far from perfect in my spirit. Ruffled at times. Master keep and lead."[20]

Second, the diary reveals that Simpson, like his friend George Muller and many of his evangelical contemporaries, felt that his Lord would guide his life in a direct and immediate way. Shortly after arriving in New York he encountered difficulties finding a house for his family. Finally, on November 25 he recorded in his diary, "After having committed it to Him to get one for me, led at length to feel he would send me word through the Herald. Went down to advertise."[21] He prayed constantly for ordinary things, from misplaced items and subscriptions to his magazine, to physical strength. "Relying on the Lord" did not always come easily. One night he wrote, "Much burdened all day. Much reproved for letting work drive me. *Lesson—this is God's work.* Never rush. Be still. He will see it all through, neglect nothing else for it. Systematic sleep, quiet spirit and humble obedient confidence. Simple Christian reflection."[22] Despite the turmoil of these early weeks in New York, Simpson characteristically drew strength from a sense of closeness to his Lord: "Jesus has been to me a Husband today and yesterday, and has often ravished my soul with his love. He has strangely given me the sense of begetting or His begetting souls, and I have found the power and prayer of their conversion in the meetings afterwards. We had many conversions today in all the services."[23] On December 23 he complained about attending too many social affairs—"not enough retirement and leisure with God."[24] On another day he rejoiced, "Heard the sweet voice of God today several times and filled with such intense desire to follow anywhere."[25]

If the quest for an ever closer relationship with God was one of the major motifs of Simpson's life, his passion for missions was another. He had looked forward particularly to working in New York because it was the headquarters for American missionary activity. By December 1879 he was already putting together the first issue of a new missionary magazine, *The Gospel in All Lands,* intended to attract a wider audience than existing missionary magazines. Working on the initial issue, he wrote, "I believe the Lord is leading me and will make it easier for illustrations and less elaborate for writing, needing less heavy and labored pieces, and being more simple and popular."[26]

Simpson's intense preoccupation with foreign missions seems to have originated earlier in his life, with a dream, which he recalled in 1894:

> Never shall I forget how, 18 years ago, I was awakened one night from sleep, trembling with a strange and solemn sense of God's overshadowing power, and on my soul was burning the remembrance of a strange dream through which I had that moment come. It seemed to me that I was sitting in a vast auditorium, and millions of people were there sitting around me. All the Christians in the world seemed to be there, and on the platform was a great multitude of faces and forms. They seemed to be mostly Chinese. They were not speaking, but in mute anguish they were wringing their hands, and their faces wore an expression that I can never forget. I had not been thinking or speaking of the Chinese or the heathen world, but as I awoke with that vision on my mind, I did tremble with the Holy Spirit, and I threw myself on my knees, and every fibre of my being answered, "Yes, Lord, I will go."[27]

Simpson had wanted to fulfill this promise to become a China missionary, but his wife refused to accompany him. When he spoke to her of his desire to go to China, she exclaimed in exasperation, "Well Bertie—Go! And heaven be praised if I can rid myself and the children—of a lunatic!"[28]

Thus barred from the foreign fields, Simpson found two outlets for his missionary fervor. First, he turned to strenuous evangelization at home, and, second, he established a training school for others who could become foreign missionaries in his place.

The evangelistic impulse already apparent in Simpson's Louisville revivalism had become so strong by the time he reached New York that he felt troubled even about accepting a settled parish. As he looked ahead to his installation as pastor at Thirteenth Street Church he was plagued by the idea that God might want him to do "a wider work" as an itinerant evangelist rather than to confine himself to one church.[29] Even after he had settled into his duties at Thirteenth Street, he wrote in his diary, "Much thought today about a Christian Evangelization Society in my church to reach the masses. Lord guide."[30] Whether or not he succeeded in organizing such a society at that point is unclear, but it is apparent that with or without formal organization he himself went into the immigrant quarters of the city seeking and winning souls. When he asked that one hundred of his Italian converts be allowed to join the church, his genteel congregation demurred. As Simpson recalled it, "What they wanted was a conventional parish for respectable Christians. What their young pastor wanted was a multitude of publicans and sinners."[31]

Though at the time Simpson reluctantly acceded to his congregation's wishes, the next year perhaps not coincidentally he complained of depression and ill health. In 1881 he heard physician-turned-faith healer, Charles Cullis, at Old Orchard, Maine and was suddenly cured. Then he made a momentous decision: he resigned from Thirteenth Street and withdrew from the Presbyterian ministry.

Friends were convinced he had lost his sanity to thus leave a comfortable church and salary. No doubt his practical-minded wife thought so too, though no record remains of her reactions on this occasion. Simpson's explanation of his action was somewhat contradictory. First, clearly, he no longer believed in infant baptism and thus was turning away from Presbyterian doctrine. Second, he wanted to work with people different from those comfortable Christians who constituted his Thirteenth Street congregation. But just who he thought would make up his future constituency was unclear. In attempting to justify his decision to a disappointed and puzzled congregation at Thirteenth Street, he turned to biblical texts about preaching the gospel to the poor (Luke 4:18 and Mark 16:15). He explained,

> I believe this system in New York of having churches exclusively for the rich and exclusively for the poor is all a mistake, though it be well intended. . . . I believe, too, that our system of financial support is a great hindrance to the success of the Gospel. Under the best management, pew rents keep many people away. Then, I believe that Christians could greatly help if they would come to the house of God in very simple attire, and lay aside all idea of social style. Then in the city of New York are churches where the poor are not wanted, and where even some are told that the church is full, and has all the people it needs.[32]

He suggested measures such as Sunday night meetings in theaters and halls, and house-to-house visitation, to reach people who were not welcome in respectable churches. Elsewhere he commented, "My plan and idea of a church are exemplified in the great London churches of Newman Hall and of [Charles] Spurgeon, comprising thousands of members of no particular class, but of the rich and poor side by side."[33]

But other evidence suggests that Simpson had in mind middle class people who had been raised in a church, but then had fallen away because of boredom and dissatisfaction with the lack of spiritual vitality. He told a *New York Times* reporter that "I have been very impressed with the fact that a vast number of people, even those who have once been church members, cannot be induced to attend an organized church. Having reached hundreds of such persons by preaching for two years in a public hall in Louisville, Ky., I felt that the same work could be done here."[34]

On another occasion he added, "Among the middle classes we were convinced there exists a great necessity for a revival movement of this kind [i.e., the kind he was even then in the process of organizing]."[35] Whatever Simpson intended—whether to reach out to the poor or the middle classes or to both—it seems plain that, like other evangelists, he enjoyed greater success among the latter.

For several years after his break with the past, Simpson held Sunday and weekday services in shifting locations in New York City, building up a devoted following. The early services were simple and brief affairs, in the style of Ira Sankey and Dwight Moody, with gospel songs, a short sermon, and a twenty-minute inquiry meeting afterwards for those who had been moved by the service and wanted help to explore its implications for their lives. At the services, Simpson's assistants sat in the audience, welcoming strangers and appealing to the unsaved. The service was free and there was no solicitation of funds. In 1882 he organized an independent congregation which charged no assessments or pew rents. Following the example of George Muller, he accepted no salary.

The very next action he took after establishing a congregation was to found a school, the New York Missionary Training College for Home and Foreign Missionaries. Even before his break with the Presbyterian Church, Simpson had used an editorial in *The Gospel in All Lands* to argue the necessity of a school to train lay missionaries. Now, with a growing band of followers aflame with their master's missionary zeal and begging to be allowed to serve, the need for some place to train them became all the more pressing. The school opened in 1882, to "a few enthusiastic followers of the founder."[36]

Two years later, in 1884, Simpson introduced a "convention" in Old Orchard, Maine, "to gather Christians of common faith and spirit for fellowship; to study the word of God; to promote a deeper spiritual life [i.e., sanctification] among Christians." This was the first of many national and regional conventions which took place in the following years. The gathering held in 1887 was typical; it lasted ten days and had as its program four days of "teaching and preaching with reference to our spiritual life in Christ," a fifth day devoted to the theme of Christ's coming, a sixth to divine healing, a seventh to "Christian work," and an eighth to foreign missions. From eight to ten each morning, five hundred persons participated in Bible study.[37]

In 1887 Simpson organized his followers into two "alliances," the first focused on work at home and the second on activity abroad. The first, the "Christian Alliance," took as its purpose "the wide diffusion of the Gospel," "the promotion of a deeper and higher Christian life, and the work of evangelization, especially among the neglected classes by highway missions and other practical methods."[38] The second group, the "Evangelical Missionary Alliance," aimed to "use thoroughly consecrated and qualified laymen and Christian women as well as regularly educated ministers" to "send the Gospel ... to the most needy, neglected and open fields of the heathen work."[39] In 1897 these two groups merged to form the Christian and Missionary Alliance.

In 1888 Simpson founded a newspaper, the *Christian Alliance,* editing it until his death in 1921. It contained essays explaining Alliance doctrines, interpretations of Scripture, a column intended for children, testimonies to healing and sanctification from Alliance members, news of Alliance activities and persons, and, above all, information on foreign missions and missionary lands. About the same time as he began the newspaper, Simpson initiated a "Colportage Library" which published, sold, and distributed inexpensive Christian literature. The newspapers and the publishing company worked in tandem, as did the other institutions and agencies; the very first issues of the Alliance paper advertised books available from the Library.

The Christian and Missionary Alliance rapidly went national, as Simpson and his associates launched conventions, local Bible classes, churches, Sunday schools, and missions in every region of the United States. Bible training schools modeled after the first school, the Missionary Training Institute, were established in Toccoa Falls, Georgia; St. Paul; Seattle; Beulah Beach, Ohio; and Boston.[40] Similar schools were planted in the foreign mission fields.

Simpson's was the guiding hand in all these enterprises. He pastored the mother church in New York, edited the Alliance paper, traveled to conventions, fulfilled speaking engagements all over the nation, wrote hymns, authored books on religious topics, and taught at the Missionary Training Institute. Yet despite myriad administrative preoccupations, Simpson does not appear to have shifted much of his energy from spiritual concerns; to judge from accounts, his students at the Training Institute saw him foremost as a model of the consecrated life.

Adoniram Judson Gordon and F. L. Chapell

A. J. Gordon (1836–1895), the founder of the Boston Bible Training School that was to take his name shortly after his death, appears to have been endowed with a more serene temperament than his contemporary and friend, A. B. Simpson. In other respects, however, he adhered to much the same pattern of Protestant piety and activism. He was born in rural New Hampshire and attended Brown College at a time when it possessed a Baptist revivalistic atmosphere. Next he prepared for the ministry at Newton Theological Institution, a Baptist seminary, and then became pastor of a church in Jamaica Plain, at the time a prosperous Boston suburb; in 1869 he advanced to the wealthy Clarendon Street Baptist Church in Back Bay Boston. In both of these churches he experienced what was for him a disconcerting amount of success and popularity; like his friend A. B. Simpson, he felt his congregations judged their pastor's efforts by excessively worldly standards. He balked at the formalism, conventionality, and complacency of his churches, and strove to substitute congregational response and singing for well-trained and well-paid professional musicians. Over the years he stripped down his preaching style, gradually moving from one rich in literary allusions to one that was by comparison biblical and plain. And he railed against fund-raising methods in the church that he claimed took people's minds off God and wheedled from them money they should have contributed freely. He also fought against the system of pew rentals that kept poorer people from becoming church members.

Reform came slowly—pew rentals were abandoned only in 1893—but either Gordon was a more patient man than Simpson or loyalty to his denomination did not collide as badly with his ideals, for he apparently never contemplated leaving the Baptist fold. Indeed, he accomplished much in his twenty-seven years at Clarendon, even by his own high standards. By the time of his death in 1895, his church supported twelve foreign missionaries and twelve local evangelists, whereas it had sustained only one of each before his arrival. Church membership had increased from 358 in 1869 to 1,083 in 1895. In addition, the church under Gordon had taken on many activities characteristic of an institutional church, supporting an "Industrial Temperance Home" for the unemployed, a young people's group, women's missionary organizations, and missions programs directed toward black and Chinese Bostonians.[41]

Many of Gordon's convictions about the role of churches and pastors had grown out of his formative religious experiences. A revival led by Dwight Moody near Clarendon Church in 1877 had reinforced his conviction of the importance of evangelism. He became a close associate of Moody and, beginning in 1880, a participant and speaker at Moody's Northfield, Massachusetts Conferences. (During Moody's absences in 1892 and 1893 he ran the conferences.) As a young pastor, Gordon had embraced premillennialism and from 1878 on he edited the *Watchword,* a paper for those who, like himself, expected the second coming at any moment. In the late 1870s or early 1880s he had apparently undergone sanctification. As a result, he possessed what his son called "the greatest assurance of God's intervention in practical matters."[42] Gordon applied this conviction in the running of the school he started, for an early catalog laconically disposed of the matter of the institution's support, "There is no endowment and no pledged support. Yet the Lord provided."[43] Probably Gordon's strong holiness persuasion helps account for the fact that he avoided theological controversy, setting an example followed by the school's leaders in succeeding decades of doctrinal strife among Protestants.

Gordon, like his friend Simpson, was much exercised about foreign missions and became chairman of the American Baptist Missionary Union, the chief northern Baptist missionary agency, in 1888. At about the same time as he assumed the chairmanship, the Union accepted responsibility for missionary activity in the Congo from British Baptists. This new commitment was not easy to fulfill, for qualified volunteers did not seem to be forthcoming. In 1889, when the British Baptist, H. Grattan Guinness, was touring the United States, arguing the cause of missions, he persuaded Gordon that a "recruiting station" and training place would help start a stream of missionary workers for the Congo. The school—for that was what the two men had in mind—would resemble Guinness' own East London Institute for Home and Foreign Missions, founded in 1872, in purpose and methods. Thus, the Boston Missionary Training School was opened in 1889 in Gordon's church. Gordon, already facing numerous demands upon his time, sought help from F. L. Chapell, a fellow Baptist pastor, who apparently had a special affinity for teaching. "Confiding to him his conception of the work he committed it largely to his hands and trusted to his ability to carry out the details."[44] Gordon became president of the new school, his wife secretary and later treasurer, and Chapell full-time resident instructor.[45]

F. L. Chapell (1836–1900), was born in Waterford, Connecticut, and educated at Yale College and Rochester Theological Seminary, a Baptist institution. Like so many other evangelistic pastors he was a church builder; in Evanston, Illinois, it is said, "he found a new, weak church in an out-of-the-way situation and left a well-organized flourishing body in a handsome and complete building on a main avenue."[46] As pastor of a Flemington, New Jersey, church in the early 1880s, Chapell organized revivals and a temperance crusade. In New Jersey he came into contact with the work of A. B. Simpson's Christian and Missionary Alliance. A premillennialist like most Alliance people, he was also drawn to the Alliance's divine healing tenets.[47] Like Alliance members also, he believed in relying upon God in other areas besides health: "his faith was as large as though he expected everything done for him."[48] Though he remained a Baptist pastor, his ties with the Alliance were strong; he taught at the Missionary Training Institute summers while he was resident instructor at the Boston training school, and served as a member of the Alliance's board of managers.

Gordon died in 1895, only six years after the school's founding; Chapell's passing followed in 1900. Their influence was therefore more limited than that of Simpson, who guided the Missionary Training Institute for almost four decades. Yet the two of them made possible the school's survival during its first few years; shaped its policies according to their missionary, premillennialist and other interests; and Gordon in particular conferred upon it his considerable stature among conservative evangelicals.

Dwight L. Moody

Dwight L. Moody (1837–1899) was an entrepreneur and promoter par excellence, endowed with the ability to recognize and exploit an opportunity. These characteristics were to flourish in the school he set up, the Moody Bible Institute. Though his contemporaries, A. B. Simpson and A. J. Gordon, possessed these talents also, they exercised them in a quieter and less exuberant manner.[49]

Before taking up Christian work, Moody had worked as a shoe salesman. Like many of his contemporaries, he had abandoned the limited opportunities of small town life for the big city, leaving his native Northfield, Massachusetts for Boston as a young man. After a period selling shoes in his uncle's Boston store, he had migrated to the developing town of Chicago, hoping there to make his fortune. A zealous salesman, he had indeed done very well. "When customers did not readily appear in the store he would stand outside, or even walk the streets, hoping to drum up trade."[50]

Then abruptly at the end of four years in Chicago, he abandoned business for full-time Christian work. But he did not forget what he had learned as a salesman, bringing the same organizing and promoting talents to his efforts for his Lord. He started a Sunday school in a poor immigrant section of Chicago. In recruiting students for the school, he sometimes stayed on the streets until ten or eleven at night looking for prospective pupils. For the parents of his pupils he organized prayer meetings and evening classes "in the common English branches."[51] Displaying a characteristic expansiveness, he wrote, "I have the best school there is in the West, anyway it is the largest school there is this side of New York."[52]

When it turned out that his Sunday school pupils and their parents were unwelcome in conventional middle-class churches, Moody organized and pastored a new, more informal church. And in 1865 he became president of the Chicago Young Men's Christian Association. But as in the case of Gordon and Simpson all this success had an unhappy side. In the midst of these achievements, he began to wrestle with worldly ambition in much the same manner as they; an acquaintance recalled, "He had become mixed up with building Farwell Hall [the Chicago YMCA building] and was on committees for every kind of work and in his ambition to make his enterprises succeed because they were his had taken his eyes off the Lord and had been burdened in soul and unfruitful in his work for months. He longed for deliverance."[53] Evidently this crisis was resolved by the experience of a second conversion in 1871.

In 1873 Moody began the widely acclaimed evangelistic tour of Great Britain that was to catapult him into fame and mass revivalism in his own country. After he returned home he conducted giant meetings in every large city of the United States. By the 1880s, however, the American appetite for religious revivals on a grand scale had slackened somewhat, and Moody himself began to doubt the efficacy of mass meetings that were not followed up by less dramatic, day-to-day work. Perhaps he also realized that he was reaching mostly a middle class audience, rather than the working classes he had hoped for. As a result, he seems to have lessened his emphasis on mass evangelism and to have turned to other vehicles for reaching "the masses." He broached, for instance, the idea of a body of lay Christian workers—"gap-men"—trained but not over-educated, who could labor among the unchurched and unconverted in the large cities.

Moody was given to the large and sweeping vision; details sometimes bored him. Often others had to execute his visions. In the case of Moody Bible Institute, the early executor was a woman, Emma Dryer, who was the principal of the Illinois State Normal University until the Chicago fire of 1871 drew her to works of mercy in Chicago. With Moody's encouragement she conducted a "Bible Work" there during the 1870s and early 1880s. Dryer's efforts had many facets, one of which was to train women as Bible teachers and city missionaries.[54]

By 1886 Moody had determined to expand the "Bible Work" if he could find the funds. In that year he issued a challenge to the citizens of Chicago to raise $250,000 for the purpose of training lay workers, explaining the need for such training:

> I believe we have got to have gap-men—men who are trained to do city mission work. Every city mission in this country and Europe has been almost a failure ... because the men are not trained. If a man fails at anything put him in city mission work. We need the men that have the most character to go into the shops and meet these hardhearted infidels and skeptics. They have got to know the people and what we want is men who ... go right into the shop and talk to men. Never mind the Greek and Hebrew, give them plain English and good Scripture. It is the Sword of the Lord that cuts deep. If you have men trained for that kind of work, there is no trouble about reaching the men who do not go into the church.[55]

The $250,000 was raised and in 1887 the Chicago Evangelization Society was organized to conduct a series of brief training institutes. In 1889 these successful efforts were expanded to a year-round program called the "Bible Institute for Home and Foreign Missions."[56]

Moody, ever the salesman, set the tone for the new institution. Writing in 1889 to members of the Chicago Evangelization Society, he exhorted,

> I see you have got the training school advertised now I want you to get it into all the papers you can and let it go the length and breth [sic] of the country and say if men and women will give a little time to training they can find plenty of fields to work in and let it be known that all can

come and the teaching will be something like the conference at Northfield but let it be pushed for all it is worth.[57]

Moody's aggressive approach to selling the Christian message, his optimistic boosterism, and his determination to reach wider and wider numbers of people by any methods at his disposal, set the tone for his Bible school, for the Bible school movement in general, and for fundamentalism as a whole. Though he was not the sole source of these elements, he was a major contributor.

Moody did not originate the idea of brief training for lay workers to achieve missionary goals. As we shall see, the idea was common currency in the late nineteenth century. And the basic institutional form was already in place before he began talking about training "gap-men." Other conservative evangelicals—Gordon and Simpson, for example—were employing it to teach the Bible and to transmit evangelistic skills at the same time he was. But Moody was easily the most renowned of the Bible school founders, and therefore his choice of the institution as the training ground for lay Christian workers gave it a visibility and a legitimacy it would otherwise have lacked.

V

BEGINNINGS
THE RELIGIOUS TRAINING SCHOOLS

When late nineteenth century Protestant leaders such as Simpson, Gordon, and Moody turned their attention to founding schools for the training of lay people in Bible knowledge and evangelistic methods, they usually had in mind as models certain European institutions that trained missionaries and other religious workers. The conservatives were not alone in their admiration of the European Schools. American Protestants of diverse persuasions—motivated by a common interest in missions—acclaimed the European schools for being fast, effective, and practical, and began establishing similar institutions in the United States. The first known American school of this type was the Baptist Missionary Training School for women (1881), in Chicago. The earliest Bible training schools—Simpson's Missionary Training Institute, Moody's Bible Institute, and Gordon's Boston Missionary Training School—followed shortly afterward, between 1882 and 1889.

Observers did not usually differentiate the early Bible schools from the more general group of American religious training schools. Even as late as the teens, Moody Bible Institute and Bible Institute of Los Angeles (1908), for example, typically figured in surveys of training schools, despite the phrase "Bible institute" in their names.

At least as early as 1888, A. B. Simpson had recognized the existence of the new religious training movement, in which he located his own school. In an article entitled "Missionary Training Colleges," he offered a definition of the type of religious training school that was just emerging upon the American scene. Missionary training colleges, he said, were "Institutions less technical and elaborate than the ordinary theological seminary, and designed to afford the same specific preparation for direct missionary work, and to meet the wants of that large class, both men and women, who do not wish formal ministerial preparation, but an immediate equipment for usefulness as lay workers."[1] He went on to refer to several such institutions in Europe and England and also a handful of fledgling schools that had been started in the United States earlier in the decade.

The first European religious training schools had appeared before the mid-nineteenth century. Undoubtedly they had a high mortality rate; many disappeared shortly after their founding, leaving little or no record. But certain successful schools survived to become well known to American missionary leaders, receiving frequent mention in books and articles on this side of the Atlantic. In fact, it seems that occasionally leaders of these European training schools could effectively appeal to Americans for funds which were not forthcoming closer to home.[2]

Among the celebrated European schools, none drew more frequent attention than the East London Institute for Home and Foreign Missions, established in 1872 by the Baptist clergyman, H. Grattan Guinness, and his wife. Guinness, through his trips to the United States and through the visits of Americans to England, wielded great influence upon Bible school founders such as A. B. Simpson, A. J. Gordon, and others. Gordon, of course, had founded his own training school in consultation with Guinness; Simpson as a young man had heard Guinness preach and had been much impressed by his activities. In 1888 Simpson hailed Guinness's institution as "the most widely known" of the missionary training colleges, claiming that it "has already sent out several hundred most honored laborers to every part of the foreign field; and has practically originated the Central African and North African missions, . . ."[3] Another much admired institution was the Pastors' College founded in the 1850s by the celebrated conservative English Baptist preacher, Charles Haddon Spurgeon. He designed his college for dedicated and devout young men who had been preaching for at least two years, but who had not had adequate opportunities for schooling or sufficient money to make up their educational deficiencies. At a time when educational qualifications and financial means were generally required at other English Baptist colleges, even the semi-literate and the indigent found welcome at Spurgeon's College.[4] An American premillennialist and missionary leader, A. T. Pierson, wrote that "Spurgeon, working on an independent basis, sends out from his own college, in thirty years, nearly a thousand ministers, missionaries, and evangelists, after one to three years of study."[5]

American missionary literature also expressed amazement at the accomplishments of two German pastors, Johannes Gossner (1773–1858) and Louis Harms (1808–1865). Neither of these men maintained a regular school, but rather each offered brief informal missionary training. A. J. Gordon praised Harms:

> Pastor Harms, of Germany, because he could get no sympathy from men in his missionary idea, was constrained to turn his own peasant church of Hermannsburg into a missionary society. He was appalled at the greatness of his undertaking; . . . [but] His church of poor artisans and farmers took up the work in prayerful co-operation with their pastor; and at the end of forty years they have put into the foreign field more than three hundred fifty missionaries, supporting them in their work, and building a ship for transporting them to and from the field; and they had nearly fourteen thousand living communicants whom they had won from heathenism.[6]

Of Gossner, Gordon reported, "He sent out and maintained one hundred and forty-one missionaries—two hundred including the wives of those married—who did a work among the heathen second to none."[7]

Gordon also praised the training school Johanneum, conducted by Theodor Christlieb in Bonn:

> Professor Christlieb sorrowfully recognized the fact that the German clergy, with all their high culture, were utterly failing to reach the lower classes, especially in the great cities. Therefore he conceived the idea of calling into service plain men—artisans, clerks, and laborers—who, with a simple knowledge of Scripture, might be able to address these people in their own dialect. He gave himself to the work of raising up such a class, teaching theology in the university, and at the same time humbling himself to instruct in the Bible these lay workers.[8]

American missionary leaders also drew inspiration from the particular group of training institutions established for the preparation of deaconesses, where training was brief, practical, and spiritually lively. The progenitor of all nineteenth century deaconess training institutions was Kaiserswerth, founded in 1836 by a German Lutheran pastor. But, perhaps because they traveled frequently to Great Britain, American missionary leaders referred most often to the Mildmay institutions set up in the mid-nineteenth century near London. Mildmay included a conference center, a deaconess training school, and a zenana training school. Gordon and his wife toured Mildmay in 1888; A. B. Simpson may well have done so on a trip to England; certainly he was acquainted with the Mildmay activities and spoke highly of them. The influence of Mildmay's example is particularly clear, however, in the case of Moody Bible Institute. Dwight Moody had become familiar with Mildmay during his travels in the British Isles and kept that model in mind when he conferred with his co-worker, Emma Dryer, about the educational activities in Chicago which were to culminate in the Bible Institute. Dryer herself spent time observing at Mildmay during 1879.[9]

Other lesser-known European schools received occasional mention. Simpson in 1888 referred to Chrischona Institute in Basel, to a school conducted by "Dr. Kraft" in Berlin, and to some unnamed training institutions in Denmark and Sweden. He praised particularly a "training college" in Bethshan, England, presided over by a Mrs. Baxter. The school, which had been founded three years earlier, enrolled fourteen students. Simpson found this school much like his own in its "happy, simple life—the same fellowship, the same gathering around the mercy seat after the evening meal, the intercourse and prayers so alike."[10]

Supporters of the European schools had a well-developed rationale for their existence, from which American advocates borrowed. They typically started by pointing to the lack of Christian workers, particularly in foreign missions. "Look at the largeness of the field," ran the typical lament, "and the fewness of the labourers in it. Is it to be hoped that this great harvest will ever be gathered in?"[11] The goal of the training schools was to help supply this lack, by recruiting and preparing workers for missions and other forms of Christian endeavor. The particular value of these schools, according to publicists, was that they drew prospective workers who—though dedicated and zealous—would ordinarily have been discouraged from entering such work by lack of education and the refusal of official church missionary agencies to accept them. The special advantage of such workers, in addition to their more than ordinary zeal, was supposed to be the fact that they came from "the masses"—the laboring classes—and therefore could be expected to function more effectively among their own people at home and among the unlettered and unchristian on the mission fields than the better educated, upper class missionaries. Proper subordination was to be observed, of course; the graduates of training schools, in theory at least, were to serve as assistants to missionaries and pastors, or in other auxiliary positions such as colporteurs and catechists. In addition to their religious work they could be expected to ply whatever trade they had learned prior to their missionary training and therefore would largely support themselves.

For the most part the European training school abandoned the language-oriented classical curriculum—standard in European education of the time—in favor of Bible study, usually in the vernacular, and the acquisition of skills such as preaching, catechizing, and methods of evangelizing the unchurched and the unchristian. The principal of the Pilgrim Institution of St. Chrischona, a Swiss training school, described his curriculum at mid-century:

> The Institution has hitherto paid no regard to the study of the classics, but only to the study of modern languages. The chief reason for that course of study lies in the persuasion of such Christian friends as deem it desirable that young men should be prepared for the service of the Church on a plan less scientific, in point of philology, than that which is generally pursued in the education of youths purposing to enter the ministry—without leading them through all the toilsome and expensive soil of the ancient heathen classics; and yet a plan not only Scriptural, but solid enough to encourage the hope, that youths thus educated may become useful labourers in the Lord's vineyard.[12]

Equal in importance to the acquisition of knowledge and skills that went on at the European training schools was the cultivation of student piety and missionary enthusiasm. At Chrischona, students were encouraged to gather in groups of two or three or more for prayer during their free time. Each Thursday and Sunday evening they met in a "conference" "for the furtherance of brotherly union and sanctification," "in which every brother is expected to open his heart freely, in a brotherly and evangelical spirit." Saturday evening was devoted to a missionary meeting "to nourish the spirit of missions, and to keep up a proper knowledge of missionary operations, . . ." On Sundays students meditated, read scripture, visited the sick and poor, and of course went to church. Each weekday they attended both morning and evening services.[13]

Most of the European arguments for the virtues of the training school were taken over by Americans, who often employed the same rhetoric of urgency about the size of the potential missionary "harvest," the need for many more laborers, and the necessity to provide training for those who would ordinarily have received no preparation. For instance, A. T. Pierson, in his 1886 book, *The Crisis of Missions,* advanced the plea for foreign missions; he declared the need for a "grand campaign for Christ" and "the immediate occupation of all unoccupied fields."[14] At home, Dwight Moody lamented over the "hundreds of families in cities . . . never coming in contact with churches or their representatives,"[15] and warned of the cataclysm to come if nothing were done: "Either these people are to be evangelized or the leaven of communism and infidelity will assume such enormous proportions that it will break out in a reign of terror such as this country has never known."[16]

The chief obstacle to the fulfillment of the vision of a converted world and a harmonious and Christian America appeared to be the lack of trained workers. Pierson had figured that at present each trained missionary must "assume an average responsibility of one hundred thousand souls," an impossible task.[17] And Moody had written in the 1880s, "Many city pastors have asked me to find laymen for them who would be skilled helpers in the Sunday-school and mission work; but I could not do it, for there was no school to train them. The call for such men is greater today then ever."[18]

All those who pointed to the desperate need for "laborers" assumed the existence of a pool of potential recruits who were eager to serve the cause of missions but were blocked from doing so by their inability to afford the long and expensive education consisting of high school or academy, college, and seminary. Pierson put it this way:

> a pastor whose heart and tongue are on fire urges the claims of a lost world, and there are a few who respond, "Here I am, send me"; but they are generally for the most part from the poorer and less-educated classes. . . . The few dormant consciences that do awake under our appeal are generally found in people to whom wealth and learning do not open attractive doors at home. How disheartening, when one offers to go to these regions to be told at the outset that from five to ten years must be spent in preparation.[19]

A writer in the *Baptist Quarterly Review* championed "many a devout candidate who has long felt the call to mission service, but whose heart until now has failed him because so often told, 'None but regulars need apply.'"[20] And A. J. Gordon in his capacity as head of the American Baptist Missionary Union reflected, "I think of those whom we hesitated over and at first rejected because of a want of the qualifications which we considered of first importance. And then to see how God has rebuked us by showing how wonderfully he could use them."[21]

So a broad call went forth for trained lay people. Moody issued his famous plea for "gap-men to stand between the laity and the ministers."[22] A Baptist writer pronounced, "this is the age of laic activity in spiritual things,"[23] and Cyrus Ingersoll Scofield echoed, "This is a layman's age."[24] A. J. Gordon wanted "to call out our reserves—to put into the field a large force of *lay* workers."[25] A. B. Simpson asked for "irregulars," saying "God is building windows for the cathedrals of the skies out of the rejected lives and fragments of consecrated service for which the wisdom of the world has not room."[26] Methodist Sunday school teacher and leader Lucy Rider Meyer spoke anxiously of the need for lay religious workers who knew their Bible to staff the Sunday schools.[27] Even the biblical scholar Charles A. Briggs of Union Seminary, New York, not known for his populist sentiments, pointed out the need for trained lay people:

> The evangelization of our cities, of our outlying populations, and of the heathen world is the greatest religious problem of our time. We need an enormous army of evangelists for this task. It is impossible to train them all in theological courses of our seminaries. We must either have new institutions for the purpose, or our theological seminaries should have sufficient elasticity to adapt themselves to the work.[28]

What part of the population were these lay people to come from? From the romantic rhetoric one would have expected them to come from the farm and factory—"men from the anvil and the plow, from the carpenter's shop and the shoemaker's bench, in short, from all the crafts and callings in which the humble poor pursue their daily toil," as one writer described them. He continued his plea on behalf of those who

> are utterly barred by their social situations and limited culture from our higher institutions of learning. There are large numbers among the toiling masses of our people who possess intellectual aptness, good health and a strong desire to labor for the salvation of souls, who are kept back by the feeling that they are not qualified to tell men the good tidings of good which they have tested and in which they glory.[29]

But the reality diverged from the rhetoric. Actually the "recruits" for home and foreign missions training usually hailed from the middle or lower middle classes. Such skills as they brought with them from the workaday world were more likely to have been acquired from their experiences as salesmen, store clerks, teachers, secretaries, skilled craftsmen, and small businessmen, than from manual toil in factories and shops. True, training school students often were not particularly well educated by present-day standards, but then, in the late nineteenth century, very few Americans were graduating from high school, let alone from colleges and seminaries.[30] The class-conscious language about training school students as "humble" and "poor" members of the laboring class, able to support themselves on the mission field by honest manual toil, may have applied to Europe, where it originated; but, however inaccurate on the American scene, it had its uses, appealing to Protestants who had begun to worry about the increasing alienation from the Protestant churches of what they called the "laboring masses."

In point of fact, the most easily identifiable group of potential workers was women. The first known United States missionary training school, the Baptist Missionary Training School in Chicago, was established for women, and most training schools admitted women. (This was at a time when women were barred from the vast majority of seminaries.)

Over the decades of the nineteenth century, women had proved themselves effective workers in religious causes. Before the Civil War they had organized local and regional foreign missionary societies; after the war they had expanded and consolidated these smaller societies into nationwide denominational organizations which paralleled the male-run ones. Through this missionary activity, the women facilitated the recruitment, training, and sending of the first unmarried women as foreign missionaries. In the post-Civil War decades, women—Lutheran, Episcopal, and Methodist particularly—sought vocations as deaconesses, serving as nurses in hospitals, as pastors' assistants, and as workers in city missions. Women did not need to put on the deaconess garb, however, in order to enter various kinds of religious work; they became Sunday school teachers and superintendents, at first dominating the new field of religious education; settlement workers; Bible teachers; evangelists; church visitors and church secretaries; YWCA workers; missionaries; and church musicians. The opportunities in Protestantism for women's usefulness seemed to be almost unlimited. But all these callings demanded more skills, more knowledge, and more training, which for the most part theological seminaries were unprepared to give women.[31]

If American lay men and women were to be quickly readied in sufficient numbers for the struggle ahead, a different kind of education was called for. First, it must be abbreviated. Said Pierson, "If we would largely increase the missionary force, we must in some way lessen the time and cost of the preparation of the average workman."[32] The first schools which set out to train home and foreign missionaries required only one or two years of attendance, occasionally even less. In addition to turning out the troops fast, the shortness of training was also intended to keep up their ardor. One of Pierson's arguments for a shorter training time was that "We have often observed that the seven years of our college and seminary life not infrequently leave candidates with a chronic chill. Long withdrawal from active work, and absorption in mere study, are not favorable to burning zeal. Intellectual standards often displace the higher spiritual ideals."[33]

This cry for brevity did not go uncontested. A. J. Gordon was criticized for "short cut" methods in his Boston Missionary Training School, opened in 1889.[34] The leaders of the Student Volunteer Movement generally favored college-educated missionaries, while the work at most training schools was below the college level. John R. Mott of the SVM cautioned, "The ultimate success of the missionary enterprise does not depend primarily upon vast numbers of missionaries so much as upon thoroughly furnished missionaries."[35] Nevertheless, despite the skepticism in some quarters, the assumption prevailed generally that there was more than enough work to occupy all helpers of good will, whatever the extent of their educational background, and the founding of training schools continued well into the second decade of the twentieth century.

Another watchword of the new education was that it should be "practical." Practicality had a particularly American ring. It demanded that classroom teaching concentrate only on those attainments which students needed for their missionary work. Liberal or general education was considered an unwanted extravagance given the exigencies of the time. Practicality also dictated that students were to get plenty of actual experience in service to the poor, the immigrant, and the criminal.

Because the new kind of education was briefer and more to the point, its supporters could claim that it was more efficient. The pervasive enthusiasm for "efficiency" in the late nineteenth and early twentieth centuries reflected the almost universal admiration of businessmen and business methods. Said Pierson, "A spirit of concentrated enterprise should apply to this giant problem [faced by missionaries] the best and soundest business principles; a system should be designed which shall prevent waste of time, money and men, and economize and administer all the available force of the Church."[36] Efficient training of religious workers meant that they were to be taught only what they needed to know in order to perform their functions quickly and confidently.

All these elements—brevity, practicality, efficiency—were summed up in the word "training." What "training" involved in part was a revolt against the older classical learning, a revolt which was in progress elsewhere in education. Nothing was inherently wrong with learning Latin, Greek, and Hebrew and with reading classical literature; many of the training school founders had themselves received classical educations. But it was not appropriate for recruits to the mission fields; it took too long and sometimes dulled their zeal. A. B. Simpson in 1897 described what he considered the older kinds of education: "How often it is merely intellectual, scholastic, traditional and many of us have found by sad experience that God has to put us to school again to unlearn what man had crammed into our brains."[37] Pierson also spoke against it. On the mission field, he said,

> Men who have no college diploma, and could not furnish that supreme test of scholarship, the "Latin essay," if found capable, willing, and winning are licensed and ordained. . . . Facts show that scholastic training is not necessary for effective service. There are scores of heroic men doing valiant battle for the Lord and the faith, who never were in college or seminary.[38]

And Moody warned that "ministers are educated away from" the people they should be attempting to reach. A boy, he said,

> is kept at school until he is ready to go to college and then to college, and from college to theological seminary, and the result is he comes out of a theological seminary knowing nothing about human nature, doesn't know how to rub up to these men and adapt himself to them, and then gets up a sermon on metaphysical subjects miles above these people. . . . What we want is men trained for this class of people.[39]

Here again, rhetoric did not always match reality. Rudimentary Greek, Latin, or Hebrew instruction sometimes crept into the most elementary training school curriculum if there was someone willing to teach it, for it persisted even among the most zealous evangelicals as the mark of a thoroughly educated person.

For all their anticlassicism it should not be assumed that the new breed of educators opposed longer and better training when it was feasible. Nor did they judge that the theological seminaries had outlived their day. On the contrary, despite their criticisms, they still felt the seminaries should and would continue to turn out most of the leaders of the church. They simply wanted to open up other shorter, more accessible avenues to Christian service, and feared that the church would forfeit potentially valuable gifts and talents by rigidly insisting on a long course of instruction.

The Missionary Training School in America

The missionary or religious training schools served a variety of sponsoring groups with diverse purposes, but they all shared certain characteristics. First, their main goal was to equip workers for home and foreign missions. Second, whatever other skills they taught, they made a thorough acquaintance with the Bible central to their purposes. Third, the training schools shared a distinct constituency: women who were not admitted to seminaries or were not admitted on equal terms with men (women made up the majority in the training school student population); and lay men who did not desire ordination or who did seek ordination, but belonged to denominations not requiring the full four years of college and three years of seminary. Often lay men had received the call to Christian service late in life.

The little corps of men and women who turned to the training schools at the turn of the century were of disparate educational backgrounds, and the school leaders recognized this by providing a variety of routes for those with college, high school, or only grammar school educations. Training school graduation might mean earning a certificate, a diploma, or, later on, a degree (usually a bachelor of religious education, or of missions, or of theology). No onus attached to those who dropped in and out. Finally, brevity was a training school hallmark: the student should not get entangled in what Jane Addams called the "snare of preparation," and thus be kept unduly long from the mission field until all fervor had been burned out.[40]

Because of their practicality, flexibility, and brevity, the training schools answered the pressing needs of new religious groups at the turn of the century for skilled workers. Thus, the Christian and Missionary Alliance depended on A. B. Simpson's Missionary Training Institute to turn out home and foreign missionaries quickly; the YMCA secured trained organizers from its two-year school in Springfield, Massachusetts; and the Salvation Army sent "cadets" to its "garrisons" for six-month training periods. By purporting to teach special skills needed by deaconesses, Sunday school teachers, Y workers, church musicians, Bible teachers, lay foreign missionaries, pastors' assistants, and church secretaries, the training schools also fostered new roles for lay Christian workers, and gave more substance to old and familiar ones. In general, the seminaries, intent on the education of ministers, lagged behind training schools in introducing preparation for lay positions in the church.

Study of the English Bible headed almost every training school curriculum. That version was taught as a matter of principle, for it enabled students to grasp the whole of scriptures and encouraged them to preach or teach the English Bible rather than to strive to sound learned by means of a sprinkling of Greek and Hebrew terms. Next in importance came practical experience, in activities such as settlement work or conducting street meetings. Training in "evangelistic," "revival," or "personal work" methods was common. Such courses as sociology or training in social work, pedagogy, foreign missions, church or sacred music almost always appeared in the catalogs, though under a variety of designations. In addition, some schools offered special "how to" courses in medicine, nursing, bookkeeping, handcrafts, and domestic science.

Many courses such as those mentioned above had not appeared in the theological curriculum before. In this sense, training schools pioneered in the field of religious education—however rudimentary a training school course in "sociology" or "pedagogy" might appear compared with later standards. But the pioneering grew out of judgments about the needs of new constituencies and new missionary fields, not out of any interest in curricular innovation for its own sake. In fact, training school curricula tended to include a number of old and traditional theological offerings. Side by side with the novel skills classes, training school catalogs listed subjects old-fashioned enough to have appeared in theological seminaries and colleges of the 1850s and before—for example, "Christian evidences" (natural theology), apologetics, and personal ethics. And despite the importance of the English Bible, study of Greek, Latin, and Hebrew occasionally cropped up, especially when the training of pastors was attempted.

Theology and doctrine received greater emphasis in the conservative schools than in the rest of the training school group. The more "liberal" schools—most of the training schools for women and the YMCA school at Springfield, for instance—showed greater interest in the emerging social sciences and also in areas connected with social Christianity, such as "social ethics" and immigrant problems.

At most schools an informal curriculum coexisted with the formal one. Students schooled themselves in the piety of faith and good works as much as in pedagogy and methods of missions. They met in prayer meetings; listened to missionaries on furlough; perused letters from their peers who had preceded them to the mission fields; received support from each other during spiritual crises; and regaled each other with accounts of their trials and triumphs in city mission and settlement house activities. The faculty encouraged and participated in this strenuous and dedicated atmosphere.

The faculty generally taught part-time, with the exception of the founder or head of the school, and perhaps one main instructor. They were often underpaid or unpaid, and frequently had some other calling in addition to their teaching, such as the ministry or public school teaching; some were former missionaries. They often did not hold college degrees, let alone graduate ones. Most teaching staffs, particularly in the training schools for women, included an unusually high proportion of women. These female teachers had often graduated from normal or religious training schools; frequently they were alumnae of the training schools where they now taught.

Training Schools and Theological Seminaries

In their rhetoric at least, most early Bible school or training school founders and leaders regarded their institutions as complements rather than as competitors to theological seminaries. Bible and training schools, they claimed, were serving a different kind of student: lay men and women, who would not ordinarily have attended a seminary anyway. A. J. Gordon in founding the Boston Missionary Training School denied any intention of competing with theological seminaries or colleges, and took pains to emphasize the low social, economic, and educational status of the training school students:

So far from intending to interfere with any higher schools of Biblical learning, or to encourage a short-cut into the ministry, the work was undertaken
solely for the benefit of such as could not, by any possibility, avail themselves
of these advantages; . . . the distinct purpose of all these schools is to recruit
men for missionary service who could not otherwise get any preparation.
The applicants for admission have come from the carpenter's bench, from
the painter's pot, from the tailor's shop, some of them confessing to a desire
which had burdened them for years to give themselves to missionary service,
but seeing no chance for themselves till this door opened. They are all
poor, and have undertaken, while emerged in study, to work for their board
in such places as the [Bowdoin] Tabernacle Office may furnish them.[41]

The training school graduates would perform at a modest if indispensable
level—rather than becoming theologians or accomplished preachers they
would be "men and women, who know enough of their Bible to lead
souls to Christ, and to instruct converts in the simple principles of the
gospel." Because of their humble background and preparation, they
"would consent to go on a limited salary," and thus help conserve the
scarce resources of most missionary boards. Furthermore, Gordon emphasized that he was not underestimating the value of advanced education;
he would be glad, he said, if some of the most able training school students
eventually wound up going on to a seminary or college course; he intended
"to test them by a year's experience in mission work, and if we find those
whose age and circumstances warrant them in going to college or seminary,
to help them in their way thither; and to give to others the best practical
and biblical instruction we can."[42] The founders of the Bible Institute of
Los Angeles made a similar argument: they

believed there were young men and women desirous of engaging in the
various forms of Christian activity who had been denied advanced educational privileges. Without discounting the desirability of such training where
possible, it was nevertheless felt that a wide field of usefulness could be
made available to these young people by providing such facilities for training
as would fit them by a few years of intensive work under qualified, experienced teachers, to engage in labors suited to their varying abilities.[43]

It is unlikely that distrustful seminary educators and supporters were
greatly mollified by protestations such as Gordon's, and probably they
were justified in their skepticism. First, training or Bible school leaders,
whether intentionally or not, often exaggerated the low social, economic,
and educational status of their students. It is not clear that the pool
of prospective students for seminaries and training schools was quite
as distinct as training school proponents argued—except in the case of
women (and even this circumstance gradually changed as theological
seminaries incorporated the field of religious education into their curricula, thereby opening their institutions to female students). Second, de-

spite the avowal of many early Bible school leaders that they were training lay workers rather than ministers, in fact would-be pastors did use them as routes to the ministry, especially in denominations with lenient educational requirements for ordination. Much to the dismay of denominational leaders, for example, scores of Baptists—including Southern Baptists— chose Moody Bible Institute as a path into the ministry, or, if they were already pastors, used their attendance there to strengthen their credentials and augment their knowledge. From the Baptist point of view not only were pastors being trained in inferior institutions; perhaps even worse, they were being prepared in *non-Baptist* institutions. Third, the very existence of the training schools was often understood—probably correctly—as veiled criticism of theological seminaries—for emphasizing the "academic" at the expense of the practical, for deadening the spiritual lives of their students, and for shutting out worthy students who if given the chance might have contributed greatly to the missionary effort. (Such criticisms of the seminaries were quite common at the turn of the century and did not come solely from training school advocates.) The competition-with-seminaries theme is particularly resonant in the history of Gordon's training school. Gordon himself had more misgivings about the effectiveness of theological seminaries than he cared to admit to certain audiences; on one occasion at least he had criticized the seminaries quite sharply:

> Here, I solemnly conceive, is one of the most serious perils to which our Protestant ministry is exposed to-day, viz., that it shall be impoverished by excess of learning, and that it shall attach the first importance to German learning and to Greek philosophy, instead of going forth with the humble equipment of the Word of God. I am perpetually chagrined to see how much better many of the unschooled lay preachers of our time can handle the Scriptures than many clergymen who have passed through the theological curriculum. I do not undervalue the seminary in saying this, but beg that we should consider the point at which it is most conspicuously failing. I wish, for one, that no more chairs might be endowed in our theological institutions for teaching the relations of Christianity to science; that those courses in polemics, which stuff men's heads full of the history of all the heresies which have afflicted the church from the beginning, might be shortened more and more, and that the time thus saved might be given to studying the Bible and practising with the "sword of the spirit."[44]

In light of this sentiment it is hard not to see the Gordon school as in some sense an alternative to seminaries, or at the very least as a prod to them to do better.

Whatever Gordon himself may have intended, many Baptist leaders certainly interpreted the Gordon school as a threat to the strength and prestige of existing Baptist theological seminaries. Even those who freely admitted that the seminaries lagged behind in meeting new religious train-

ing needs feared that the existence of the schools like Gordon's would
sap any dawning seminary impulse toward reform.

The suggestion of competition implicit in A. J. Gordon's comments
above grew stronger later on (1907) after the Gordon school was affiliated
with Newton Theological Institution. It is clear that the Gordon school
used the affiliation to raise its academic sights. Its 1909–10 catalog asserted
that its "position with a great theological school behind it, and the interest
which many prominent friends take in it, make possible a level of instruction worthy in many respects of a theological seminary."[45] The arrangement between the two schools broke down in 1914; part of the reason
for the split was Newton's resentment over the Gordon school's expanding
role in the training of Baptist ministers. (Widening theological differences
also came into play.) Apparently before the rupture, a leader at Newton
had urged the Gordon school to limit itself to women students, probably
on the model of the missionary training school for women that existed
in conjunction with the Southern Baptist Theological Seminary in Louisville, Kentucky. The suggestion was self-serving; such a change would
have safely curtailed the Gordon school's movement toward training for
the ministry, thoroughly subordinating it to Newton and eliminating it
as a rival. Not surprisingly, Gordon leaders rejected this proposal and
went their own way.

By the teens and twenties many Bible and training schools such as Gordon had begun openly training pastors in three-year "Pastoral Courses."
Even earlier than these decades, some schools had taught subjects smack-
ing strongly of ministerial preparation. In 1885, for instance, only three
years after its founding, the Missionary Training Institute included "Pastoral Theology" in its curriculum. Training and Bible school leaders may
honestly not have seen themselves in competition with seminaries, but
their schools were certainly attempting to perform many of the same functions as the older institutions.

Within fundamentalism, it should be noted, the theme of competition
was muted, especially by the twenties, by the fact that there simply were
not many theological seminaries for the Bible schools to be seen in competition *with*. Nevertheless, the possibilities for tension between Bible schools
and seminaries were there and have tended to surface in recent years;
in the eyes of many, Bible schools have represented an orientation toward
practice, evangelistic zeal, and lively faith, whereas fundamentalist seminaries have sometimes attracted the age-old charge of being overly concerned with scholarship and too little occupied with spiritual vitality or
evangelistic effectiveness. When a new Nazarene Bible school was founded
in the early 1970s, the first such school in this denomination, the understanding was that it was to produce a different kind of graduate, more
devout and more activist than those who had come out of the longer-
established Nazarene theological seminary.

Continuing the Training School Tradition

Until about 1920, no hard and fast division separated a "training school" from a "Bible school" or "Bible institute." In the 1920s and 1930s, however, the Bible schools emerged decisively as a group of institutions distinct from the general category of religious training schools (see the list of Bible schools following this chapter). One reason for this emergence is that Bible schools simply turned out to be survivors, while most other training schools either closed down or ceased to exist in recognizable form. These yielded either to financial hardship, particularly during the Great Depression, or to waning interest in foreign missions in their supporting denominations, or to sharply reduced funding for religious education. Some training schools failed when their major functions were duplicated by the theological seminaries, as after 1910 more and more of the latter reformed their curricula to offer studies outside the group of traditional ministerial subjects, and enrolled women and men bent on lay training. Furthermore, some training schools for women used the flush years of the twenties to admit men and introduce pastoral training; by so doing they placed themselves in unequal competition with the well-established seminaries. (To emphasize the point made earlier, Bible training schools could add pastoral training to their lay education efforts without much danger of duplicating seminary functions.) Thus, in summary, most training schools, with the exception of the theologically conservative ones, lacked any further reason to be and therefore ceased to exist in recognizable form; some simply closed their doors, while others merged with seminaries, losing their separate identities; a few evolved into liberal arts colleges; and one or two even became theological seminaries.[46]

A more important reason for Bible schools to emerge as a distinct educational type lay in the sudden rise to prominence of fundamentalism itself in the twenties. In the scramble to choose sides, it became important for fundamentalists and nonfundamentalists alike to pick out those institutions they could readily identify with the new conservative religious movement. Bible schools stood out. Probably more than fundamentalist colleges or seminaries, they became the educational standard bearers for the movement.

But the emergence of the Bible schools in the twenties as distinct entities did not lead to a break with older training school traditions. Like the earlier institutions, Bible schools continued to regard the training of lay persons as a central purpose, and their student bodies therefore included a large number of women, as before. At most schools, in fact, women constituted a majority. Also in keeping with their training school origins, Bible schools remained preeminently practical institutions, furnishing students with actual skills. They prepared graduates for most of the same roles as had training schools: Bible teachers, pastors, evangelists, Sunday school teachers, home and foreign missionaries, Y workers, Christian Endeavor leaders, and church musicians. Like the training schools, they accomplished this by requiring or encouraging students to engage in various kinds of actual religious work while attending school and by offering them classroom subjects that heavily emphasized the "how to" aspects of knowledge. The demand for Bible school graduates was fostered by a vigorous fundamentalist network that was organizing rapidly and efficiently throughout the twenties and thirties in the areas of local congregations, Bible conferences, and foreign missions.[47]

The Bible schools also inherited the training school commitment to providing American Protestantism with foreign missionaries. While mainline denominations were drastically cutting their foreign missionary endeavors in the thirties under the pressure of the Depression and confusion about the nature of the missionary's task (in the Northern Baptist Convention, for instance, missionary giving in 1936 reached only 55% of the 1920 amount), conservative foreign missions were growing in size and number. The China Inland Mission sponsored about five hundred missionaries in the first half of the thirties and established one hundred new mission stations without closing any, despite almost constant turmoil in China. Many Bible schools established foreign missions organizations. The Missionary Training Institute was the model for the numerous Christian and Missionary Alliance Bible schools in mission fields. C. I. Scofield, founder of the Philadelphia School of the Bible (1914), was also the chief organizer of the Central American Mission. Bible Institute of Los Angeles personnel were responsible for the Orinoco River Mission and the United Aborigines Mission in Australia, and also funded a sister Bible school in China. Whether or not a particular Bible school actually involved itself in organizing foreign missions, however, all of them sent out missionaries. Moody Bible Institute alone had prepared some 1,800 foreign missionaries by 1934.[48]

Post-1920 Bible schools served as centers for the cultivation of piety, just as had the training schools. They also maintained the informality of the earlier schools, admitting students from varying educational backgrounds, and helping them to make up their educational deficits. At many schools students could enter and leave any time they wished. Like the training schools, the Bible schools continued to operate with a large proportion of part-time faculty and staff who accepted minimal remuneration. The chief strengths of Bible school teachers, as of those at training schools, lay in their religious dedication and their experience in Christian work, not their academic credentials.

Bible school leaders in the twenties located the roots of their institutions in the European training schools and in early American training schools. The existence of such an educational tradition provided the Bible schools a legitimacy they could not otherwise have claimed, and which they sorely needed. The tradition also suggested some desirable educational directions, encouraging a common sense of purpose among Bible school leaders long before the forging of any formal ties.

Partial List of Bible Schools Founded by 1945

Name of School	Founding Date	Sponsoring Group	Comments
Missionary Training Institute, N.Y.C. & Nyack	1882	C&MA	became Nyack College
Union Missionary Training Institute, Niagara Falls and Brooklyn	1885	inter.	merged with National Bible Institute, 1916
Moody Bible Institute, Chicago	1886	inter.	
Northwestern Bible Training School, St. Paul, Minn.	1889	inter.?	closed in 1899
Boston Missionary Training School/Gordon College	1889	Baptist/ inter.	
Western Baptist Bible College	1890		trained black ministers
Cleveland Bible Institute	1892	Friends	
Johnson Bible College, Knoxville, Tenn.	1893	Churches of Christ	
Toronto Bible College	1894		
Boston Bible School/ New England School of Theology/Berkshire Christian College	1897	Advent Christian	closed during 1980s
Free Church Bible Institute and Seminary	1897	Evang. Free Christian	
Training School for Christian Workers, Los Angeles	1899	Friends	became Azusa College
Providence Bible Institute/ Barrington College	1900	inter.	merged with Gordon C., 1985
God's Bible School, Cincinnati	1900	inter.	
Practical Bible Training School, Johnson City, N.Y.	1901	inter.	

Partial List of Bible Schools Founded by 1945 *(continued)*

Name of School	Founding Date	Sponsoring Group	Comments
Northwestern Schools, Minneapolis, Minn.	1902	Bapt.	
Ft. Wayne Bible Institute, Ft. Wayne, Ind.	1904	inter.	
Grayson Normal School/ Christian Normal Institute, Grayson, Ky.	1906	Churches of Christ	
National Bible Institute, N.Y.C./Shelton College	1907	inter.	
Bible Institute of Los Angeles	1908	inter.	
Hesston College and Bible School, Hesston, Kans.	1909	Mennonite	
Chicago Evangelistic Institute/Vennard Coll.	1910	inter./ holiness	
Trinity Seminary & Bible Institute, Minneapolis	1910	Evang. Free Church	
Colorado Springs Bible Training School	1910	Pilgrim Holiness	
Toccoa Falls Schools, Toccoa Falls, Ga.	1911	C&MA	
Metropolitan Bible Institute, North Bergen, N.J.	1912	A/G	
Albany Bible School, Albany, N.Y.	1912	inter.	founded for women
Minnesota Bible College	1913	Churches of Christ	
Bible Institute of Pennsylvania, Philadelphia	1913	inter. ⎫	merged to become Phila.
Philadelphia School of the Bible	1914	inter. ⎬	College of the Bible, 1951
Winona Lake School of Theology, Winona Lake, Ind.	1914		
Denver Bible College	1914	inter.	
Bethel Bible School, Newark, N.J.	ca. 1916		closed in 1929

Partial List of Bible Schools Founded by 1945 *(continued)*

Name of School	Founding Date	Sponsoring Group	Comments
St. Paul Bible Institute	1916	C&MA	
Hope Bible School, Chicago	1916	inter.	
Midland Bible Institute	1918	C&MA	closed in 1923
Cascade College, Portland, Oreg.	1918	inter./ holiness	closed in 1923
Baptist Bible Institute of New Orleans	1918		became New Orleans Bapt. Theol. Sem., 1946
Lutheran Bible Institute, Minneapolis	1919		
Glad Tidings Bible Inst., San Francisco	1919	A/G	later, Bethany Bible College, Santa Cruz
Simpson Bible Institute, Seattle, Wash.	1921	C&MA	
American Home Bible Inst., Washington, D.C.	1921	inter.	merged to form Washington Bible Inst., 1938
Omaha Bible Institute	1921	inter.	
Central Bible Institute, Springfield, Mo.	1922	A/G	
American Seminary of the Bible, Brooklyn, N.Y.	1922	inter.	
Boston Bible Training School	1922	C&MA	closed about 1938
Prairie Bible Institute, Three Hills, Alberta	1922	inter.	
Columbia Bible Institute, Columbia, S.C.	1923	inter.	
McGarvey Bible College, Louisville, Ky.	1923	Churches of Christ	
Cincinnati Bible College	1923	Disciples	
Berean Bible Institute, San Diego, Calif.	1923	A/G	

Partial List of Bible Schools Founded by 1945 *(continued)*

Name of School	Founding Date	Sponsoring Group	Comments
Canadian Bible Institute	1924		closed 1929
Zion Bible Institute, East Providence, R.I.	1924	Pentec.	
Bible Institute of Washington (D.C.)	1924	inter.	
Harrisburg School of the Bible, Harrisburg, Pa.	1925	inter.	started as evening school
Manhattan (Kansas) Bible College	ca. 1927	Churches of Christ	
Atlanta Christian College	1928	Churches of Christ	
North Central Bible Institute, Minneapolis	1930	A/G	
Olive Branch Missionary Training School, Chicago	1930		
Washington (D.C.) School of the Bible	1930	inter.	
Baltimore School of the Bible	1931	inter.	
Trinity College	1932	inter.	
Kansas City Bible College	1932	inter.	
Baptist Bible Seminary, Johnson City, N.Y.	1932		
People's Bible School, Greensboro, N.Y.	1932		
Chattanooga Bible Institute	1933	inter.	
Fundamental Bible Institute of Kentucky, Corbin, Ky.	1933	inter.	
Lancaster School of the Bible, Lancaster, Pa.	1933	inter.	
Bay Cities Bible Institute, Oakland, Calif.	1934	inter.	
Altoona Bible Institute	1934	inter.	
Canton Bible Institute, Baltimore	1934	?	

Partial List of Bible Schools Founded by 1945 *(continued)*

Name of School	Founding Date	Sponsoring Group	Comments
Colorado School of the Bible, Denver	1934	inter.	
Southeastern Bible School, Birmingham, Ala.	1935	inter.	
Atlanta Bible Institute	1935	inter.	
Fundamental Bible Institute, Los Angeles	1935	inter.	
Western Baptist Bible Coll., Oakland, Calif.	1935		
Keystone School of the Bible, Pittsburgh	1936	inter.	
Mt. Lake Bible School, Mt. Lake, Minn.	1936	?	
Multnomah School of the Bible, Portland, Oreg.	1936	inter.	
San Diego School of the Bible	1937	inter.	
Midwest Bible and Missionary Institute, St. Louis	1938	inter.	
Buffalo Bible Institute	1938	inter.	
Eastern Bible Institute, Green Lane, Pa.	1938	A/G	
Akron Bible Institute	1939	inter.	
Lutheran Bible Institute	1939		
Milwaukee Bible Institute	1939	inter.	
Dallas Bible Institute	1940	inter.	
Reformed Bible Institute, Grand Rapids, Mich.	1940	Christian Reformed	
Allentown School of the Open Bible, Allentown, Pa.	1941	inter.	
Baptist Bible Institute and School of Theology, Grand Rapids, Mich.	1941		
Birmingham Bible Institute, Birmingham, Ala.	1942	inter.	

Partial List of Bible Schools Founded by 1945 *(continued)*

Name of School	Founding Date	Sponsoring Group	Comments
Faith Bible Institute and Academy, Camdenton, Mo.	1942	inter.	
Temple Missionary Training School, Ft. Wayne, Ind.	1942	inter.	
Ozark Bible College, Joplin, Mo.	1942	Churches of Christ	
Freewill Baptist Bible College, Nashville, Tenn.	1942	National Assoc. of Free Will Baptists	
Martur Bible Institute, Grand Rapids, Mich.	1942	inter.	
Baptist Bible Institute of Cleveland	1942		
Carver Bible Institute, Atlanta, Ga.	1943	inter.	
Grace Bible Institute, Omaha, Nebr.	1943	Mennonite	
Southern Bible Institute, Knoxville, Ky.	1943		
Lincoln Bible Institute, Lincoln, Ill.	1944	Churches of Christ	
Lutheran Bible Institute, Seattle, Wash.	1944		
Pacific Bible Institute, Fresno, Calif.	1944	Mennonite	
Detroit Bible Institute	1945	inter.	
Piedmont Bible Institute, Winston-Salem, N.C.	1945	Baptist	
Port Mission Bible School, Baltimore	1945	?	
South Baltimore Bible Institute	1945	?	
Southland Bible Institute, Pikesville, Ky.	1945	?	

ABBREVIATIONS: A/G—Assemblies of God; C&MA—Christian and Missionary Alliance; inter.—interdenominational.

SOURCE: Much of this information comes from Hubert Reynhout Jr., "A Comparative Study of Bible Institute Curriculums" (M.A. thesis, University of Michigan, 1947), pp. 43–54.

VI

A TYPOLOGY OF BIBLE SCHOOL DEVELOPMENT

In 1930 *The Sunday School Times,* a prominent fundamentalist publication, listed fifty-one "Bible Schools That Are True to the Faith."[1] Though no formal organization of Bible schools *as Bible schools* was to appear until the late 1940s, and though before that decade Bible school educators lacked regular and official channels through which to exchange ideas and devise uniform educational standards, it was possible to discern the existence long before 1945 of an informal movement made up of schools with similar goals and curricula, common cultural and religious outlooks, and similar histories. Despite the variety of circumstances, locations, personalities, and denominational affiliations (or lack thereof) involved in the foundings and histories of Bible schools, these institutions followed remarkably similar paths of development. By the 1920s and 1930s, for example, one could almost count on the division of a given Bible school curriculum into at least five departments or "courses": General Bible, Missions, Pastoral, Christian Education, and Music, with the names for these courses varying very little. No matter what the affiliation of a particular Bible school, one could usually find allusions in its catalog or other literature linking it to the heroes of conservative evangelicalism—Taylor, Muller, Spurgeon, Moody, and Gordon—to the early Bible and prophetic conferences, and to crucial documents—the King James Bible, of course, C. I. Scofield's notes on Scripture, and *Jesus Is Coming.*

How does it happen that these schools developed so similarly in the absence of standardizing agencies? For one thing, the institutional form had been established in the oldest Bible schools, those that had grown out of the missionary training school tradition. Furthermore, Bible school leaders and instructors found frequent opportunities to exchange ideas informally; they met during Bible conferences, revivals, and visits to each other's institutions. For instance, the Bible Institute of Los Angeles received visits from Elmore Harris, president of Toronto Bible Institute, and James M. Gray of Moody Bible Institute in 1911; in 1915 W. B. Riley, head of the Northwestern Schools, spent a month there. The lines of communication among Bible schools were also kept open by the students, who often migrated from one school to another. Finally, the graduates of one school often taught at another Bible school, and it was not unusual for the same person to teach at several Bible schools during his or her lifetime.

But surely one of the most important reasons Bible schools shared so much in common was the existence of Moody Bible Institute as a model. Other Bible schools took their cues from what the Institute was doing in the areas of curriculum and evangelism. Don O. Shelton, founder and president of the National Bible Institute in New York City, echoed the general consensus when he hailed Moody as the institution "to which all other Bible institutes are constantly indebted."[2] Moody may not have been the sole model for younger and less established Bible schools, but it was certainly the most prominent and the most assiduously studied.

The histories of Bible schools started between about 1880 and 1915, then, share many common elements, enough so that their stories, read one after the other, would sound a bit repetitive, whatever the unique events and persons in each institutional history. It is possible, in fact, to discern three stages of development that most schools seemed to pass through, during roughly the same time periods.

Stage One, Foundings. 1882–1915

This stage applies to the period, approximately 1882–1915, during which most Bible schools were included in the larger genre of religious training schools. At this time schools were usually housed in makeshift and frequently temporary locations. The Boston Missionary Training School opened in the vestry of A. J. Gordon's church. The Bible Institute of Los Angeles was housed in a couple of rooms over a pool hall in downtown Los Angeles; the Missionary Training Institute founded by A. B. Simpson started out on a theater stage of 23rd Street in Manhattan. In the following years it moved frequently, from 22nd Street to 49th Street, and then to 54th Street.

Ordinarily, Bible schools opened with a small student body. In the third year of operation of the Boston Missionary Training School, 1891–2, the catalog reported that eight students had returned for a second year, thirty new students had appeared for day classes, and twelve had presented themselves for evening classes. In addition, there were twelve "occasional" students, presumably ones who, as they were able, attended lectures that interested them. But even this modest enrollment was impressive, compared to that of the Boston Bible School, which started out in 1898 with twelve students and rarely attracted more than a total of twenty until the 1930s.

Most students at the early Bible schools were relatively mature men and women, usually in their early or mid twenties, or even older. Either they had decided on a Christian work vocation later in life, or, owing to family responsibilities or lack of money, they had not had a chance to acquire an education until then. Many had already held jobs—as salespersons, farmers, railway employees, printers or printer's assistants, secretaries, teachers, and mechanics—before deciding on training as Christian workers. The first regular student at Biola had been trained as a printer and in fact early put his skills to work at the Institute, setting up a print shop there and producing Biola's first publications. In the training school tradition, most of the early Bible schools were lay oriented; women often were in the majority, or at least accounted for a substantial portion of the student body. One exception was Boston Bible School, which started out by training prospective ministers (mostly male) for its denomination; it enrolled women and lay men also, but in smaller numbers. Since at the beginning Bible schools did not have sleeping and eating accommodations for students, most lived either at home with parents or spouses or in nearby rooming houses. An exception is the Boston Missionary Training School, which right from the start opened a residence home for its women students (Carey House also doubled as a temporary home for departing and returning foreign missionaries). But the school did not provide housing for its male students until later.

Only a few subjects were taught at most early Bible schools: Bible study, missions, music, and teacher training, usually; the entire course of study normally took only one or two years. The first course of studies at the Missionary Training Institute, for instance, lasted one year and consisted of instruction in English, Christian Evidences, Bible Study and Interpretation, Church History, and Christian Life and Work. As a rule, the primary emphasis was not upon classroom activities but rather upon the "practical work" students did outside of school. For instance, at Biola the school's publication, *The King's Business,* had very little to say about what the students were learning in the classroom and a great deal to report on their evangelistic activities. Right from the beginning Biola had a department of "shop work," which sent out evangelists to work with employees in factories, railway carbarns, and fire houses; a department of "Spanish Work," which oversaw evangelistic activities among the many Mexican immigrants in the Los Angeles area; a department of "Seamen's Work," which directed evangelistic efforts among crews and passengers in Los Angeles harbor; and a department of "Jewish work," whose purpose was to proselytize the Jewish residents of Los Angeles.

At Biola and other Bible schools success was typically measured in the number of people converted, tracts distributed, or Sunday school classes taught, rather than in number of degrees earned or examinations passed. For early faculty, teaching at a Bible school was primarily an act of love or dedication, for they were paid little or nothing. The faculty might include two or three or four full-time people, but much of the teaching was done by part-time instructors and by visiting evangelists and Bible teachers (some of them well known) who might offer a series of lectures.

The founder and leaders typically had other roles besides that of educator. Recall, for example, that A. B. Simpson at the Missionary Training Institute was also busy overseeing the Christian and Missionary Alliance, editing the Alliance paper, pastoring the Gospel Tabernacle in New York City, conducting speaking tours across the United States, and writing books and hymns. Generally, faculty were admired for their piety and their experience and zeal as Christian workers and leaders rather than for academic degrees and achievements (though some had graduated from theological seminaries). Even as late as 1914–15, the Gordon Bible Institute's catalog read,

> The ideal instruction is given, not mainly by beginners, however talented, nor by those retired from all active affairs, nor by men immersed in books and out of touch with life. The highest instruction is given by those who are themselves thinkers and leaders in the lines of which they teach. The true teacher, in a school which fits men and women to deal with life and affairs, and to think in terms of reality, is one who is himself in active life, is doing the things which he teaches and is living in the world of men as well as of books. The teacher who develops power as well as knowledge in the pupil must be one who is a center of power. The teacher of religious truth should be one who is an active leader in spiritual things. All of these things mean a curriculum of life and power as well as of knowledge.[3]

Often students did not stay the usual course of two years; they might feel compelled to answer a call to enter some line of Christian service, or possibly respond to a relative's summons for help at home. At the Boston Bible School an early departure like the following one in January 1913 seems to have been regarded as quite ordinary: "Mr. Harold Patch of Morrisville, Vt., who has been a student in the Boston Bible School since the opening of the fall term, feels it his duty to enter the ministerial field at once; and to enter doors which have providentially opened before him."[4] The catalogs of many Bible schools made it clear that students were free to come and go as they wished or needed to. Said the 1903 Boston Bible School catalog, "It is very desirable to begin the year and stay till it ends. But, when this is impossible, students are welcome to begin the year and stay as long as they can."[5] And the 1892 catalog of the Boston Missionary Training School advised, "it is desirable that students remain, if Providence permits, for two years. Yet numbers have found themselves greatly benefited by one year's training."[6]

Students came from a variety of academic backgrounds, but in the early days few were turned away because of their lack of educational preparation. The literature of the Boston Bible School encouraged prospective students, "No matter how poor may have been your opportunities and how limited your present achievements.[sic] You can begin at the very bottom and acquire a good English education."[7] In 1905–1906 the school offered an extra year for those "who lack preparation in English."[8] Two years later the catalog explained, "Experience has shown that we must provide training for many who have not enjoyed the benefits of a high school course."[9] At Biola not much was said about educational prerequisites at all until 1920, and then only a common school education or its equivalent was specified. And the founders of the Boston Missionary Training School explained that it was a school for "young gentlemen and ladies, who are called of God to enter Christian service, but who may, for various reasons, find it impractical to take the more extended course of College or Seminary instruction." The founders went on to prescribe as academic prerequisites only a "fair knowledge of the English branches of education," which could and did mean anything from a year or two in grammar school to high school graduation. Beyond that, the students were to possess "sufficient gifts and consecration" to guarantee they would give themselves "wholly to the Lord's service." A pastor or church "or some other responsible party" was to vouch for the applicant's "character and intention."[10]

To be sure, Bible school educators were always glad to receive applications from high school graduates and even sometimes from students who had attended college (who apparently felt the need to supplement their academic preparation with practical experience and immersion in a devout atmosphere), but they recognized that the major part of their constituency was made up of those with limited educational backgrounds and modest academic aspirations. Stage one, then, was characterized by small beginnings and maximum latitude about who could attend and under what circumstances. This attitude is nicely summed up in the reassuring tone in the publicity for the Phillips Bible Institute, Canton, Ohio, which opened in 1912: "No matter who you are, or what you do, or where you live—if you desire religious instruction, there is an opportunity for you, a course to supply your need, a way to solve your financial problem. This we guarantee."[11]

Stage Two, Expansion. 1915–1930

After a time successful Bible schools acquired or built a permanent school building or buildings, often including space for a dormitory. In 1897 the Missionary Training Institute left its quarters in the Gospel Tabernacle in New York City for Nyack, New York, where a campus was built. After spending a few years in its rooms over a pool hall, Biola finished construction on three buildings in 1915, two thirteen-story dormitory structures—considered "sky scrapers" at the time—joined by a 4,564-seat auditorium. In 1917 Gordon Bible College moved into new and larger quarters on Boston's Fenway.

In stage two the tendency was for the course of study to be extended to three or even four years. Finishing the course became more important; now students often earned a diploma or certificate upon completion of prescribed studies. As the normal length of study increased, so did the number of subject offerings, though they remained basically practical and vocational in purpose and orientation. Whereas before all students had followed the same course of study, now they could choose from a number of programs, depending upon what kind of Christian work they anticipated doing. The most common choices were "General Bible," "Music," "Missionary," and "Christian education." This was a period during which a "Pastoral Course" might appear, as the school began formally and deliberately to train prospective ministers. Subject offerings became more specialized: students could take a class teaching them how to work with children or women or young people, or they could explore a single Bible book, or they might acquire special skills for evangelizing Jews, Italians, or Spanish speaking immigrants, or they could study "missionary medicine" to gain skills appropriate for foreign missionaries. Stage two usually brought a number of permanent and full-time faculty, though the roster continued to include numerous part-time instructors as well. And Bible schools in this period were more likely to have leaders who made education their primary role; "career educators" like Nathan Wood who headed Gordon for several decades following 1910 became more common.

Furthermore, as Bible schools got command of more resources, they tended to reach out to larger numbers and varieties of students: they might start an evening program (if, indeed, the school had not begun with such a program) or a summer institute. In addition, they might offer correspondence courses, put out journals carrying Bible study, missions information, advice to Sunday school teachers, and news of the school itself. They published Christian literature from their own presses; sponsored annual Bible conferences; put on radio programs, or, in the case of Moody Bible Institute and Biola, even owned radio stations; and sent out touring musical groups—quartets, octets, glee clubs, and choirs. Some even supported "branch" Bible schools in missionary lands. During the twenties, for instance, Biola leaders poured many of their resources into the Hunan Bible Institute in China.

It was usually during stage two (though sometimes earlier) that the first statements of faith, which faculty and trustees were required to sign, came into being. For instance, the 1922–23 Gordon College catalog printed a clear statement of doctrine,

> The Board of Trustees of Gordon College of Theology and Missions officially records the absolute loyalty of the College to the great evangelical doctrines of the Deity of Christ, the Only-begotten Son of God; his miraculous Birth; his sinless Life; his vicarious Death; his bodily Resurrection; his triumphal Return; the Holy Spirit as the third Person of the Trinity; and the Bible as the supernaturally inspired Word of God;—and in accepting the confidence and the gifts of evangelical Christians they thereby pledge the College to such loyalty as its permanent policy, and agree that the Trustees will now and hereafter engage or retain as regular officers, professors or instructors only such persons as affirm genuine loyalty to these principles.[12]

The promulgation of such statements was spurred by the doctrinal battles of the teens and especially the twenties, in which the staking out of conservative and liberal theological positions figured so prominently. Not all of the disputes were with liberal Protestants, however. Some Bible school statements of faith were designed to forestall the activities and influence of those whom Bible school educators regarded as fundamentalist extremists. When he became dean at Biola in 1912, R. A. Torrey immediately authored a statement of faith that seems to have been aimed not primarily at potential liberals on the faculty but rather at the ultra-dispensationalist Bullingerists who had been teaching at the school.

There is what might be called a little sub-stage in the thirties, during the Great Depression, when at best much Bible school development stood still. Often, in fact, these schools had to cut back programs that had come into being during the relatively flush decade of the 1920s. Several points ought to be made about this era, however. First, in surviving the rigors of Depression, Bible schools were aided by the fact that they were still informal, flexible institutions which could be run quite cheaply. Most Bible school educators had never gotten accustomed to commanding lavish resources anyway and were capable of improvising according to what funds and other kinds of support came their way. Teachers had never been well paid, and now many of them went for months with salaries cut or delayed, making up for the lack by pastoring churches or finding other supplemental income. The thirties were lean years for Bible schools, surely, as for other educational institutions, but their leaders managed to carry on remarkably well in the circumstances.

Second, some Bible school educators proved themselves quite adept at raising funds during a time when it seemed few people had any extra money. Louis Talbot, head of Biola during the thirties, was able repeatedly to rescue his school from mortgage foreclosures and similar financial perils by desperate appeals to his congregation and to his radio audience.

The third point that needs to be made is that despite the deprivations of the thirties, Bible schools continued to be founded. In fact, at least twenty-nine new Bible schools appeared during the thirties, compared to seventeen in the previous decade. Again, probably the relative inexpensiveness of the Bible schools worked in their favor during a time of serious economic hardship; Bible schools were affordable, whereas other types of "higher education" were beyond the scope of most founding groups, especially during a time of economic hardship.

Stage Three, Toward Academic Respectability. 1940–Present

This is a time when Bible schools began to offer degrees, a bachelor's of some sort—eventually a B.A. or B.S. Bible schools and institutes became Bible colleges (or simply colleges). They demanded higher educational prerequisites of students; high school graduation became a requirement at most of the older institutions. Bible schools acquired bigger and bigger libraries, faculty boasted more and more advanced degrees. A larger number of liberal arts subjects entered the curriculum. At many schools tuition came to be charged for the first time, and the older schools achieved a greater degree of financial stability. Ultimately these schools earned accreditation, either through the Bible school association established in the late forties, or, in the case of some, through the same regional associations that accredited liberal arts colleges. As many Bible school educators paid greater attention to the quality of the regular academic program, they found it difficult to find the extra resources and personnel for correspondence courses, extension classes, radio stations, and the like. Frequently, therefore, the scope of their outreach diminished. This happened at Biola, for instance. Like other Bible schools, it had multiplied its evangelistic outreach efforts during the twenties, then cut back in the thirties because of economic depression. When relative prosperity returned in the late 40s and the 50s, Biola never attempted to restore the full array of evangelistic and outreach activities, for by this time its leaders had resolved to bring the school up to a certain level of academic quality. During the fifties, for instance, the Biola directors decided they should sever the longstanding ties with the branch school in China, and that "Biola should concentrate all its efforts and its resources on its educational program, especially since the School had become fully accredited."[13]

Another characteristic of this stage was for many schools to move from downtown to the suburbs in order to purchase cheaper land for expansion and also to escape from urban blight. Biola, for instance, moved from downtown Los Angeles to suburban La Mirada in 1959; in the 1950s Gordon switched its campus from Boston to Wenham on the north shore of Massachusetts; in 1958 Boston Bible School (by then known as the New England School of Theology) moved from Boston to Lenox, in western Massachusetts; in 1965 Trinity College (a product of the 1946 merger of the Evangelical Free Church Seminary and Bible Institute of Chicago and the Trinity Seminary and Bible Institute of Minneapolis) left Chicago for suburban Bannockburn, Illinois.

This schematization is admittedly rough. Change happened at different rates at different schools. Gordon, for example, moved quite rapidly along the route to academic respectability; its dean was already uneasy with the Bible school label in the teens and the school was offering standard degrees by the early twenties. On the other hand, the New England School of Theology, hampered by antischooling feeling in its denomination and poor financial backing, proceeded slowly, only becoming a degree-granting college in 1959. A large number of schools, of course, closed before they got beyond stage one. And Moody Bible Institute has been a law unto itself. Bolstered by Dwight Moody's impressive fundraising abilities, it started out big and strong compared to other Bible schools. Furthermore, it has never moved from its original site in Chicago's Loop, nor has it become a college, though through arrangements with other institutions Moody students can earn standard college degrees. At the same time it has served as a model to other schools, it has also played a maverick role, refusing to follow what sometimes have seemed like "inevitable" patterns of institutional evolution.

The notion of stages is still relevant in the present, as the founding of Bible schools proceeds apace. To be sure, some of the new schools, endowed with relatively lavish resources, have entered stage two or three immediately; others, however, have started out in stage one as evening schools or Bible classes in church basements. Then eventually, if circumstances permitted, they moved on to the next stages as had Gordon and Nyack before them.

VII

INSIDE THE BIBLE SCHOOL
CLASSROOM TEACHING

The Teaching of the Bible

During the twenties the principal of the New England School of Theology proclaimed that "The Bible is the foundation of instruction and emphasized in every department."[1] Similarly, the catalog of the Central Bible Institute pronounced the Bible to be "the chief text-book of the Bible Institute."[2] And the 1920 catalog of the Bible Institute of Los Angeles echoed, "The Bible is the only text book of the Bible Institute." Furthermore, Biola leaders made it clear that this dictum applied to all Institute classes; under the description of the department of "Psychology and Sociology," the same catalog declared, "The best text book on psychology is the Bible. The Bible sets forth man as he really is, and not as speculative philosophers imagine him to be."[3] When Bible school educators called their institutions "Bible-centered," they were not exaggerating.

To be sure, the Bible had had a central place back in the missionary training schools, but then the fact that a particular school taught the Bible implied little about the way it was taught, except that the English translation was employed, and that the text was approached with reverence and attention to its practical uses. Beyond this, it is difficult to make general statements about methods of teaching the Bible in the early training schools, since the theology of such schools varied considerably; some training school leaders had incorporated the higher criticism, while others had shied away from it. It is easier, on the other hand, to identify certain techniques and approaches that Bible school educators widely shared.

Though Bible school Bible study was designed for conservative religious purposes, many Bible school educators in fact considered themselves reformers in the area of Bible instruction. They had some justification for this attitude; it was true that Bible school approaches to the teaching of Scripture constituted a reaction to the older practice, common in theological seminaries during most of the nineteenth century, of dealing with the biblical text mostly by exegesis—that is, the close reading of a selected passage in the original language, with minute attention to philological distinctions. Bible school teachers disparagingly referred to such an approach as the analysis of "fragments" of Scripture. Rather, they argued, the student ought to master the entire Bible before attempting to study its parts. Accordingly, Scofield in his Reference Bible advocated "A Panoramic View of the Bible"; and James M. Gray of Moody Bible Institute recommended his method of "synthetic Bible studies" as "giving a Bird's-eye View of the Bible."[4]

One theological basis for a holistic approach to Scripture study lay in the dispensationalism of the majority of Bible schools. Dispensationalists interpreted the Bible as a series of divine offers of salvation and a corresponding series of rejections by human beings; in their view the Bible when considered as a whole revealed God's grand and progressive scheme for human redemption, and was unified by the unchanging nature of God's purpose and by the consistency of human resistance. Moreover, as suggested earlier, dispensationalism made study of the Bible in its entirety feasible as well as theologically desirable, since it claimed to reconcile the seemingly contradictory parts of Scripture, rendering a "panoramic view" comprehensible rather than perplexing and bewildering.

The views of Bible school educators about studying Scripture as a whole should be considered as part of a larger picture, for they could not claim to have a monopoly on this "reform." Higher critics too argued that the Bible must be viewed in its entirety, though for different reasons. They claimed that the Old and New Testaments taken together showed the marvelous progressive development of human religious experience and humankind's gradual maturation as ethically responsible beings. Higher critics also claimed to be able to account for the contradictions and discontinuities of Scripture, but they accomplished this by explaining that various parts of it were created by diverse writers in different historical contexts and for various purposes. If, for example, the Old Testament idea of justice differed from that of the Christian era, this disparity showed a growing ethical sensitivity in human beings, not a confusion in Scripture itself.

Bible school teaching was also reformist in its rejection of the idea that students must acquire Greek and Hebrew in order to be able to grasp the meaning of the Bible. Instead, Bible school classes concentrated upon study of the Bible in English, which made it possible for larger numbers of students to gain familiarity with the whole sweep of the Scriptures in a relatively short time.

In turning primarily to the English Bible, Bible school educators again had company; higher critics in their capacity as college and seminary teachers were also placing increased emphasis on study of the Bible in English translation. They had come to the conclusion that the degree of language mastery demanded of anyone who was going to study the original text in a truly serious way was so great that it lay beyond the capacity of most students. Therefore, said the higher critics, let those who were intending to become experts in biblical studies spend long years in concentrated language study; let the others read it in English. As a result, advanced Greek and Hebrew increasingly became electives rather than required subjects in the theological seminary Bible departments dominated by biblical critics.

Bible school educators also departed from older teaching practices in their opposition to the use of commentaries on the Bible, at least at the beginning level. Earlier students of the Bible, they complained, had sometimes spent more time in reading commentaries than in studying the text itself. James M. Gray, dean of Moody Bible Institute, claimed that one "great advantage" of his synthetic method lay "in getting the people to read the Bible for themselves." He added, "To master the English Bible you must begin by getting your own individual impression of the contents or outline of each book."[5]

In the attempt to encourage students to think about Scripture for themselves, without the aid of commentaries, Bible school teachers often borrowed a familiar pedagogical technique; they posed study questions intended to focus students' reading of Scripture. This was the approach used by R. A. Torrey, a dean at Moody Bible Institute and later at the Bible Institute of Los Angeles. His purpose was "'not to save the students the necessity of personal thought and study, but to stimulate thought and Bible searching.' His method for accomplishing this goal was to provide the reader with a series of questions and numerous Bible references which the student could look up and study in order to arrive at personal answers."[6] At the Missionary Training Institute, A. B. Simpson also taught by means of study questions, for much the same reason. And Columbia Bible College, established in 1923, supplied its Bible students with "question sheets" of "thought-provoking research questions."[7]

In their eagerness to make the point that their Bible study techniques encouraged students to arrive at independent conclusions after careful investigation, Bible school educators frequently chose the adjective "inductive." Torrey, for example, entitled his lessons an "inductive study guide." Biola's 1920 catalog claimed that in the Institute's course on "Bible doctrine"

> the method of study is entirely different from that usually pursued in theological seminaries. The doctrine is never stated and then proof texts hunted up to prove the doctrine. The method is rather that pursued in our day in all other branches of scientific study, the INDUCTIVE METHOD. Every passage of scripture bearing upon the doctrine is examined and its exact meaning in the light of the context determined, . . .[8]

When Bible teachers used the word "inductive," then, they meant to convey the idea that their students began Bible study with an open mind and arrived at their conclusions only after ruminating exhaustively upon the "facts" or "evidence" of Scripture. The Bible student, they insisted, proceeded in much the same careful and objective manner as the scientist. Precisely in the scientific overtones carried by "inductive," in fact, lay its virtue. Bible school educators, like others of the twentieth century, prided themselves upon emulating the methods of science as they understood them.[9]

In eschewing commentaries and stressing independent study, Gray, Torrey, and other Bible teachers emphasized their faith in the ability of students to make sense of the context of Scripture with only a modest amount of help. The title page of Gray's *Synthetic Bible Studies* advertised "concise, clear and valuable expositions of Scripture, . . . made so plain that the ordinary Bible reader can comprehend it." In a similar spirit, Ashley S. Johnson of Johnson Bible College offered a text, *The Self-Interpreting New Testament.* In this respect higher critics and Bible school teachers parted company, for the critics did not share this confidence in students' ability adequately to understand the Bible without extensive and expert historical, archaeological, and linguistic information.

To judge from their expressions of desire for independent students, Bible school educators also appeared serenely confident that average students, with only a modicum of guidance, would inevitably arrive at "correct" interpretations of Scripture. Of course, the students were not as completely free to choose their understandings as their mentors liked to suppose. First of all, most were unlikely to have enrolled in Bible schools unless they possessed certain presuppositions about the nature of Scripture which made scientific objectivity—in the sense usually understood by the twentieth century—problematical. Second, many elements in the Bible school ambiance reinforced those presuppositions and coaxed them into articulate form. Third, the "inductive" approach to Bible study as practiced by Bible school instructors was scarcely as unbiased as was sometimes implied. As any pedagogue knows, questions are usually framed to lead the respondent in certain directions. Simpson's queries to his students will illustrate. When he asked, for instance, "What do we learn about the earth's future nations from Genesis, chapter 9, 10, and 11?" he was assuming that students *could* learn something factual about "earth's future nations" from these chapters, in other words, that they contained reliable prophecy. Simpson was implicitly taking prophetic statements literally, as liberal Christians would not have done, and encouraging his students to do the same. "Nothing" was not a possible answer to this query. Or when Simpson asked, "What special lessons may we learn from Isaac's life?" he was urging students to apply moral and spiritual examples from the Old Testament to their own lives.[10] Biblical critics would probably have frowned upon this sort of question; to them it would have sounded like an anachronistic and overly moralistic imposition upon historical events and persons.

Every Bible teacher touted a favorite "method" of studying the Bible.

Most of the approaches were similar, however, and incorporated the basic assumptions behind the "reforms" outlined above. A Miss Miller at the Missionary Training Institute espoused the "Berean Method," or the "Scripture searching method."[11] Her purpose was "for the student to obtain firsthand, personal enlightenment in the Scriptures," which she felt could be accomplished "by taking the Scriptures as self-explanatory to the diligent, prayerful student, without recourse for personal understanding to outside 'help,' but only to the Lord Himself directly in His own oracles." She resorted to "'Search Questions,' which, while conveying no information, still serve to direct in a definite, orderly and successful way the student's search for understanding of the portion under study." After Miller's students had answered the "Search Questions," she assigned them a theme, which was intended to "assemble and organize the material acquired in a comprehensive and original way such as to exercise and prove the student's ability to make the Scripture speak clearly to others."[12]

A method of Wilbert W. White at Biblical Seminary in New York City (originally the Bible Teachers Training School) proved popular in many Bible schools. He advocated studying the English Bible as literature, using then-standard techniques of literary scholarship. Because literary study during White's time was primarily appreciative and also less historically oriented than the approach of the biblical higher critics, it could be considered "safe," assuming the student was devout. Moreover, the literary approach did not require any particular expertise such as knowledge of ancient languages; anyone could undertake it; and yet it required enough intellectual rigor to be academically respectable. Of course, White—very properly in the view of Bible school educators—warned that the Bible was more than literature; it was the word of God. Through White's writings and those of his successors at Biblical Seminary, his ideas filtered into many Bible school classes.

Probably no approach to learning the Bible was more popular in Bible schools than James Gray's method. As early as the first half of the 1890s it was in use at Moody's and Gordon's schools; Gray himself employed the technique in classes he conducted at the Missionary Training Institute in 1900. In succeeding decades his method spread to many Bible schools, whose teachers were not always aware of its source. Not all of Gray's ideas originated with him; many permeated the air. For instance, a number of teachers—and not only at Bible schools—were advancing one of his principles, the study of the Bible by books rather than by random passages.[13] Probably Gray's prominence as longtime dean and president of Moody Bible Institute help account for the popularity of his method at other Bible schools.

Gray had begun using the method in Boston with large adult audiences assembled for Bible study; later he organized the material into fifty-two lessons, one for each week of the year. These were published in *The*

Union Gospel News in Cleveland, and finally in 1900 in book form as *Synthetic Bible Studies*. In the book's introduction, Gray defined the term "synthetic study": "the study of the Bible as a whole, and each book as a whole and as seen in its relation to the other books. The word 'Synthesis' has the opposite meaning to 'Analysis.' When we analyze a subject we take it apart and consider it in its various elements, but when we synthesize it we put it together and consider it as a whole . . ."[14] Gray instructed students to read a Bible book—or, in the case of a very long book, a large chunk of it—in a single sitting. After that, assuming students had a few days to complete the assignment, they were urged to reread the same book several times, again in one sitting per rereading. The ideal regimen was to read through the given book once a day. Students were discouraged from spending much time puzzling over difficult passages or absorbing minor details; rather, they were urged to read rapidly through the book in the attempt to grasp its overall themes. They started with Genesis and went on to each book in the order of appearance in the Bible.[15]

Gray made Bible study seem a remarkably simple, matter-of-fact affair. As he described the task of Bible study, "The object now before us is to get hold of the facts of the lesson. . . . The facts must come first and interpretation afterwards. To a great extent if we get the facts the interpretation will take care of itself, for the Bible is wonderfully self-interpretive."[16] Scripture, then, was simply a series of "facts" to be learned in orderly fashion. This argument, besides making the Bible seem refreshingly accessible, also put it on much the same footing as the data of science, and implicitly compared the role of the Bible student to that of the scientific investigator. Again, a Bible school educator was appealing to the luster of science to reflect upon his own field.

To explore the way Gray's method worked in practice, it might be worthwhile to see how he directed a student to approach the first lesson, Genesis 1 to 11. He started by pointing out what he called "the great outline facts" of these chapters: "Creation," "Fall," "Deluge," and "Nations." As subcategories under the first "outline fact," Creation, he proposed the various groups of creation events: Light, Firmament, Dry Land, Lightholders, Fish and Fowl, and Cattle and Man. Under one of these subcategories, the creation of man, he further subdivided the biblical narrative into the topics of "Nature," "Location," "Moral Test," and "Helpmeet." Similar divisions and subdivisions occurred under each of the other three "great outline facts." The class was expected to jot down each of these memory cues in their notebooks in outline form. Gray intended these catchwords to help students fix the most important events in their minds. Along the way students were urged to employ other aids to memory; in studying "Nations," for instance, they were encouraged to consult maps of the Middle East to locate places mentioned in the biblical text.[17]

The second lesson, on Genesis 12–28:15, took a slightly different tack. In this section Gray's attention focused upon the persons of Abraham and Isaac. He urged students to outline the main events of Abraham's life, again in catchwords by means of which students could readily reconstruct the highpoints of the patriarch's career: Call, Egypt, Lot, Covenant, Hagar, Circumcision, Sodom, and so forth.[18]

But Gray was interested in more than simply identifying what he considered the main outlines of the biblical narrative and fixing them in the students' minds. He also offered definitions of biblical terms, added apologetic notes that supported the biblical account of history and natural events, put forth general principles of interpretation, and in fact interpreted the text. To demonstrate his central point that all the parts of the Bible were interconnected, he often picked out passages from other books of the Old Testament or from the New Testament which, he claimed, corroborated, paralleled or explained passages or themes of Genesis. For instance, he urged students to compare what human beings were made of in the Genesis account with what 1 Thess. 5:23 had to say on this subject.[19] Using a time-honored technique borrowed from the Church Fathers, he interpreted Old Testament people, objects, and events as precursors of New Testament people, objects, and events. Thus, he saw Isaac as a "type" of Christ, pointing out shared elements such as their supernatural birth, their sacrifice, and their restoration to life. As these statements suggest, Gray's protestations that the Bible is self-interpreting ought not to be taken literally; in fact, he had definite opinions about how students of the Bible ought to understand Scripture, opinions that others might not have found self-evident.

Some of the interpretive lines adopted by Gray were decidedly dispensationalist. For instance, he incorporated the central dispensationalist idea of the "rapture" of the church in his discussion of Isaac: "Isaac's going out to meet his bride and bringing her into his mother Sarah's tent, is emblematical of Christ coming out from Heaven to meet the church, and the rapture of the latter in entering with Him into millennial glory, as we find in such places as John 14:1–3 and 1 Thessalonians 4:13–18."[20] The strong interpretive purpose manifested itself in social commentary as well. In his view, Genesis held out some stern warnings for the present: "Notice carefully the cases leading up to what has been called 'the antedeluvian apostasy,' and observe that the fearful progress of wickedness was coincident with a rapid advance in civilization (4:16–22) and that the female sex came into peculiar prominence in connection with the disregard of the primal law of marriage (6:1–2)."[21]

The interpretive lines also touched upon issues of personal morality. In thinking about Abraham, the student was encouraged to catalog the patriarch's positive and negative charactertistics, thus:

Good	Bad
Faith	Fear
Obedience	Falsehood
Unselfishness	Unbelief
Courage	
Sympathy	

Unlike the higher critics, Gray had no interest in explaining Abraham's character in terms of his historical context. Instead, he treated it primarily as a model for the behavior of present-day Christians. Finally, Gray was always anxious to add notes that demonstrated how "science" or archaeology corroborated the biblical record. He noted, for instance, that one reason some scientists had contested the Genesis account of creation was because, they said, light could not have been created before the sun. Not so, countered Gray: "later scientific discoveries indicate that there is a light separate from the sun—that the earth itself is luminous."[22]

Gray's strong insistence on "facts," "laws," and the Bible's agreement with the evidence of science nicely illustrates George M. Marsden's point that fundamentalists were strong advocates of Baconian science and saw Scripture in that context. In their opinion, true science consisted not of theories but rather of "facts," observable data, and proven laws. As Marsden argues, Baconians were taxonomists, categorizers, and classifiers, not theorists. So also were fundamentalists, and not least of all when they turned to the word of God. Their frequently repeated quotation of 1 Timothy about *"rightly dividing* the Word of Truth" (my emphasis) well accorded with this view, as did the dispensationalist classification of scripture into seven (or six or eight) periods, and as did Gray's predilection for outlines with their careful orderings of biblical names, dates, and places. Treating Scripture as scientific data, given by God in much the same way as he presented scientists with the data of nature, served an important apologetic purpose. Regarded as a scientific fact book, the Bible partook of some of the seeming certainty of Baconian science with its fixed classifications and laws.[23]

Student reminiscences indicate that Gray's method made a significant impact on them. One woman who attended Moody's Bible Institute in the early 1890s recalled,

> God bless Dr. Gray of Boston and his synthetic method! It was he, who told us to read Genesis at one sitting, then re-read two or three times, if possible, before meeting him. In the lecture room he drew *from us* a crisp word-analysis, which fastened the chain of ideas in mind, then elaborated it somewhat, adding general suggestions and a mention of striking texts, types or lessons. Next day, Exodus, and so on, nearly through the Old Testament in three weeks,—rapid yet thorough work. So we gathered up the outline facts—sure foothold for all to follow. It is wonderful what

mere continuous and repeated reading reveals. With each reading a book shines out the clearer as if from a dissolving cloud-mist, until it stands a bold outline in memory; the relation of book to book grows plainer, and the Bible, as a unit, is ours in a new way.[24]

Goals similar to Gray's were reflected in the practice of other Bible schools. Columbia Bible College advertised

Scientific, critical study of the Bible by the student for himself. The Bible itself is the main textbook in these courses rather than any commentary on the Bible. . . . The general plan is to give the student a detailed through the Bible book by book study in the Old Testament the first year, in the New Testament and in special book studies the second year.[25]

A 1911 graduate of the Boston Bible School credited his instruction with helping him see Scripture as an entirety. He recalled that "The Bible was once an unorganized mass of unrelated incidents in my mind. It now seems to be woven into one grand, complete whole." He had learned in Bible school to reject a narrow exegetical approach: "It jars on me to hear a man drag a Scripture passage out of its setting and build some hobby or notion of his own upon it. If I cannot come to a reasonable interpretation of any passage that will harmonize with the context and sum of other Scripture, I would better let it alone until I can."[26]

The holistic approach to Scripture—designated in Bible school catalogs as Bible Synopsis, Book Study, Synthesis, or Bible Survey—did not exhaust the ways the Bible could be studied in these schools. Since the majority of classroom hours were devoted to Bible study, due attention could be given to other methods once it could be assumed that the student had mastered the biblical text as a whole. Scripture could also be approached topically; classes which followed this method were sometimes entitled "Bible Doctrines." Evangelist George Pentecost described this method:

By topical reading I mean, take up a subject and follow it through from Genesis to Revelation. For instance, take the word Faith, and follow it through the Bible with the aid of a concordance. You will find about two columns in Cruden's Unabridged Concordance devoted to "faith." What a study it is in all its phases—its mighty workings, its relations to the life that now is and is to come! Then all its cognate words, and its opposite words, "unbelief," "faithless," &c. . . .[27]

That this technique was practiced at Moody's Bible Institute is attested to by a student reminiscence: "Sometimes, with the guidance of different teachers, we track one thought or doctrine throughout the Bible."[28] Or students could concentrate their attention upon particular Bible characters. Charles Stelzle recalled doing this under Wilbert W. White's tutelage at Moody's Bible Institute in the early 1890s: "Dr. W. W. White, now President of Bible Seminary in New York, was the teacher of Old Testament at the Institute, and his sanity and enthusiasm spurred me on to make a number of highly interesting original studies—and I often spent most of the night chasing an Old Testament character through the Bible."[29]

Alternatively, students could focus upon single books, "great chapters," "key words," "biblical prophecy," or the various "names of God."[30] The list was limited only by the imagination of instructors or interpreters. Once the whole Bible was mastered, students could also engage in the traditional technique of exegesis, usually referred to as "Analysis" in the catalogs. A woman student at Moody Bible Institute commented that, "after such 'telescopic' work [as Gray offered], Prof. Weidner and his 'microscopic' study of Genesis is delightful."[31]

To imply, however, that all Bible school Bible study had been planned and coordinated by reforming instuctors would be misleading. Many of the approaches to Bible instruction undoubtedly resulted from happenstance: who taught at a particular school and what kind of Bible instruction these teachers themselves had received. For instance, the approach of William P. Pinkham, at the Training School for Christian Workers, seems to have harked back to the methods of the mid-nineteenth century theological seminary rather than to the ideas of Gray and his fellow reformers. Pinkham "emphasized ascertaining the meaning of words in the original text. Sometimes it would take two class periods to cover one verse."[32] Similarly, George Pardington at the Missionary Training Institute was a scholar of Semitic languages and "One of his favorite ways of expounding the Scripture was to give the original and literal meaning."[33] Nevertheless, as Bible school educators communicated with each other more and more frequently, and as Moody Bible Institute increasingly became the standard for other schools, it is reasonable to assume that the teaching of the Bible grew more uniform and less subject to the idiosyncracies of individual instructors.

Whatever decade we discuss, Bible study at Bible schools included a great deal of memorization. Those evangelists were considered most effective who could quickly pull Scripture passages out of their memories at will. Louis Talbot, a student at Moody Bible Institute during the early teens, remarked in a letter home that he was thankful that he had "a good memory" and for that reason "study so far hasn't been as hard as I expected."[34] Instructors sometimes taught mnemonic techniques to help students commit Scripture to memory more efficiently. Outside of classes students themselves sometimes learned additional passages on their own initiative. Some schools kept elaborate tallies of how many verses had been committed to memory by various groups, such as the men and women students, or the junior and senior classes.

Other Bible classes served as auxiliaries: "Bible Geography," "Bible Atlas" (both studies of the geography of the Holy Land), and "Bible Introduction," which usually had an apologetic purpose. At Moody Bible Institute this subject dealt with "the authenticity of the Bible including its history, the formation of the canon, and current criticism."[35] In classes bearing titles like "Blackboard Drawing," students learned to illustrate their talks on the Bible with quick sketches. The idea was that, equipped with such skill in drawing, Christian workers could extend the audience's interest and comprehension. For instance, the Bible Institute of Los Angeles described its class in "The Use of the Blackboard":

> Every Bible teacher, and especially the workers in the Sunday-school, should be able to sketch off-hand maps or illustrations that will get and hold the attention of the class. Elaborate blackboard drawings are not attempted, but any students with some natural gift for drawing will get sufficient training in the fundamentals to develop the gift along correct lines.[36]

Bible school students learned to put Scripture to intensely practical uses. First, there was the personal dimension. Familiarity with Scripture was said to mold good character; in achieving virtue, it was thought, the model of biblical heroes could be particularly useful. (Recall Gray's catalog of Abraham's faults and virtues.) The example of the Bible was also thought to lead as a matter of course to the formation of "pure" and "wholesome" literary tastes. Further, the right Bible verse, located or remembered at an opportune moment, could help a Christian resist temptation. Certain psalms seemed designed for particular emotional states or special occasions. H. W. Pope, Superintendent of Men at Moody Bible Institute in the early teens, tendered this advice:

> In the morning read Psalm 19, and at even, Psalm 8. If you are going on a journey, Psalm 121 is appropriate. If it be Sunday, Psalm 122. If in perplexity, read Psalm 37. If you are grateful, choose Psalm 105, or 106, or 107. If your heart needs searching, Psalm 139 will accomplish it: . . . If it is comfort you need, you will find it in abundance in one or another of the following Psalms—34, 91 or 103.[37]

But above all, the Bible had the power to persuade students of their sinfulness and to teach the truth of salvation through faith. At Bible schools, nothing in life surpassed this function in importance.

Still, the Bible was even more than a guide to individual salvation; its usefulness extended to personal work with the unconverted or the Christian who had "fallen away." This personal work, conducted through the vehicle of Scripture, was a skill which teachers at Bible schools professed actually to teach. One woman told of watching a Moody Bible Institute student adroitly lead her friend, a "lapsed" Christian, back into the fold:

> How was it all done? I had talked and tried to win him [the friend] back, had recognized my failure and retreated to my prayers, afraid lest they, too, lack prevailing power. Here was a task for thinking. Knowledge of God's Word had done it,—applied knowledge—*usable* knowledge. I had talked but my own talk. This worker talked only *God's Words*. He presented a Saviour *whom he knew,* and to the sick soul a cure *he had taken.*[38]

Not long after, as a Bible Institute student herself, she was able to effect the conversion of a Norwegian immigrant who had lost her faith. All it took, she recalled, was the chance to speak with the woman for an extended period of time. Given such an opportunity, the student evangelist read biblical passages which she thought applied to the woman's situation: Jeremiah 2:5, 13; 1 Kings 11:9–11; Amos 4:11–12; "David's cry after two years of unconfessed sin: 'Restore unto me the joy of thy salvation' and its answer, in Ps. lxvi, 10–20, and the traitor Peter's loving recognition by our Lord: 'Go tell my disciples *and* Peter.'" She continued with Isaiah 13:5, 6 and Jeremiah 31:3 and finished with Jeremiah 29:11–13. The sacred word did its work; the woman rejoined the fold, a zealous Christian worker.[39]

Similarly, one of Reuben A. Torrey's assistants recalled dealing with a ragged and hopeless man who claimed he had committed the "unpardonable sin" and therefore planned to kill himself. The worker invited the sufferer to his hotel room, where he instructed him to read Revelation 22:17 and John 6:37 (". . . him who comes to me I will not cast out"). As the worker related it, "The time for decision had arrived. 'Are you willing to come?' The simple query received an affirmative answer. 'Then you have proven you have not committed the unpardonable sin. If that had been the case the Spirit of God would not have prompted you to come. You must decide for yourself.'" In an outcome typical for this genre of conversion tale, the man reappeared several days later with shining face, decent clothing, surrounded by his grateful family.[40]

Bible school personnel often wrote, as in the foregoing narrative, as if reading or quoting Scripture wrought a miraculous effect on hitherto indifferent sinners. H. W. Pope, in arguing for the memorization of Scripture, reported, "I know of a case where a wife committed two verses at an afternoon service, and at the supper table she used them on her husband. He was so affected that he knelt right down and accepted Christ without waiting to finish his supper."[41] An unidentified person at Moody Institute told the story of a similar, almost instantaneous conversion:

> One night one of our students in the Bible Institute was going down West Madison street. He saw another young fellow going along, and stepping up to him he said, "Are you a Christian?" "No sir, I am not." "Why are you not a Christian?" "Because I think the whole thing is humbug—there are so many hypocrites in the church." "Look here," said the student, stepping under a lamp and opening up his Bible to Romans xiv: 12, "Every one of us shall give account of himself to God." That went like an arrow to the young fellow's heart. He dropped on his knees right there on the sidewalk and accepted Jesus.[42]

It is striking how often in the accounts of conversions and successful counseling the troubled seeker or inquirer had been raised an evangelical Protestant (typically by a devout mother) but had "fallen away." Many of the objects of Christian workers' solicitude had had a childhood familiarity with the Bible and had once learned a few verses by heart. Sometimes if a worker approached such a person equipped with enough familiar scriptural passages, one or another would strike home. The properly prepared worker had either memorized such strategic verses or could readily locate them in the Bible.

The proselytization of Jews presented particular challenges for evangelists. Here again workers' success was thought to depend upon their familiarity with Scripture, particularly with certain Old Testament passages such as Deut. 28:37, 63–66; Num. 23:16; Isa. 53; Psalm 22; and Dan. 9:26. Judging from accounts, evangelists found it easiest to engage Jews in discussions of the meaning of Old Testament verses, though it is not clear that such conversations often resulted in the creation of "Hebrew Christians."

In addition to its uses in personal work, Bible study was critical because it supplied material for biblically oriented sermons. After about 1920, if not sooner, most Bible schools prepared preachers alongside lay people. A type of sermon known as "expository," based on a close biblical reading or series of such readings, was widely considered by fundamentalists to be the best spiritual fare conscientious ministers could offer their congregations. Only pastors trained at Bible schools, it was claimed, had the knowledge of Scripture necessary for the construction of expository sermons day in and day out.[43]

But not only ordained ministers were called upon to explicate the Bible; fundamentalists emphasized the role of lay people, both male and female, in leadership as well. Any active religious worker therefore had to be prepared to speak in public as well as in private—often extemporaneously—on the subject of Scripture. Bible school graduates, it was claimed, could do so with ease.

The test of success in Bible study as in other areas of the Bible school curriculum, then, was practicality: could Bible study be applied? Could students quickly locate verses they wanted, either for personal or evangelistic purposes? Did they know the Bible well enough so that if they were wrestling with a problem, their own or another's, they could recall passages which applied? Could they impress inquirers with the thoroughness of their acquaintance with God's word? Could they grasp another's needs and sense which verse would most likely meet them? Wrote a student at the New England School of Theology in praise of what she called a "practical working knowledge of the Scriptures":

> Suppose a person comes to you and asks, "How may I become a Christian?" Could you lead him to your Christ? Could you lead him to a place of assurance? Can you now suggest a verse to which to call the attention of the unsaved questioner, which would help him to see his sinful condition, the need of Christ and how to find Him? "But," you say, "I do not need

to know the Bible to lead a person to Christ. I could just tell him my experience—how I found Him." Wait a minute, my friend, are you sure that would do? Is it certain that the questioner's experience will be the same as yours and that you can satisfy him? God has not promised to use *your* words. . . . The Word of God is the only means by which God has promised to convict sinners, therefore, it is necessary to have a practical working knowledge of the Scriptures.[44]

The Bible school represented a twentieth century apotheosis of American Protestant biblicalism. In these schools Scripture became not only the center of the curriculum, but also the focus of the student's life. For the Bible school student to think, feel, react, and speak biblically was the ultimate goal. In the introduction to his *Synthetic Bible Studies,* James Gray asked rhetorically, "Do we not want this great Bible class to be something more than a feast of intellect?"[45] At the Bible schools the Bible class was indeed much more.

Personal Work Classes

Notwithstanding the numerous accounts in which sinners experienced instantaneous and miraculous changes of heart upon hearing scriptural passages, the Bible could not always be depended upon to accomplish its healing work unaided by human agency. In addition to their Bible classes, therefore, most Bible school students attended classes in what was variously referred to as "Personal Work," "Personal Evangelism," or "Personal Soul-Winning"; under an assortment of titles these classes taught students how to approach individuals in the attempt to convert them. Whatever the variations from school to school, these classes shared elements in common with a class in sales techniques: a goal of both kinds of classes was to identify certain sales pitches suited to the psychological makeups of prospective "customers."

Specifically, teachers in personal work classes outlined the most frequent objections raised by potential converts and suggested standard responses for evangelists to try; they identified scriptural passages that might prove effective in given cases, sometimes requiring students to memorize a large number of such verses; and they rehearsed operational principles that had proven effective in the past.[46] Certain precepts were standard in these classes. For example, students might be exhorted to proceed by listening carefully and then initiating conversational subjects closest to the potential convert's heart. Overzealous evangelists would be warned against criticizing and therefore alienating those they hoped to win over. Above all, students were cautioned against getting embroiled in endless theological and intellectual arguments with candidates for conversion; it was appeal to experience and to Scripture that was considered to bring about conversion, not pointless wrangling over ideas or doctrines.[47]

The organizing, classifying impulse so prominent among conservative evangelicals came into play in personal work classes: possible candidates for evangelism were grouped into character types, and members of "unorthodox" religious groups were studied with the view to identifying the most effective methods of approaching them. A good proportion of the four-term Moody Bible Institute "Cycle of Study" in Personal Work concentrated upon the various "classes" of people students might encounter and how to deal with them:

First Term Dealing with the Uninterested and Unconcerned; the Interested but Ignorant.

Second Term Dealing with Those Who are Interested but have Difficulties; the Self-Righteous; the Backslider; the Fearful and Despairing.

Third Term Those misled by Erroneous Views of the Truth; Roman Catholic; Unitarian; Universalist; Seventh-Day Adventist; Spiritualist; Jew; Christian Scientist; Milennial [sic] Dawnism.

Fourth Term The Procrastinator; the Obstinate; the Skeptic.[48]

Similar points were covered in a Personal Work class at Biola:

(4) How to begin a conversation (5) What instructions to give a new convert (6) How to deal with those who realize their need of a Saviour, and really desire to be saved. (7) How to deal with those who have little or no concern about their souls. (8) How to deal with those who have difficulties (. . . the various passages of Scripture that have been most used of God in delivering men from these difficulties, are brought forward). (9) How to deal with those who entertain false hopes. (10) How to deal with those who lack assurance. (11) How to deal with backsliders. (12) How to deal with professed skeptics, infidels, atheists, and agnostics. (13) How to deal with those who wish to put off decision until some other time. (14) How to deal with the deluded. Under this head all the modern delusions, such as Christian Science, Russellism, Seventh Day Adventism, Spiritualism, Theosophy, etc., are considered, . . . (15) How to deal with Christians who need counsel, rebuke or encouragement.[49]

Despite the attempt to reduce personal work to sets of principles which could be committed to memory and applied at the proper time, perhaps the most important pedagogical tool used in these classes was that of anecdote. To illustrate their points, instructors told edifying and inspiring stories of successful encounters between evangelist and prospective convert; from their own daily experiences students brought accounts of their attempts, both effective and failed, to proselytize, which could be used in class for the purpose of illustration and discussion.

Specialization

The majority of students at Bible schools selected a program called the "General Bible Course" or some similar title. Those enrolled in the general course took classes in Bible, evangelism, some theology, and perhaps a smattering of music or pedagogy. At most schools that were at least a few years old it was also possible to specialize; those who desired could learn special skills associated with such roles as pastor, Christian educator, religious musician, and foreign missionary. Students in these specialized courses often built their programs upon the same core of Bible and evangelism courses as the rest of the students. In addition, however, prospective foreign missionaries might study the history and principles of missions, elementary medical information and techniques, the linguistic principles thought to underlie most languages (a subject often called "phonetics"), biographies of missionaries of the past, and characteristics of particular mission fields. Christian educators-to-be were likely to attend classes in child psychology, principles of pedagogy, storytelling techniques, and Sunday school teaching methods. Prospective religious musicians took classes in music theory and lessons on their chosen instruments.

Later on, at the largest and wealthiest schools, students could choose subspecialties. For instance, at Moody Bible Institute the missionary course came to include special preparation in aviation for "missionary aviators" who would be using their expertise to transport themselves and their fellow workers to out-of-the-way mission stations. At both Moody and the Bible Institute of Los Angeles prospective "medical missionaries" could take a variety of classes in medicine from doctors and nurses. At many Bible schools the Christian education course came to provide additional classes for students who expected to concentrate their efforts upon work with youth, for example, or young children. This kind of development accelerated as fundamentalist organizations became more complex and sophisticated, and therefore required workers with more specialized knowledge and skills.[50]

Many of the classes taught under the headings of Foreign Missions, Christian Education, and Church Music were new on the religious educational scene—practical and created to meet a certain need. The pastoral course, however, often injected a traditional element into an otherwise untraditional curriculum; pastoral studies were likely to contain a number of subjects straight out of the nineteenth century theological curriculum: apologetics, Christian evidences, systematic theology, homiletics, pastoral theology, Greek, and Hebrew. Inertia partly explained the retention of these subjects; so did the fact that the ideal of the nineteenth century "learned minister" lingered among fundamentalists; for many of them,

the conviction persisted that the best-prepared minister was one who possessed a grasp of biblical tongues and of classical ministerial studies—in
addition to a warm style of evangelism and a thorough familiarity with
the biblical text in English. Thus, the nineteenth century theological seminary curriculum maintained a foothold, even in the unorthodox educational setting of the Bible school. The old curriculum, it was true, might
be quite changed or attenuated, owing to financial or educational exigency.
Instruction in Greek or Hebrew, for instance, was likely to be conducted
on a very elementary level, and homiletics classes might be altered in
part for women and lay men who were more likely to be teaching Bible
classes or giving Bible talks than delivering sermons from the pulpit.[51]

Classes Outside the Religious Curriculum

When, as often happened, a large portion of the student body possessed
only an elementary educational background, basic academic skills—reading, speech, composition, history, and arithmetic—had a place in the curriculum. At a few schools even penmanship and hygiene found their way
in. In some schools, the most elementary subjects were separated into
a "preparatory department," as was the practice in nineteenth century
colleges, and ill-prepared students had to pass them before embarking
upon the rest of the curriculum; the Central Bible Institute, for instance,
had a preparatory course between 1926 and 1931. In other schools the
rudimentary classes were dispersed throughout the whole curriculum.

If students were poorly prepared, the need for instruction in the basics
of reading, writing, and arithmetic was usually self-evident. Often, however, Bible school educators were cautious about introducing more advanced liberal arts subjects. One reason is obvious: the more liberal arts
subjects in the curriculum, the less time and energy students and faculty
would have left to learn or teach Bible and missions. But, in addition
to encroaching upon traditional Bible school curricular interests, the liberal arts could seem to endanger institutional goals in more fundamental
ways.

The social sciences—political science, economics, psychology, and sociology—posed the greatest threat to the Bible school view of the world, for
they tended to place humanity and human concepts in the foreground,
and offered naturalistic explanations of human behavior, with little or
no reference to divine activity and divine history. Furthermore, they employed the language of gradual development not favored by fundamentalists, who preferred to speak of discontinuities and crises in the individual
life, world history, and in geology and biology; they also depended heavily
on historical relativism. Then, too, the habit of "separation from the
world," practiced particularly among holiness advocates, discouraged extensive exploration of political, social, or economic phenomena.

Even when the social sciences were taught, it was their direct application to the tasks of evangelists and teachers that mattered. The Boston Bible School, for instance, offered one year of psychology in 1913–14: "This study is of great value to those whose business it will be in later years to deal with and persuade men. As the whole subject leads up to and centers in the cultivation of the will, one can see at a glance its importance in any course of study."[52] Bible school teachers of Christian education concentrated more on effective and proven pedagogical techniques than on the psychological theory—if any—undergirding them. The "how" rather than the "why" predominated, the practice rather than the theory.[53]

In some schools as time went on study of the social sciences most useful to missionary goals became more thorough and sophisticated, as Bible school educators discovered that by means of serious study of psychology, evangelists and teachers could truly understand their potential converts better—their motivations, hopes, and anxieties—and therefore could know how to approach them more effectively. Similarly, careful study of anthropology could aid prospective foreign missionaries in appreciating the possible points of connection between Christianity and the indigenous religions of the people they planned to evangelize. One eventual sign of this increased interest in anthropology, for instance, was the establishment in 1960 of the graduate level Jaffray School of Missions at the Missionary Training Institute in Nyack, New York; the new school specialized in two areas: advanced study in theology and, significantly, cultural anthropology. Such developments, however, belonged to the later history of Bible schools.

Contrary to what might be assumed, science was not necessarily regarded as threatening, because it could be learned in its Baconian version, as facts, information, and techniques, rather than as theories or as a skeptical, inquiring approach to the world. Nevertheless, most Bible schools simply lacked the time, personnel, and demonstration equipment necessary for teaching any kind of science until late in their development. History was acceptable, too, because it could be taught as some form of sacred or church history. But often the teaching of history simply had to wait for the expansion of the curriculum and the hiring of additional instructors.

English literature at one level or another usually found its way into the Bible school curriculum quite early on, partly because the subject was usually linked with the task of improving students' writing. Because teachers could carefully select the reading for its "wholesomeness" and its "Christian" content, literature was safe. Moreover, literary studies had the advantage of bestowing a little polish upon students whose small town backgrounds often did not include much acquaintance with literature or the arts. Such students were, after all, typically upwardly mobile and eager to acquire the marks of gentility.

At Gordon College under Nathan Wood, particularly, the liberal arts were valued for the "culture" they could transmit to students. "Culture" in fact was a favorite word there; in catalogs and letters the school's head, Nathan R. Wood, praised "college culture," referring admiringly to "the high type of culture" at the "great English universities," and cited it as an essential ingredient in Gordon education. There, it is clear, "culture" was to be gathered from classes surveying English literature, up to and including Victorian writers such as Arnold and Tennyson, and from instruction in rhetoric, philosophy, science, history, French, and mathematics; all these subjects were added to the curriculum soon after Wood became dean in 1910. In part these classes functioned to transmit a more cosmopolitan aura to unsophisticated students who had lately poured down into Boston from the rural towns of maritime Canada and northern New England.[54] At Gordon, enculturation involved encouraging a dawning appreciation of genteel literature; it meant broadening students' horizons with at least a smattering of philosophy and history; and perhaps above all, culture meant enabling them to express themselves correctly and even with grace and polish.[55] To be sure, literature at Gordon (and at other Bible schools) was more likely to be "edifying" than thought-provoking; the frame of reference supplied by history and philosophy was to teach an appreciation and defense of Christianity—and "Christian civilization"—rather than a critical stance toward it. Culture like knowledge was to be prized and preserved, not improved, created, or changed.

Gordon College's efforts to incorporate the liberal arts were more vigorous and successful than those of other Bible schools, and in fact not all Bible school educators would have wanted to emulate Gordon's romance with culture, which in their view too easily verged into "worldliness." But the model existed in the Bible school group as well as in higher education generally, and pointed the way for any other schools whose future leaders might wish to follow.

There were many consistencies and constancies in the Bible school curriculum, whatever the time period or the school: the unprecedented emphasis on Bible study and certain understandings of Scripture; a preoccupation with the *practice* of evangelism and missions; and the five-course division (General Bible, Pastors, Christian Education, Missionary, and Music Courses). Yet it is also true that the individual Bible school curricula were shaped by a liberal amount of happenstance. After all, the schools were young and relatively free of educational tradition; for a long time they escaped the oversight of accrediting and other regulatory agencies; they belonged to no formal organization of Bible schools; and if they were to survive they needed to be responsive to the particular needs and visions of founding and supporting groups and individuals. For this reason, except for a basic agreement about the content of the curriculum and the kinds of roles for which students were being prepared, there was no standard pedagogical style. To be sure, rote memorization was popular with instructors, as was recitation. In many classes students listened and took notes while instructors lectured. It is improbable that free-ranging discussions were much encouraged. And yet, when one recalls that many of the Bible school subjects were not the usual high school or college fare, it seems unlikely that classroom approaches were uniformly old fashioned. Rather, teachers of novel subjects—child pedagogy and personal evangelism, for instance—had to improvise. And, above all, room had to be left in all classes for what Bible school leaders sometimes called the guidings of the Spirit.

If we were to end our exploration of what happened inside Bible schools with this examination of the curriculum we would wind up with a grievously incomplete picture of school life. The "extracurriculum" played at least as important a part in what students learned as what went on in the classroom; in fact the extracurriculum undoubtedly altered the nature of the classroom experience itself, and it is to that aspect of Bible school life that the next chapter turns.

VIII

INSIDE THE BIBLE SCHOOL
BEYOND THE CLASSROOM

Practical Work

Bible school students typically spent several hours a week in actual religious work outside the school, much of it involving evangelism. In fact, it was not unusual for Bible school educators, apparently mindful of prestigious medical school and science education, to speak of this practical work as the "clinic" or "laboratory" for Bible school students.[1] These "clinics" supplemented the "how to" instruction of the classroom. Or, rather, so important was practical work in some schools, especially early on, that it might more properly be argued that the classroom learning supplemented the practical work experience. During the early years at the Bible Institute of Los Angeles, for instance, evangelistic activities seem to have taken priority over those in the classroom. Even as late as 1915 the Bible institute was being described not so much as a school as "a soul saving station whose workers were busy night and day reaching unsaved people in all walks of life."[2]

The practice of requiring students to obtain practical training served several purposes. First, it obeyed the principle of then-current educational theory that students learned best by doing. The practice also insured that students from working classes would not lose touch with the "men in the shops"; perhaps more to the point, since it is unclear that many students came from the working classes, it helped middle class students to develop sympathy with blue collar workers and the knowledge of how to deal effectively with them. Fundamentalists, including Bible school educators, were well aware that Protestantism had not succeeded very well in attracting the laboring classes, and that a more effective approach was required. As a Moody Institute writer warned,

> If you do not know how to make a twenty minute speech in about six and one-half minutes you had better not go to a "shop Bible class." If you cannot make a "corking good speech" from a soap box; if your vocabulary is only understood at the Ibsen Club; if you do not know the problems

of the working class and cannot speak of them without the use of personalities or abuse, you had better not go.[3]

Clearly work outside the school was designed, among other things, to produce evangelists who could speak the language and respond to the needs of working people.

Practical work also provided a welcome outlet for students who were, as they might have put it, "on fire for souls." Many eagerly regarded it as the core of their training, the most challenging part; such students would likely have engaged in some form of personal evangelism even if it had not been part of the school's program. Finally, practical work tested students, allowing them to see their weaknesses and enabling Bible school instructors to spot those who were too lukewarm or too tactless to evangelize effectively.

A. B. Simpson, founder of the Missionary Training Institute, could have been speaking for other Bible school educators when in an 1897 article he set forth the assumptions underlying the emphasis on practice. Criticizing the churches' traditional method of educating the ministry—he must have had theological seminaries in mind—he argued that what was needed was men and women who knew their way around the real world: "the age needs practical men, men that are in touch with their fellowmen, men that understand the real needs of the sinful and sorrowing, men that have been taught to go down into the depths and, hand to hand and heart to heart, pluck sinners as brands from the burning." What was required, he added, was "actual soul winning and wise effective methods of reaching men."[4]

Generally students could choose from a variety of practical work assignments. At the Bible Institute of Los Angeles, these were purposely rotated so that students would acquire a variety of experiences. As part of their practical work it was usual for Bible school students to lead church choirs, teach Sunday school and Bible classes, or organize and advise young people's groups. The focus for some, however, was not churches but rather religious and philanthrophic institutions of other kinds: students worked in asylums, almshouses, old people's homes (as they were called), hospitals, prisons, industrial homes, rescue missions, settlement houses, and city missions. In these settings they sometimes did social service work, feeding and clothing the destitute, for instance, or teaching immigrants English and practical skills. Concomitantly, however, they acted as evangelists, conducting personal work, teaching the Bible, and leading evangelistic meetings with hymn singing, testimony, and short talks on the Bible. Still other students took to the out-of-doors; individually, in pairs, or in groups, they distributed Bibles and tracts; they conducted "house-to-house visitation," that is, they knocked on the doors of householders or tenement dwellers and tried to witness to them; still other students led open air meetings, services in tents, or impromptu street services, often with the aid of a portable organ and a plentiful supply of tracts. Finally, Bible school students could usually be drafted to assist in mass revival meetings, as ushers, choristers, and personal workers. In 1917, Gordon College students turned out in force to assist at the Billy Sunday meetings in Boston.

A 1912 feature in the *Alliance Weekly* allows a fairly detailed picture of the activities of students at the Missionary Training Institute. It reported that work with prisoners "has borne some fruit, though there is much to discourage, most of the inmates being sin-hardened and gospel-hardened." Students walked fifteen miles round trip to the New City Jail, and visited the hospital in Nyack, as well as the one in Tarrytown across the Hudson. One student had organized a Christian Endeavor Society in the "colored" Methodist church in Nyack; a Finnish student had been conducting services for his fellow countrymen in Nyack and Englewood, New Jersey, and reported twenty-eight conversions. Women students at the Institute set up and staffed a night school for Italian immigrants in the Nyack YMCA. Adopting a practice of American temperance workers, Institute students entered saloons in Nyack and the neighboring towns of Piermont and Sparkill, handed out copies of Scripture, and exhorted the drinkers to abandon the saloons for the Nyack Gospel Mission. Sometimes they succeeded, sometimes not: "in a few instances the workers were ejected from the premises and asked not to come again."[5]

At Biola students worked in railway carbarns and firehouses, singing and leading short worship services during the breaks between shifts. At this school the most difficult assignment of all was considered to be duty on weekend nights in a rented building on Los Angeles' skid row. Male students would go there, taking doughnuts and coffee. They would invite vagrants to come in, attracting perhaps four, five, or six. Then they would try to get the men to sing; one student would preach. This was discouraging work, since a portion of the small audience usually nodded off. It could be rough work also, and was the one practical work assignment closed to the women students.

At most Bible schools newcomers to the United States were a central concern, especially since most of them were at least nominal Catholics. As one of their assignments in 1910, Moody Institute students evangelized the children of immigrants:

> the plan being to send out a band of four to six students, men and women, among the Italian, Polish and Bohemian children on Sunday afternoons. They carry a banner containing a picture descriptive of the Sunday-school lesson for the day, a crowd is gathered by singing, and then they tell the story of the lesson, using the picture to make themselves better understood. After the meeting they do such personal work as they are able, and distribute cards giving in miniature the picture on the banner, and also the Scripture teaching of the lesson in the language of the different nationalities, which the little ones bring home to their parents.[6]

Work with immigrants was considered particularly germane for the numerous students with foreign missionary aspirations. If evangelists could prove effective with Mexicans in Los Angeles or Italians in Chicago who knew neither the English language nor the message of the Gospel, surely they could successfully proselytize Chinese, Sudanese, or South Americans. Upon occasion work with urban immigrants also served to spark students' interest in foreign missions. In his first year at Moody Bible Institute one student did work in a Chinese mission which was said to have "marked the beginning of his interest in foreign missions."[7]

When a school was located near a harbor, sailors attracted particular solicitude, perhaps because of their reputation for foul language and dissipated lives. Students eagerly sought out missions for seamen. Gordon students selected a battleship in the Charlestown Navy Yard as a site for their evangelistic efforts; Biola students had been given a boat by a well wisher so that they could easily board ships riding at anchor in Los Angeles harbor; there they sought out not only a ship's crew but also its passengers. To accommodate the varied nationalities usually on board, they distributed literature translated into a number of different languages.

Often students intending to become ministers engaged in more traditional forms of practical work, those long familiar to theological seminary students. They worked as temporary ministers in churches; pastored small and perhaps struggling congregations; started up new churches of their own; or substituted for regular ministers during summer vacations.

During the early days of Bible school education, practical work was considered to be educative in itself, and usually educators made little systematic attempt to supervise students' experience. Since student bodies were small, it was probably customary for students to report informally to teachers, consulting with them on how to handle problems they encountered during their practical work. Moreover, some instructors accompanied students when they went out to evangelize in missions and on street corners. As time went on, however, school leaders often made concerted attempts to regularize the practical work and to encourage students to reflect systematically on their experiences. They appointed directors or superintendents of practical work, required students to submit reports on their work, and designated occasions for them to receive comments and suggestions from their mentors.

Despite the consistently vigorous rhetoric about the importance of experience, practical work programs sometimes ran into difficulties. In fact, at some schools the appointment of a director of practical work may have represented attempts to remedy such problems. It is likely that difficulties cropped up with particular frequency when school leaders determined to raise academic standards; by increasing the emphasis on classroom studies, thereby redistributing students' time and energy, they may inadvertently have diminished student opportunities for intensive, meaningful firsthand experience.

The example of the Missionary Training Institute allows us a glimpse into the difficulties that could afflict the practical work program. By 1912 something seems to have gone awry in the Institute's efforts in this area. That year the writer of a column on Nyack activities felt compelled to refute the "common error" that "our students have been gaining little practical training while here," but nevertheless admitted that "we have deeply felt the need of a thorough system, under a regular staff teacher."[8] A couple of months later another writer conceded that "some students have had more notebooks than actual ability when leaving the School."[9]

These evidences of dissatisfaction with students' degree of practical experience should be understood against the background of the brief existence of an Alliance "Home School and Worker's Training Institute" in New York City. Established in 1907, it was designed to fill the vacuum left by the 1897 departure of the older school for Nyack, some twenty miles up the Hudson. The New York City school supplemented the more limited practical experience available to Nyack students; seniors there became accustomed to spend a month at the Home School before graduating. In 1912, however, the Home School was discontinued and absorbed into Nyack, probably as the result of a drive for "efficiency" during that year. Reports in the *Alliance Weekly* make it clear that some Alliance people were discontent or at least perplexed over the Home School's closing. It seems reasonable to surmise that the 1912 criticism of Nyack's practical training program was related to the sudden demise of the Home School in the same year. At any rate, the response to the criticism appears to have been the appointment of a "Superintendent of Christian Work" shortly before the school year beginning in fall 1912. Under his direction, it was announced, "Weekly meetings will be held with the bands of workers for conference and comparison of results."[10]

In a larger way, the suggestion of problems in the Institute's conduct of practical work may point to a surfacing of the tension between practical and academic learning that affected so much turn-of-the-century education. Certainly the evidence at the time these complaints were registered suggests that Institute leaders had newly committed themselves to raising academic standards. For instance, a writer of a 1912 column asserted that the "Schools at Nyack do not belong to the class of cheap religious institutions where there may be a good deal of religion but very questionable instruction along intellectual lines."[11] In their efforts to strengthen the school "along intellectual lines" Nyack leaders may have started downplaying practical experience, or at least have appeared to be doing so. It is doubtful that this conflict—the rise of academic standards versus the attainment of extensive practical experience—was unique to the Missionary Training Institute.

Notwithstanding the existence of problems in practical work programs, however, there is no denying that earnest students managed to get considerable amounts of actual experience in the course of their Bible school education. As a result they had the opportunity to develop initiative and leadership. In theory, at least, practical work bred individuals who had grown used to seizing evangelical opportunities, who had tested and proven themselves in the school of experience, and who as a result had added to their skill and self-confidence as evangelists. Such workers were obviously invaluable to the fundamentalist movement.

Probably the practical assignments had an unintended effect: they modified the efforts of Bible school educators to shelter and protect their charges from the corrupting influences of the outside world—efforts that grew more pronounced as time went on. Protection by itself might have produced graduates who were too naive and impressionable to conduct effective evangelism—hothouse evangelists; practical work, on the other hand, rendered students worldly, knowledgeable, and "street wise" in acceptable and practical ways.

One of the most significant contributions of practical work to the education of students was seldom emphasized by Bible school educators themselves: since most early Bible schools were located in cities, Bible school students usually conducted their practical work assignments in urban settings. Since so many Bible school students came from farming and small town backgrounds, one result of practical work was to introduce rural Protestants to the city. Through practical work, Bible school students gained an awareness of typically urban groups—immigrants, blacks, Jews, working class people—they might not otherwise have known. Presumably, they learned about their problems, histories, and aspirations and came to know effective ways of evangelizing them; whatever their nostalgia for the agrarian America of their pasts, they came to appreciate the enormity of the evangelical tasks to be accomplished in the cities. Thus, through their practical work, Bible school students hastened the adaptation of fundamentalism to the conditions of urban America and thereby contributed in no small measure to the movement's educational effectiveness.

Cultivating Consecration

In addition to encouraging students to acquire useful knowledge and practical skills, Bible school educators also hoped to shape their spiritual and emotional lives: to help them resolve their spiritual conflicts, deepen their righteousness, strengthen their faith, broaden their religious experience, increase their steadfastness, and promote their self-assurance. Not infrequently, to be sure, the atmosphere of Bible schools intensified emotional and religious conflicts that students had brought with them, or touched off new upheavals. But this was supposed to be temporary, a prelude to an abiding and activist faith.

Many entering students had not had a chance to mature spiritually.

Some had not even been converted; they had often had been sent by worried parents in the hope that the atmosphere and regimen of the Bible school would effect a change in their yet unsaved offspring. Many students who had experienced conversion by the time they reached school found themselves struggling with troublesome doubts or a nagging sense of sin and worthlessness.

Bible school students also faced vocational dilemmas. Even if they had long before determined to "labor in the Lord's vineyard," as they might have put it, many students struggled with difficult decisions about exactly what form that labor should take. Agonizing questions about personal identity were often involved. One circumstance which made the decision particularly trying was that by common consent a "definite call" to the foreign mission field was considered by far the most noble. But not every Bible school student felt qualified for that kind of service; or, in the case of some, practical considerations stood in the way. Relatives might have to be cared for, and even devout parents were sometimes reluctant to relinquish their children to the danger, privation, and long absence involved in foreign missionary service. A spouse might refuse to go overseas. Even when the way lay open to foreign missionary service, the choice of *which* missionary field sometimes became an occasion for additional soul searching.

The autobiographical account of Christina E. Lang, who attended New England School of Theology in 1922, illustrates some of the problems students faced. Before entering the school, Lang had grappled with a number of spiritual and vocational conflicts. God had "spoken" to her several times, she said, before she finally responded by converting at age fourteen. As a high school student facing a particularly worrisome examination, she had promised to become a missionary if God helped her to pass the test. Though she passed, "[I] tried to forget the promise I had made, but the Lord did not let me." After considerable indecision about what to do after graduation from high school, she had entered the New England School of Theology. There the old struggles intensified. Her mother had begged her to become a home instead of a foreign missionary, and for a while she had determined to accede to the maternal wish to keep her daughter close by; but in the charged atmosphere of the school the thought of foreign service would not die. By her senior year, the cost of her prolonged struggle over her goals appeared to have been anxiety and religious apathy. "I felt restless and dissatisfied with what I was doing," she recalled. "I could not go to church, nor listen to a sermon, without feeling very uncomfortable and nervous, and could not get at all interested in the message." The turning point came when a fellow student happened to mention the need for a missionary to work at an orphanage in India. This casual remark revived Lang's uneasiness about her unfulfilled promise; another period of turmoil followed, but

finally two circumstances gave her rest by convincing her that God wanted
her in the Indian orphanage. First, apparently coincidental references
to India kept cropping up around her, and, second, random passages
she opened to in the Bible seemed to point in a veiled way toward India.

Even then resolution gave way to another period of agonizing—"the
Devil got busy and began to tempt me to do different things"—but Lang
finally determined to "let God be first in my life!" The result was inner
peace and a revival of religious vitality:

> Praise God, when I obeyed his call he came into my life in all fulness.
> Since my decision I have grown into closer companionship with my Lord,
> and he is talking with me through his Word, and by the still, small voice,
> telling me of his desire for my life; and I have his precious promise with
> me every day: "Lo, I am with you alway, even unto the end of the world!"[12]

As if the problems of faith and vocation such as those faced by Lang
were not formidable enough, students often imposed upon themselves
rigorous moral guidelines which were reinforced by the Bible school ethos.
Sometimes a partial moral transformation had already taken place before
students arrived at Bible school. Some students were in the process of
renouncing the pursuit of fame and fortune; others had turned their
backs on disreputable habits. Some made good on longstanding debts
even if they had to conduct a lengthy and strenuous search in order to
locate old creditors. Usually the ambiance of the Bible school strengthened
and intensified these initial impulses toward moral reform and purity.
An alumnus from Moody Bible Institute recalled, for instance, "As soon
as the new student begins to sense the atmosphere of the school his standard of character and conduct begins to rise. In some cases the change
is so radical that he begins to write letters of apology and confession
to people whom he has wronged, and not infrequently to make restitution
of money."[13] At Biola a female student told of being kept awake by the
fact that she had accepted a job offered her, even though she knew another
student needed employment more than she. After tossing and turning
for hours, she finally decided to turn the job over to the needier student
and then immediately fell into a peaceful sleep.[14]

The generalized perfectionist atmosphere, devoid of concessions to
human weakness, which left it to individual students to search their con-
sciences in order to determine if they were obeying God's will "to the
fullest," could be very demanding. Gordon students, for instance, were
expected to pattern their lives according to resolutions like the following:
"I will subordinate all my temporal interests to the one great work of
honoring God, in winning men to Christ." For students who interpreted
the resolution literally—and some tried—this behest demanded nothing
less than total self-sacrifice. Any who attempted to heed it would, in the
very nature of things, fall short. At its most stringent, the Bible school

definition of righteousness permitted very few occasions for self-satisfaction or peace of mind.

Furthermore, as part of their education in righteousness, Bible school students learned to make the most of every moment to engage in useful activity. Ideally, they rose early and retired early (unless they labored late in the business of their Lord); they studied the word of God in every spare minute, and they kept constantly on the lookout for opportunities to speak to strangers about Christ. Not much value was placed on fun, frivolity or relaxation. Even organized athletics was ignored, at least until much later. The strain upon students must have been considerable.

Finally, most Bible school students experienced a great deal of stress while witnessing in a hostile world. Their practical work usually involved proselytizing the uninterested, disenchanted, or resistant; and they were expected to take advantage of chance encounters with strangers on streetcars or in stores without knowing what kind of reception their overtures would receive. In their attempts at evangelism, students had to learn to cope with the unpleasantness of dealing with people who at best judged them old-fashioned and perhaps amusing, at worst crazy, offensive, and even dangerous. New Bible school students were apt to feel particularly anxious when they faced their first practical work assignment; some students never overcame their shyness and nervousness, despite much practice. Even those for whom personal work had become routine sometimes became discouraged when their efforts met with repeated rejection or derision.

These struggles, common to Bible school life—for more meaningful spiritual experiences, for a worthy vocation, for greater righteousness, and for the boldness required by evangelists—were encouraged, even if the attendant strain made the Bible school something of an emotional pressure cooker. Many elements of life at the Bible school were designed to promote and intensify those strivings but also to foster satisfactory resolutions.

In helping students to spiritual maturity, nothing was more important than emulation; the faculty, occasional speakers and lecturers, graduates, and the biographies of admired evangelicals of the past all served the end of inspiring students and of demonstrating what roles they too might play in furthering "the King's business." Generally speaking, the faculty of Bible schools were chosen for the quality of their spiritual lives. Those teachers endowed with vital faiths could transmit their visions to their students, as a description of A. B. Simpson suggests:

> suddenly a hush falls, for down the aisle comes the dignified form of Dr. Simpson. The massive head upon the broad shoulders is bowed as one who enters a holy place. . . . he takes his chair, opens his Bible, and smiles in delightful comradeship upon his class. "Will you not sing another chorus?" he asks "Song is a little of heaven loaned to earth." He is one of us, young as the youngest. One feels that he knows every thought and

desire of the most wayward heart, yet his face and voice betray the fact that he has been caught up into the third Heaven and has seen things unlawful to utter. . . . We can only sing, "My Jesus, I Love Thee, I Know Thou Art Mine," or some similar hymn of adoration. Then follows the prayer as he talks about us to Christ Jesus at his side. We breathe softly and listen for each word as it is uttered. It would not surprise us much to hear an audible answer because the Lord seems so near. In such moments our petty sorrows and little selfish plans wither and are gone. Deep in the soul is born a desire to please in all things, not Dr. Simpson, but that Living One, whose voice whispers to us, and whose hand we feel upon our hearts. As the Scriptures are expounded, the same Presence lingers and many a splendid point of truth is not only intellectually grasped, but is personally applied as some convicted one takes a practical step of obedience and whispers, "Lord, I will."[15]

The faculty also served as models of the activism characteristic of fundamentalist Christianity. It was not unusual for Bible school instructors to carry on a number of religious functions in addition to their teaching; they served simultaneously as pastors, evangelists, administrators, missionaries, writers, editors, and founders and organizers of religious institutions and agencies. Some faculty members had served as foreign missionaries. A. E. Thompson, a prominent teacher at the Missionary Training Institute, had spent much of his life in Palestine, while Robert Glover, instructor of a class in missions there, had worked in China. Many teachers, particularly those who had of necessity become involved in building new evangelical institutions, had demonstrated a high degree of initiative and organizational ability. The students under their tutelage were encouraged to emulate their practical exploits and achievements as well as their piety.

More than emulation was involved, however. Bible school teachers served their students as counselors; in fact, they did more, often acting as spiritual mothers and fathers. Bible school leaders customarily described their institutions as "homes." This was not unusual; administrators of schools of many varieties advertised the domestic virtues of their institutions. In the case of the Bible schools, however, this ascription was particularly justified. To begin with, many Bible schools were small enough for all members of the community to know each other well. Bible school teaching was often a family affair; husband and wife both taught, or worked for the school in some other capacity. Among the full-time faculty, few felt that their duties were discharged when they left the classroom. They usually tried to be present at worship services, prayer meetings, and school social events, and they made themselves available to individual students who needed academic or spiritual help. This was possible because faculty often lived at the Bible school or nearby (often they were required to). Students responded by bestowing nicknames such as "pappy" and "mother" upon their mentors.

Students in Bible schools were also exposed to a stream of visitors, who, in addition to providing information, inspired faith and activism as well. Students at the Missionary Training Institute, for instance, heard both city and foreign missionaries. One of the most colorful Alliance city mission leaders was "Mother" Whittemore, who in 1890 had founded the "Door of Hope," a mission in New York City intended for the rescue of "fallen" women. Mrs. Whittemore, a converted socialite, had donned a Salvation Army-like uniform and wore a "P.B.F." pin (signifying "Past, Buried, Forgotten"). She scoured the seamiest streets of New York in search of disreputable females. One of Mrs. Whittemore's prize converts was "Delia the Bluebird of Mulberry Bend," a reformed drunkard and drug addict. On a Friday night in 1891, "Mrs. Whittemore gave, before the sermon, a very interesting address to the students of the Training College—dressing herself in the dress in which she visits the slums, and gave many touching incidents to which she had been an eye-witness."[16] A couple of decades later, "Brother Crawford," representing a considerable Alliance presence in Boone, Iowa, offered a series of addresses, one on the text from I Corinthians 4:9, "Appointed to death": "it was a very simple, clear, but solemn talk on the condition of being a minister of Christ after the apostolic type."[17]

One of the greatest inspirational resources a school possessed was its graduates. Alumni/ae who had undertaken evangelistic tasks stirred special interest in Bible school students. If those who had gone before could accomplish such deeds, then so could they; in fact, it was incumbent upon them to measure up to the standards which had been set by their predecessors. Bible schools retained especially close ties with their alumni/ae who were in religious areas of work. Such graduates usually demonstrated great loyalty, returning to their alma maters as often as geography would allow; in lieu of actual visits they might correspond with former teachers and with students or write articles for the school journals and yearbooks. School publications usually carried detailed information on what graduates of the school were accomplishing on the home and foreign missions fields.

The reaction to the example of C. W. McDonald, a former student at the Missionary Training Institute, was extreme, but shows how the sacrifices of graduates could stir the student body. McDonald had left the Missionary Training Institute after one term to become a "Christian Evangelist" in Ohio. His sudden death shortly after he arrived there was announced in the January 16, 1891 edition of the *Christian Alliance*. A week later, an article in the same paper reported that the news of McDonald's death "was followed by a season of deep heart searching on the part of all who knew him, and the result was that on Thursday morning, Jan. 16, during morning prayers a very remarkable outpouring of the Holy Spirit began, and for several days the college was again transformed into a place of very sacred communion and a very gate of heaven." The revival continued, and on February 6 the *Christian Alliance* followed up its initial report:

> The precious outpouring of the Spirit, so wonderfully given a few weeks ago at the morning prayers, has not yet been withdrawn. It is no infrequent thing for the constraining power of his presence to be so felt in these morning gatherings that they are prolonged even to the mid-day meal, and that hush which speaks so plainly of God is noticed in very many of the young people in a more marked manner than formerly.[18]

Graduates departing as foreign missionaries often received impressive sendoffs that heartened not only them but also those they left behind. At the school there might be a reception in their honor; or the school community might offer prayers for their success and for the evangelization of the world in general; the missionaries might give testimony, telling how they had come to the decision for foreign service; if the school was located near a major harbor, the entire faculty and student body might gather on the pier for the sailing. Once the graduates had arrived at their destinations, students back at the school followed their progress with great interest. Finally, students were encouraged to pattern themselves after leaders and heroes whom they could never know personally. Hudson Taylor and George Muller have already been mentioned; both men inspired untold numbers of pages written for the edification of the faithful. Dwight L. Moody was another subject for inspirational biographies. The Missionary Training Institute and Gordon's training institute each had their own patron saints, Simpson and Gordon, whose exemplary biographies influenced students at those and other schools. Many of the other leaders of the early generations had their chroniclers: the well-known British Baptist, Charles Haddon Spurgeon; the British missionary leader, H. Grattan Guinness; and the dedicated young missionary, William Whiting Borden. Conservatives also reached further back into a number of divergent Protestant traditions for additional heroes: Martin Luther, David Brainerd, Adoniram Judson (and his wives, Ann Hasseltine Judson and Sarah Boardman Judson), Charles Grandison Finney, John Wesley, and John Woolman. Thus, the world of the Bible school student was populated with heroes, both living and dead, who taught the lesson that all things were possible to those with faith.

Other facets of Bible school life educated the students in piety. Probably nothing did more to set the Bible school off from all other educational institutions than the pervasiveness of evangelical music, particularly hymns. Training in music was an important part of the formal curriculum of most Bible schools; accordingly, the Bible school campus constantly resounded with the strains of practicing singers, pianists, trumpeters, and organists. Almost every school had at least one chorus and perhaps also a male and a female vocal quartet or octet. But all students sang, and not just during occasions of formal worship. Anthems rang out from devotional gatherings even before breakfast; classes often began and ended with them; mealtimes became the occasions for yet more singing; picnics and other student outings would almost certainly echo with gospel songs. At the Missionary Training Institute, the "quiet hour" each night was announced "in one dormitory at least by the singing or playing softly of a devotional hymn, by a group going from floor to floor."[19] Students also customarily struck up hymns while conducting their practical work in prisons, hospitals, and saloons. And it was commonplace at most Bible schools for members of the faculty to write hymns in their spare hours; thus, each school had its own indigenous anthems.

Hymns taught the lessons of service, devotion, and piety, both through the catchy rhythms and moving melodies and also through the words that quoted Scripture and drew upon a rhetoric of persuasion and exhortation. When students at the Missionary Training Institute sang Kenneth Mackenzie's hymn, "Here am I, Oh Lord, send me,"[20] for instance, they learned the attitude considered proper for a missionary:

> I have heard my Saviour calling,
>   To the harvest rich and fair;
> Where the workmen now are busy,
>   I must take my station there.
>
> Tho' I may not with the reapers
>   Gather large and heavy sheaves,
> I, like Ruth, may catch stray handfuls
>   Which some careless gleaner leaves.
>
> Jesus, use me now and ever
>   I will give myself to Thee,
> Thine to be in body, soul and spirit,
>   Here am I, O Lord, send me.

Prayer was equally omnipresent at most Bible schools. Prayer meetings took many forms: formally scheduled daily, weekly, or monthly occasions arranged by the faculty or administration; meetings organized and presided over by the students themselves; all-day prayer meetings for special objects such as missions or the success of graduates; and impromptu gatherings involving any number of students, from a handful to the entire student body. A student at Boston Bible School recalled "gathering in small groups to take some special burden to the Lord."[21] At the Christian Workers Training Institute in Los Angeles, a Quaker institution, "Sometimes the 5 a.m. Thursday prayer hour would last until 9 a.m."[22] Biola students gathered daily in what was called the "superintendents' half hour" right after breakfast, to which the superintendents brought "whatever message for the day that God may have given them." After supper the students again met for prayer; this time they led the gathering. Finally,

Biola had daily "corridor prayer meetings," at which "The students on each corridor gather in a student's room at whatever hour is most convenient to discuss their perplexing personal problems and to present them to God for solution. It is here, as perhaps at no other gathering, that definiteness in prayer is learned."[23] At Moody Bible Institute, periodic financial crises were often climaxed by daylong sessions of prayer for the future of the school. In 1922 Institute leaders, demonstrating their customary command of statistics, reported that there were 1,324 "stated prayer meetings" per month, "besides innumerable gatherings for prayer that spring up spontaneously and cannot be tabulated."[24]

In addition to hymn singing, prayer meetings usually consisted of Bible reading (often students would follow the passage in their own Bibles), and sometimes brief remarks from the prayer leader. One of the most important ingredients of such gatherings for prayer was the giving of testimony by all participants. When students "testified," they told and re-told the story of their spiritual journeys. Testimonies usually dealt with the teller's conversion, dedication to Christian work, episodes of doubt and backsliding, and renewals of spiritual vitality. Because most testimonies had been offered many times, they often sounded as though they had been learned by heart, even rehearsed; and, because they covered common experiences, they frequently incorporated the same repeated phrases; they also quoted many of the same scriptural verses. This use of stock phrases and familiar quotations prevented the testimonies from becoming too painfully personal, while the formulistic element also facilitated their repetition and dissemination.

Unfortunately, few transcripts exist from the frequent occasions upon which testimony was given, but now and then journals printed student testimonies. Ellen Coburn, a student at the New England School of Theology in 1922–23, testified,

> My folks, though not Christians, always enforced church attendance but tolerated dancing and theatre attendance with other worldly amusements. I found enjoyment in these but many times while at a dance my thoughts were turned to something which seemed to me more satisfying, the songs of praise or the text of the Sunday before. . . . At one dance a voice seemed to say to me, "Are you going to spend your whole life in this manner?" Thoughts of how Christ had suffered on the cross, taking upon himself the iniquity of us all, helped me to decide to give up dancing. Two weeks later, in a theatre, I heard the voice saying, "If Christ should come tonight, would you be saved?" The thought of being lost troubled me, and I felt sure, that if Christ should come, He never would come into the theatre to save me. A vision of Christ standing with outstretched arms, pleading with me, remained in my mind. A week later . . . I accepted Jesus as my Saviour. My soul was flooded with happiness, and joy and peace. Everything, even nature put on a new beauty. Soon I was baptized and became interested in church life, but he had to lead me into service by bringing about my

election to the charge of our Sunday school. I did not feel at all capable of undertaking the work, but I loved God and despite my inadequate training, for two years I gave my time to work with the children. Upon the approach of hard times and the removal of some families, feeling that I was left alone with the work I became discouraged and turned to art. Prompted now by my ambition to become a great painter I broke down my health at my easel. While Christina Lang, now in India conducted the work in Sabattus, I became again interested in Christian work. True to a promise I made to her, and burdened for souls, especially children I commenced blackboard work in an effort to save them. Finding that in order to have victory I must put God first, I laid my all upon the altar in a consecration service held last August on Mechanic Falls campground. I pledged to go where he wanted me to go and to do what he wanted me to do. I hoped now to be able to train. As I waited for the way to open my eyes were on Jesus, but when I looked away or doubted I was miserable. Praying for a definite answer I received Joshua 1:9: "Be strong and of a good courage; be not afraid, neither be thou dismayed: for the Lord thy God is with thee whithersoever thou goest." This gave me light. The way did open wonderfully and most unexpectedly. When God leads, he leads through.[25]

Students facing a spiritual or vocational crisis often appealed to their fellow students during prayer meetings or worship services. When perplexed about her future, Christina Lang, described in the first part of this section, prevailed upon other students to pray for her, "that before the week was over the Lord would show me just what his will for me was." Accordingly, "during the devotional hour we all made that a subject of prayer."[26]

Occasionally something special would happen at a devotional hour; a student's remarks would elicit a particularly intense response from other students, or a sermon would move them especially powerfully. At these times, the period for prayers might be extended, classes canceled, and revival would break out. At the Missionary Training Institute the account of one such revival figured in a 1907 faculty report. The Holy Spirit, the reporter recalled, "came suddenly one Sunday noon at the Missionary prayer meeting. He wrought sufficiently pungent conviction of sin, beginning with some of the most earnest and consecrated students, to lead to confession in public of a manner before unknown among us." The Sunday service did not end until six o'clock the next morning. After a mere two-hour break, the "8 o'clock chapel-service ran on and superseded regular class and study time, not closing until noon." This activity, the report said, continued for three weeks.[27] A similar revival occurred at the Central Bible Institute, Springfield, Missouri, in 1938:

for two days He visited us in an unusual manner, during which time classes were suspended. Under great conviction, we were constrained to make numerous confessions, both public and private. Before God's visitation was

ended, we were feeling clean and refreshed in our souls, because we had
dealt with those things that were displeasing to Him; and God, just as good
as His Word, had imparted new blessing to our souls.[28]

Spontaneity was particularly characteristic of the early days in Bible
schools. Later on, revivals—fall or spring "spiritual renewal series"—might
be scheduled in a more deliberate and routine fashion around the visits
of well-known evangelists.

Rules

Often allied with the influence outlined above was a solid structure
of regulations to govern the comportment of students. This was a relatively
late development, however; at most of the older Bible schools this complex
of rules—so frequently the bane of present and recent Bible school
students—appeared only with the second or third generation of students.
The early students went largely unregulated, probably because most of
them were older—often in their twenties—and highly motivated; with their
sights set on the evangelistic tasks they hoped to accomplish, these earnest
students hardly had time or energy for the mischief frequently characteristic of younger student bodies. Besides, most lived at home or in rooming
houses and therefore spent a relatively small proportion of their time
in classrooms. Even had the early Bible school leaders wished, they would
have found it well nigh impossible to regulate students' lives.

The tendency, however, was for the student body to get younger as
a school got older. (The exception is immediately after the two World
Wars, when returned GIs flooded the schools in large numbers.) At the
Bible Institute of Los Angeles, for example, the average age of students
between the year of founding, 1908, and the early 1930s was twenty-five;
by the early 1940s the usual age had declined to twenty.[29] As younger
and younger students applied, the schools found it necessary to set minimum ages. In 1907 the Missionary Training Institute began requiring
that students be at least twenty.[30] Similarly, in 1916, Biola stipulated that
entering women be twenty years old, entering men twenty-one. Apparently
these minimums were subject to downward pressure, for in 1920 they
were lowered to eighteen for both sexes. Moody Bible Institute leaders
evidently tried to hold the age line longer, for the minimums were still
twenty-one for men and twenty for women as late as 1928, though exceptions could be approved by the faculty. Students and parents did indeed
request waivers, as the 1928 catalog explained,

> Conditions in Christendom are so affecting the teaching in many of our
> colleges and universities, that Christian parents are asking the Institute to
> accept their sons and daughters though under age, in order that they may
> be equipped with a knowledge of the Bible and a deepened spiritual experi-
> ence to meet the attacks upon their faith when they enter such schools.[31]

In addition, as time went on, Bible schools seem to have admitted more students who were there simply because their parents thought attendance would do them good. Often they were the children of pastors and missionaries, who had themselves sometimes attended Bible school. Inevitably some of these later generations of students found themselves in Bible schools against their wills. One 1919 alumna of the Missionary Training Institute, for instance, reported that she had been preparing contentedly for a secular teaching career at the University of Pittsburgh when her mother, an active Methodist deaconess, decided her daughter should go into Christian work and therefore must attend the Institute at Nyack. By her own report, the alumna was not a committed Christian when she arrived at Nyack—"it took a long time before the Lord really dealt with me."[32]

These two factors—the increasing youth of students and the presence of students who had not chosen Bible school (let alone a Christian vocation) —probably help account for the increasing regulation of student lives. (Furthermore, as time went on, Bible school educators may have perceived greater threats to student morality stemming from changes in the general cultural and religious climate.) But a necessary ingredient if school leaders were to succeed in controlling the behavior of their students was the dormitory or residence hall, where oversight could be maintained and rules enforced twenty-four hours a day. It is significant that once Moody Bible Institute had constructed dormitories, day students were required to live in them, even if their homes were in the Chicago area.

The tendency of Bible schools to assume increasing responsibility for the personal morality and conduct of their students appears to explain changes at the Boston Bible School over several decades. Whereas the 1905–1906 catalog had read simply, "Students of this School are adults and will be treated as such . . ."[33] the 1931–1932 catalog issued from an administration that was more exacting and explicit in its requirements:

> As it is assumed that students who come for Christian service do not desire to be hindered in their work by social activities, students will not be excused from study hours on Monday, Tuesday, Wednesday, and Thursday evenings unless it be to attend religious meetings chaperoned by some member of the faculty or to such meetings as are approved by the principal.[34]

The oversight now included the condition of student rooms: "All rooms occupied by students are open for inspection between the hours of 9 A.M. and 7 P.M. every day," warned the 1931–1932 catalog.[35] In late January 1940 the two male students who had kept the neatest rooms over the preceding semester received books as prizes. Making the Dean's List at the New England School of Theology involved more than high grade averages. Other criteria were "general deportment," "orderliness in person and room," "school spirit," and "unsolicited cooperation."[36] Nothing, it seemed, escaped the purview of school authorities; in 1936 students heard four lectures on "The Cultivation of a Pleasing Personality."[37] In short, the school had become more nearly a total environment where no aspect of the student's formation was overlooked or left to chance.

The same forces were at work at the Missionary Training Institute. In 1912 one of the publicized advantages offered by the construction of a new school building was that it would allow more complete separation outside classes of male and female students. (They had been segregated before this, but within the same building.) In 1912 also came the announcement of an explicit new textbook policy, "to exclude from all class-rooms textbooks that are in any way antagonistic to the spirit and teaching of God's Holy Word."[38] At around this time, A. B. Simpson and his co-workers began to envision a complete and safe school system, to be called the "Nyack Missionary University," which would embrace Alliance sons and daughters at an early age (an academy for boys and girls had been set up in 1906) and carry them through to adulthood, "to ripest results."[39] Presumably resources were lacking to accomplish all parts of this ambitious plan—no university ever came into being—but the aspiration was undeniably there to enclose evangelical offspring within a total educational system, insulated from the deleterious influence of the rest of the educational world.

As the example of Nyack suggests, the rules were especially stringent with respect to relations between male and female students, where segregation was the watchword, or, at the very least, close supervision. The codes also dictated what constituted "decent" dress, hairstyles, and other aspects of student appearance. They generally outlawed such activities as smoking, drinking, theater-going, dancing, betting, card playing, and (later) movie-going and television watching. At Biola it was even forbidden to "talk against the school."[40] A male graduate of the Missionary Training Institute recalled the strictness of Dean Cora Turnbull during the teens and twenties:

> To most of us students under Cora's reign she appeared Victorian in style and too strict a disciplinarian. She was especially rough on the girls. Skirts must reach within six inches of the floor, blouses be fully lined with sleeves to the wrist, and reach upward to the collar bone or Adam's apple, whichever came last. There was no integration of sexes in those days. Boys must walk south on the days the girls walked north, and vice versa. . . . Any couple whose courses crossed on the Nyack-Tarrytown ferry were sure to be limned in her telescopic eye.[41]

An alumna who attended Nyack during the late teens had similar recollections of Turnbull: she "used to tell us how to dress and how to look and how to act."[42]

Individual schools had their own procedures for dealing with those who broke the rules. At Biola disobedient students were summoned to the superintendent or dean, where they might hear a remonstrance like the following: "What are you here at school *for*? You come from wonderful dedicated Christian parents . . . it would break their hearts if you were thrown out. What do you think is wrong with Biola? Maybe something is really wrong with *you*?" For serious offences students might find themselves placed on probation for a year. If they transgressed again, they might receive a second chance or even a third one. Biola faculty found it difficult finally to give up on students considered "spiritually not right with the Lord," clinging to the hope that wayward ones might straighten out if only given a little more time and patience.[43]

Enveloped in such an intense atmosphere as that provided by the Bible school, students would have had a difficult time indeed remaining aloof or merely pretending piety. Those who dissented from prevailing attitudes or found the pressure too great were forced to leave or departed of their own accord. The records of most schools are unfortunately silent on this subject. Now and then, however, a glimpse emerges of students who were unwilling or unable to cope with the highly charged atmosphere. The Christian and Missionary Alliance annals report that some time between 1905 and 1918, "a revival broke out" at the Missionary Training Institute, "that flourished for weeks, evoking all kinds of confessions. Some resisting students left school; some repented and returned. A Jewish student who had fallen into gross sin wanted the confessions stopped. There was confusion."[44]

It would be a mistake, of course, to suggest that Bible school students never had fun, or that they failed to think of anything besides their spiritual condition and service to God's cause. The fun was, to be sure, expected to be "wholesome." After a turkey dinner on Thanksgiving Day 1927, for example, Biola students spent the rest of the holiday boating in Westlake Park, singing "Gospel choruses" with the aid of a saxophone accompaniment, and playing games. Bystanders, it was assumed, must have been surprised to see "a group of young people so happy without having hired an orchestra and executing a fox trot."[45]

One has also to assume that Bible school students were quite capable of highjinks, mischief, and even serious offenses, at least upon occasion, though the annals disclose mostly the innocent variety. Women students at Biola during the early twenties, for example, staged a mock wedding, complete with a bridesmaid outfitted in a gown constructed of newspapers and a wedding guest dressed to parody the current dean of the school, R. A. Torrey, who was notorious for his formal attire.[46] And it is quite apparent from the following description that Nyack students did not always have their sights set on eternity—even in chapel—nor did they consistently feel uncritical reverence toward their instructors; one Thanksgiving day all the students on campus

> climbed the hill to share a chapel union service, at which [Dean W. C.] Stevens was assigned the primal prayer. Chapel was on the second floor,

kitchen and dining room on the first, so that the tantalizing aroma of roast turkey was wafted aloft incessantly and unhindered. On the chapel wall slowly ticked an accusing clock toward which we students took furtive glances—hopefully. But Stevens was a deliberate speaker, and on this occasion he was not unlike Solomon in dedicating the temple. For twenty-four long minutes he prayed and prayed. All of us had special cause for thanksgiving when he completed his review of the past, concern for the present, and survey of the future.[47]

Further, it must be recalled that despite the restrictions keeping men and women apart, students in large numbers managed to carry on romances and later to marry. (A. B. Simpson's wife is said to have grumbled upon occasion that the Missionary Training Institute was hardly more than a marriage bureau.) Yet despite these qualifications, no other student bodies merited the adjectives "wholesome," "earnest," and "pious" more fully than those at Bible schools. In an era that tended to give more rather than less latitude to its young people, the founders and leaders of these institutions had succeeded to a remarkable degree in imposing ever greater oversight upon their charges. And the majority of Bible school students appear to have acceded to—often embraced—the vision set out for them by their elders of the proper spiritual, moral, and intellectual preparation for young Christians in the twentieth century.

IX

WORLDS WITHIN THE BIBLE SCHOOL

A Foreign Missionary Culture

If the Bible schools fostered a Bible culture they also created a foreign missionary culture. Consider the situation of many Bible school students: their parents or some other close relatives might be foreign missionaries. Not a few of their fellow students—possibly a best friend or a roommate—had pledged their futures to the foreign mission fields, and some had even gone so far as to select a particular area of the world for service. A number of students had grown up in mission stations and could describe life there firsthand.

Graduates of the school who were foreign missionaries contributed letters and articles about their experiences, and many stressed the romantic aspects of missionary life. Photographs and maps of missionary lands hung on the walls of classrooms and student rooms. Souvenirs and artifacts from missionary lands were displayed in cases in school corridors. The library and bookstore shelves offered scores of heroic accounts of missionary endeavors, written to engage a popular audience. It was not unusual for graduates to die in the field; they might be murdered or succumb to tropical disease or uncongenial climate. When news of such deaths reached their alma mater, it galvanized students, who often pledged themselves to take the place of the "martyred" missionaries.

In place of the lighthearted fare common in student yearbooks at secular colleges, the student publications at Bible schools described the urgency of missionary needs and, in elevated prose liberally interlaced with biblical quotes, exhorted students to offer themselves as foreign missionaries:

> Truly, "The field is the world, and the harvest is white, but the reapers are few." "Pray ye therefore the Lord of the harvest that he may send forth more laborers." Hear the voice of Jesus say, "Who will go and work for me?" and behold they also call us from the uttermost ends of the earth. Who, who, will answer gladly saying, "Here am I, O Lord, send me."[1]

The 1931 yearbook at Gordon carried "Messages from the Ends of the Earth to You." sobering and inspiring exhortations from missionaries to Gordon students.[2] Each Bible school campus had at least one foreign missionary organization. The student bodies of many schools were divided into "prayer bands," each of which concentrated upon a particular part of the mission field, such as Africa, China, or South America. These bands usually met weekly for an hour to study the field, keep track of progress, pray for the success of missionaries there, and raise money for the effort. Students who had signed a pledge to become foreign missionaries, "God willing," usually belonged to the campus branch of the Student Volunteer Movement. Student volunteers at Gordon College in 1923 held meetings every Tuesday evening. The first Tuesday of the month was a business meeting; the second Tuesday's meeting was convened for the purpose of "asking God's blessing upon our missionaries and our efforts here." The third Tuesday was a "Study Night," when students usually chose some textbook on foreign missions as their point of departure for discussion. On the fourth Tuesday the Student Volunteers presented "some special feature of interest for the students." Generally the speaker at these meetings was a returned missionary, or "some of our own students representing some foreign field."[3] In the Biola Student Missionary Union there were Active and Associate memberships. The Active members were actually pledged "to give their lives to evangelistic work in the Home or Foreign field," while the Associates promised "to support the cause of world evangelization by prayer and gifts."[4] This organization, like its counterpart at Gordon, met once a week:

> A large part of the time is spent in definite prayer for the definite needs of missionaries in the field, and conditions in the field. Letters from former students have a prominent place at this meeting, and there is usually an address from a returned missionary, which keeps the students in close touch with all parts of the world.[5]

Visiting foreign missionaries played a prominent role in stirring up enthusiasm for their cause; they were well aware of the romance that surrounded foreign missions in the minds of most Bible school students, and, hoping to win recruits, they regaled students with tales of hardship, sacrifice, and suffering. Sometimes they accompanied their talks with stereopticon slides. In 1921 at the Missionary Training Institute, a missionary to Africa, a Mrs. Dickinson, "amusingly, and yet seriously, . . . told how sanctification of eyes, ears, nose, stomach, was necessary and that nothing in the way of preparatory training in the death to one's senses was amiss for a missionary to Africa. Prayer-habit, long patience, and faith in the cleansing power of Jesus' blood were emphasized."[6] The overriding emphasis on foreign missions is reflected in the statistics. By 1927, less than two decades after Biola's founding, 300 graduates had gone to the foreign mission fields; in 1928 Moody Bible Institute claimed to have sent out 1,440 missionaries, 1,096 of whom were still active at that time.[7] By 1962 Safara Witmer of the Accrediting Association of Bible Colleges could write that "it is conservatively estimated" that at least 50% of the 27,000 Protestant missionaries then in the field had prepared at Bible schools. Of these some 2,700 were Moody graduates.[8] But the preeminence of foreign missions at Bible schools is perhaps best exemplified by the case of two graduates of the New England School of Theology, Vesta Clothey, '24, and her husband Frederick, '23. The Clotheys sailed for India as missionaries in late October 1924. The summer before their departure they had been married by the school principal in an Advent Christian church, with another graduate of the school serving as an usher. If their wedding was something of a school event, their departure for India was even more so. First, Frederick Clothey left a memento behind; he gave the school "a missionary banner showing the number of students in the foreign field." The leavetaking involved almost everyone at the school: "Most of the student body went to India Wharf, Friday afternoon, October 24, to bid Fred and Vesta Clothey God-speed . . . Let us remember all our class mates in prayer as they sail to their new mission." But this farewell did not end the round of good-byes and good wishes:

> Student Merritt took a number of folks from West Wareham to Sagamore and hailed the New York boat as it passed through the canal with the missionaries. Fred responded and the boat threw the searchlight on the bridge so the missionaries could see Merritt and his friends. We trust it cheered Fred and Vesta and the other missionaries on their way.

Once the Clotheys reached their destination, the denominational newspaper reported on their activities, including the births of their children. From time to time Mrs. Clothey herself contributed inspirational articles and poems to the school literary magazine.[9]

A World of Women

At the early Bible schools women students enjoyed considerable educational opportunity and a large measure of equality. Certainly they fared better at Bible schools than at most theological seminaries, where either they were not admitted at all or were relegated to subordinate status. Many of the advantages of Bible school education for women were unintended: they resulted as by-products from the nature and purposes of the institutions rather than from their ideology. When Bible school founders supported the training of lay people, they automatically advanced the idea of religious instruction for women. As noted earlier, women customarily predominated in early Bible school student bodies, and they usually were well represented on faculties. If sheer numbers of women tend to give rise to a female culture, then such a culture developed at Bible schools.

Certainly women students could find many models for female religious activism and leadership among the teachers and speakers at their schools. Some of the faculty, it is true, differed little from the familiar school-marm, devoting themselves mostly to teaching voice, elocution, English composition, and literature, but other women teachers simultaneously led lives as active evangelists, revivalists, missionary leaders, and even preachers. For example, Helen Barrett Montgomery, who taught at Gordon in the twenties, was a well known and influential leader in Baptist missionary organizations. Furthermore, a large number of visiting foreign missionaries and founders of city missions—standard speakers at Bible schools—were women. And female students could look among the ranks of graduates for exemplary women who had become successful and admired foreign missionaries, evangelists, Bible teachers, and even preachers in their own right, rather than simply adjuncts to pastor or missionary husbands. Two of the most famous evangelists produced by the Northwestern Bible and Training School were women—the team of Alma Reiber and Irene Murray. Reiber was a preacher, Murray a songleader.[10] A Gordon alumna, Frieda Bonney, was described in the school's history as "one of the best evangelistic preachers of her . . . day."[11] Probably one reason Bible schools produced women preachers was that they often included them in homiletics classes, along with the male ministerial students. At the Missionary Training Institute, for example, women sometimes took Greek and were required to do practice preaching, along with the men, in church. In the Institute's 1888 graduation, a prize for excellence in "Homiletic Exercises" went to a woman.[12] The Boston Bible School, conducted by Advent Christians, permitted women to take pastoral courses in preparation for ordination along with the men students. The fact that a school taught women preaching and speaking skills did not necessarily mean that its leaders sanctioned or encouraged the entry of women into the ordained ministry, but intentionally or not, the schools in fact enabled determined (and sometimes "Spirit-led") women to assume unconventional leadership roles in the church.

In addition, certain common characterics of Bible schools—their informality, their flexibility, the absence of a predetermined notion of what a Bible school did or did not do, even their poverty—worked in favor of women students and faculty. There was no prior male culture at Bible schools into which women had to fit or from which they could be excluded, and women could often manage to accommodate school schedules to their duties to parents and husbands. The permissive educational requirements at Bible schools and the inclusive attitude toward applicants also aided women. A prime criterion for would-be Bible school students was not their previous academic achievement but rather their demonstrated religious devotion. Measured by this standard women stood second to none. Furthermore, the poverty of most schools encouraged the retention of women on the faculty, since their services came most cheaply. Finally, the usual focuses of Bible school education—foreign missions, teaching, music—were the very interests that traditionally attracted women.

But women's favorable position at Bible schools was not simply a matter of happenstance. Conservative evangelicals were not particularly given to endorsing the women's movement, it is true; they knew better than to look for trouble. For the most part we must guess what their attitudes were from what we know about the role of women in the schools. But A. J. Gordon for one appears to have declared himself at least a moderate champion of enlarged opportunities for women. In an article he defended a preaching ministry for women on the foreign missions fields, rejoicing that women "are telling out the good news of salvation to heathen men and women publicly and from house to house, to little groups gathered by the wayside, or to larger groups assembled in the zayats." As scriptural support for these activities he appealed to Joel 17: "your sons and daughters shall prophesy" and also, "in Christ there is neither male nor female." Furthermore, he insisted on a narrow and limiting interpretation of the standard texts used against women's religious leadership (1 Tim. 2:11 and 1 Cor. 14:34). Gordon's own wife Maria was active in the leadership of the Bible school; she was secretary and treasurer for many years and also taught Bible courses there.[13]

Thus, as a result of both circumstances and intention, the early Bible schools were hospitable to the idea of women in religious service and leadership. But we must stop far short of assuming that Bible schools were cradles of liberation for women. Several important factors countered the egalitarian tendencies discussed above. Bible school administrators— often male—were far from immune to the prevailing societal sexism. And this general discrimination against women would only have been reinforced by the conservative social and cultural attitudes of fundamentalism, especially after 1920. Furthermore, the biblical literalism of fundamentalism would have sanctioned the use of texts enjoining women's silence and submission as proof texts to bolster conservative social attitudes (the very thing Gordon refused to do).

Indeed, we find plenty of evidences of sexism in Bible schools. Generally, the longer established and wealthier the school the more the signs of segregation and discrimination along sexual lines we are apt to find. This is because the older schools tended to introduce more conventional ministerial training into their schools. Such training proceeded on the assumption that the ministry was a male preserve, and it seems safe to say that its practitioners brought a conservative view of gender roles into the Bible schools. The older institutions usually attempted to raise academic standards, excluding women with marginal educational backgrounds. At times the acquisition of better physical facilities worked to the detriment of women. When a women's dormitory was built or purchased, for instance, school leaders could more thoroughly segregate male and female students, a development that in turn allowed a greater disparity between the way male and female students were treated. Finally, the older school could afford to move toward more course specialization; this meant that the leadership if it desired was able to shunt women students into courses specially designed for females. At schools where it was assumed that women students would become teachers, unordained missionaries, or pastors' wives (rather than pastors), they were often expected to take classes stressing "female" skills, such as domestic science, pedagogy, and "child evangelism." At Moody Bible Institute, for instance, under "Home Economics and Manual Arts," the catalog directed, "the subject is taken by all women students except such as have had such training before, or are definitely preparing for Christian service where it is not required." On the other hand, "Manual Training and Bookkeeping" was "intended principally for men and for those who are preparing for work in missionary lands."[14]

On at least one occasion raising a school's academic standards and prestige meant attracting more men students. Early in Gordon's history women students outnumbered men, as they did at most other early Bible schools. But in the 1920s, Nathan Wood, Gordon's ambitious dean, introduced greater emphasis on ministerial and graduate education. Clearly one of the virtues of the innovation in the mind of Gordon's administrator was that it drew more men to the school. In the 1920s and 1930s enrollment at the graduate level was almost entirely male. In 1919 Dean Wood wrote to an alumnus, "I am glad to say that in these last two weeks the enrollment has progressed remarkably, for Gordon Bible College, and *especially with men*" (my emphasis).[15] The climax of this upgrading drive came in 1930 when the trustees voted to restrict the number of women to one-third of the total student body.[16]

Clearly woman at Bible schools suffered many of the usual restrictions and disabilities imposed on them by their culture. But the fact remains that as members of largely unshaped, "pioneer" educational institutions they enjoyed more freedom to train for unconventional religious roles in unconventional ways.

A Culture of Scarcity

Money was inescapably a central concern for both students and administrators; both groups found themselves perpetually short of funds. They were not alone; difficulties with finances plagued students and leaders in other educational institutions as well. Yet Bible school personnel operated even closer to the financial margins than most. Some of the early Bible schools, it is true, were founded by wealthy individuals; the Bible Institute of Los Angeles, for instance, benefited from the oil fortune of Lyman Stewart, both at the beginning and for many years afterward.

At its inception Moody Bible Institute attracted substantial gifts from wealthy businessmen like Cyrus H. McCormick, Jr. (in fact, Dwight Moody solicited pledges before he decided to go ahead with the Institute); in 1913 Moody Bible Institute received a $100,000 legacy from William Whiting Borden, a young missionary to China who had died prematurely.[17]

However, the bulk of the money that enabled Bible schools to operate arrived in small amounts, from individuals, from graduates, and from congregations. Bible schools that were connected with denominations usually received some support from that source; for the most part, however, such church bodies—particularly those which were likely in the first place to foster Bible school education—commanded only scarce resources and therefore were unable to allocate large sums. At a few schools the labor of students, on a farm owned by the school, or in some light industry, earned extra income for the institution, and therefore reduced the cost to students. And most schools had one or more vehicles that put the name of the school before a sympathetic public: radio stations or programs, publications geared to a wide public, extension classes, correspondence programs, and touring musical groups. Many of these yielded names and addresses of people who might eventually respond to a request for funds.

Fortunately for those entrusted with making ends meet, the operating budgets of the Bible schools were unusually low. Faculty received little or no remuneration; subject offerings were limited in number, and included few electives. In many schools students performed the essential janitorial and kitchen tasks, reducing the need to pay a nonteaching staff. The faculty took on many clerical and administrative duties as a matter of course and without additional compensation. Until money became available for school buildings, many Bible schools were located in church basements or private homes and therefore had few overhead costs.

Schools such as the Boston Bible School operated on a particularly marginal basis. About 1911 an item in the Advent Christian paper, the *World's Crisis*, requesting the churches of the denomination "to observe the present week as a week of self-denial for the school," reported that "There is not a sufficient sum on hand to pay salaries for the week."[18] The school received most of its money contributions in $1.00 or $2.00 amounts. Many well wishers, however, sent payment in kind instead. In 1911, for instance, the Women's Home and Foreign Missionary Society of the Hartford, Connecticut, Advent Christian church donated one dozen silver knives, forks, and spoons; six dessert and table spoons; one "very large linen tablecloth"; twenty-four Turkish towels; fourteen washcloths; and sixteen pairs of curtains.[19] Sister Abbie Keyes of Middleboro, Massachusetts, contributed a bag of "very fine Greenings." Survival sometimes appeared to hinge upon a barrel of potatoes: "While it is cause for gratitude that all the students are enjoying good health, and possess splendid appetites, yet as those who have charge of the home, watch the receding tide in the

potato bin, they wonder where the next barrel is coming from."[20] Even
the library was assembled by means of this catch-as-catch-can philanthropy.
In 1902, for instance, the school received $50.00 for books, a set of the
Encyclopedia Britannica (presumably used), "ten volumes of English literature," and a "neat and attractive little book-case" that apparently accommo-
dated the entire library. In 1910 a former principal of the school received
thanks for his gift of the five volumes of "Geisler's Church History" and
a copy of the "Epistles of the Apostolic Fathers." Occasionally the school
advertised among its constituency for particular books students needed;
in October 1917, for instance, its leaders were looking for copies of Beet's
Manual of Theology.[21]

In their financial arrangements, Bible school leaders found themselves
in conflict. On the one hand, they, like most educators, longed for more
buildings, more equipment, greater financial stability, better teacher salaries, more programs to reach more people, and financial help for students.
On the other hand, they expressed a certain satisfaction over their modest
circumstances. Most Bible school founders and leaders believed in the
doctrine of the imminent second coming and took seriously the biblical
behest, "Lay not up for yourselves treasures upon earth." It seemed a
testimony of faith to give no thought for the morrow, like George Muller, who assumed the Lord would provide when the need arose. All
signs of permanence—buildings, incomes, full-time teachers, endowment—made Bible school leaders uneasy, because they seemed to suggest
a lack of trust in God and doubt that his son would be arriving any time
soon. In fact, very few Bible schools built up much of an endowment;
most simply did not have the opportunity, but some resisted it as a matter
of principle. Oil magnate Lyman Stewart, whose fortune helped establish
the Bible Institute of Los Angeles in 1908, had initially rejected the idea
of a permanent building—putting any money into "brick and mortar,"
as he put it:

> If the Lord's people have funds, I believe they should be transmitted as
> quickly as possible into living gospel. Putting them into an endowment
> rather suggests the laying of them in a napkin. It always seemed to me
> very uncomplimentary to the future church to think it would not take care
> of its own current work. By putting funds into immediate gospel work,
> there will be a much stronger constituency created to take care of the work
> in the future.[22]

A long-time chairman of the board of Moody Bible Institute insisted that
the Institute "must be financially dependent upon each succeeding generation."[23]

Also dampening Bible school leaders' enthusiasm for bricks and mortar
was the fact that they hated to incur debt in building. These religious
conservatives were often financial conservatives as well and besides tended
to attach a moral taint to the transactions of lending and owing money.

Furthermore, their unease with the status of borrower was reinforced by memories of how difficult it was to meet mortgage payments in times of economic depression. Even active solicitation of funds seemed to fall short of precedents set by holy men like Muller, who was celebrated for praying rather than asking for anything his orphanage required. The difficulty of many fundamentalist educators is summed up by what one writer has said of premillennialists in general: "since they refused to set dates for the return of Christ, they had to live as though Christ might return at any moment—*and,* at the same time, as though he might not come for years."[24]

Yet, the more effectively Bible schools demonstrated their contributions to the advancement of evangelism, the easier it seemed to be to justify those measures that enhanced institutional stability and longevity. Sometimes, accordingly, Bible school leaders started what amounted to small endowments, applying some euphemistic label to them. Moody Bible Institute actively and vigorously campaigned for operating funds. By the twenties, the Moody Extension Department included a team of full-time, paid money raisers who canvassed the United States. In 1927 Biola leaders overcame whatever scruples they had about active money raising and made their first "general appeal to the Christian public for funds."[25] To be sure, Bible school educators were not ready or able this early to concern themselves very much about accreditation, but the pressures for financial stability were already there in nascent form and would become steadily more powerful.

In the early days few Bible schools charged tuition; and those that did levied only a modest sum. Yet to judge from accounts, many Bible school students—like students elsewhere—were chronically short of money. Of course, even when students did not face tuition charges, they still typically had to come up with money for room, board, and clothing; older students might be obliged to contribute to the support of families. Student indigence seems regularly to have vexed and worried school leaders. In 1912 the Missionary Training Institute warned "old students,"

> The Board of Trustees feels constrained no longer to encourage students to come to Nyack whose expenses are not quite reasonably provided for. To have students come to Nyack and be unable to meet the modest financial obligations involved, either by cash payments or by work if such has been promised them, not only makes necessary the running of large tradesmen's bills by the Schools but encourages students in the formation of unscriptural habits.[26]

Some students who needed to earn a full-time income worked during the day and attended Bible school at night. (Most schools had night programs, at least by the twenties.) Many if not most day students worked a few hours a week to meet their expenses. In some lucky cases, a practical work assignment paid at least a modest stipend; this was especially true for those students pastoring churches. But often students were fortunate even to receive money for their transportation to a practical work assignment. Thus, most students could not rely on practical work assignments for financial assistance. Those in need of funds found a wide variety of remunerative jobs, which they often performed in addition to their Christian work. Students at Boston Bible School, for instance, painted houses, mowed lawns, shoveled snow, cleaned basements, washed windows, and mopped floors. One student got up at four every morning to stoke furnaces and then returned to this duty every evening after supper. Missionary Training Institute students cleaned houses, worked as clerks in stores, and did assistant or substitute teaching in the public schools. One student at Moody Bible Institute waited on tables in a boarding house for one hour a day, in exchange for his meals. Biola students often clerked in downtown department stores not far from their school. At Northwestern Bible and Training School in Minneapolis, most students held part-time jobs; the women worked as housekeepers, waitresses, and cooks, while the men served as chimney sweeps, night watchmen, and maintenance workers.[27]

Many students took advantage of the summer to strengthen their economic position. At Boston Bible School two students arrived late for the fall term because they had been digging potatoes in Maine:

> We were glad to welcome back to the student body this week, Miss Elsie MacLeod and Andrew E. Thompson. They were late in entering on account of Mr. Thompson having the oversight of gathering one hundred and twenty-five acres of potatoes in Northern Aroostook; something like thirteen thousand barrels being gathered. Miss MacLeod picked up about one thousand barrels.[28]

During prosperous times, Bible school students usually found employers happy to hire them because as Bible school students they had acquired a reputation in the neighborhood for honesty, punctuality, hard work, and sobriety. At some business establishments, in fact, certain slots had been "reserved" for students of a nearby Bible school. Most schools had employment bureaus to facilitate the placement of students in paying jobs.

For many Bible school students the combination of classes, an intense devotional life, practical evangelistic work, and a job made for a strenuous routine. One Moody student wrote a brother who was expecting to follow him at the school: "With regard to finances, I would say working your way sounds nice and romantic but I want to tell you it is hard, real hard. To be honest with you, I can tell you it shook me to pieces for a while up here as it was an awful struggle to make ends meet. Yet I knew it was the making of me."[29] Perhaps for this reason Bible school leaders sometimes seem to have been of two minds about the necessity for so many of their students to work. On the one hand it took time away from studies. The 1920 Biola catalog warned, "as a rule the men and women who work their way through the Institute are at a disadvantage and it is not advised, except where absolutely necessary."[30] On the other hand, the Protestant ethic held sway. At Biola *The King's Business* made a virtue of necessity and congratulated students for their industry: "Most students work their way through school. This makes for a sturdy type of self reliant young people who upon graduation are prepared to assume their full share of life's responsibilities."[31]

For students who did not have many financial resources, either because their families lacked them or because they were too old to appeal to parents, the Bible school offered an affordable place to get an education. The expenses were comparatively low, and no stigma clung to those who had to work, even at menial jobs, since so many other Bible school students were in similar circumstances. And those who simply had to work full-time could usually attend at night. For students with energy and resolve, then, it seemed there was always a way to combine study and earning a modest livelihood.

Because Bible school leaders sought to convey more than skills and religious knowledge—and because students sought to acquire more—the extracurriculum was critical at these schools. Of course, the extracurriculum was a major concern of students and educators at the most secular of colleges and universities, but in these institutions the view was usually pluralistic; it was up to students to choose from a number of options how to spend their time outside the classroom. Even life styles and moral values became increasingly matters of personal preference as time went on. But Bible school leaders were not interested in the cultivation of a variety of styles and values; they were bent on turning out graduates of one type: effective evangelists and zealous students of the Bible. To this end, almost every aspect of the curriculum, inside the classroom and out, worked in tandem.

Moody Bible Institute with its comparatively lavish resources particularly succeeded in creating a total environment for those within its walls. Not only were students the recipients of a thoroughgoing curriculum and extracurriculum: faculty, spouses, and staff were enveloped scarcely less completely. James Gray, longtime head of the institution, encouraged faculty to live near enough the campus so that they could participate in all facets of the school's life.[32] Many of them belonged to the Moody Memorial Church; Charles Alexander, for instance, a music instructor at the Institute, also led the children's chorus at the church. Spouses "attended" the Institute no less than did their partners. Mrs. Gray interested herself particularly in the wives of the male students, conceiving the idea of a Married Women's Guild, which had a building of its own. Under the auspices of the Guild, the wives attended classes in Bible study methods, Bible doctrine, Christian education, and personal evangelism. "They practiced leading meetings and giving devotions. They learned to sew and to be better mothers. They exchanged money-saving ideas and recipes."[33] While their mothers were thus engaged the children received care in a nursery staffed by Institute students.

The nonfaculty employees—by 1931 they numbered over two hundred—received special attention also. A one hundred-member Institute Council, composed of faculty, business staff, and "lesser officials," actually functioned more as a devotional group than a council:

> Its meetings were monthly, when all came together at a social meal. This was followed by a gathering in an upper room for song, prayer, and testimony, impromptu reports from departmental and field workers, the reading of letters from Alumni on mission fields, and a general exchange of views concerning conditions in the Institute, and the cause of Christ everywhere. An act of renewed consecration brought the meeting to a close.[34]

By the late 1920s, an annual "fellowship gathering" of all employees, attended by everyone from the president to the errand boys, and including many spouses, had also become a tradition.[35] In addition, employees were encouraged to attend 8:30 chapel meetings and put aside their usual duties at the Institute to participate in the special prayer days. Some employees belonged to the Moody Church and took part in its activities; A. F. Gaylord, long-time business manager for the Institute, also served as the church's Sunday school superintendent.

Thus, if much of Chicago outside the Institute walls seemed indifferent and even inimical to evangelical beliefs and interests, the Institute itself furnished a safe, predictable haven where young evangelists could count on receiving support and reinforcement from peers and elders. Here was no troubling pluralism to confuse students and require choices; the curriculum and extracurriculum taught the same message, and all members of the community addressed themselves to achievement of unified evangelistic goals.

X

THE BIBLE SCHOOL AND THE FUNDAMENTALIST MOVEMENT

This chapter returns to Ernest Sandeen's assertion, cited in the introduction, that the Bible schools allowed the fundamentalist movement to survive. They accomplished this in many ways, some of which Sandeen pointed out; they trained workers and leaders for the movement, helped shape its basic ethos and style, functioned prominently as symbols (recall Moody Bible Institute's reputation as the "West Point of Fundamentalism"), operated as regional organizing centers, and served as bases of operations for individual conservative evangelicals.[1]

The Bible Schools as Moderating and Unifying Influences

One of the most important of the Bible schools' contributions to the survival of fundamentalism, however, was their check on the movement's powerful centrifugal forces. As anyone familiar with fundamentalism well knows, it has exhibited a strong propensity to splinter and divide; lifelong enmities have been fomented over what others considered minor theological points or over differences of personality and leadership style. A movement hopelessly torn and disorganized would have stood a poor chance of evangelizing and educating effectively; fortunately for the conservative evangelical cause, there were also factors making for unity: the sense of urgency that many conservative evangelicals brought to the task of evangelization—that frequently allowed workers to ignore differences of doctrine, style, and personality; dispensationalist ecclesiology with its low regard for the earthly churches and their petty wrangling; and interdenominational institutions and agencies that encouraged cooperation among conservative Protestants from diverse theological traditions. Among these unifying elements were the Bible schools; they played a critical role in helping conservative evangelicalism to survive more or less intact.

Still, the Bible schools and their allies had their work cut out for them, for the conflicts in fundamentalism were many, varied, and stubborn.

There were the predictable denominational rivalries, of course; posed against these enmities was the interdenominationalism of many of the largest and most prominent schools, including Moody Bible Institute and the Bible Institute of Los Angeles. Even some of those schools that were denominational in name were actually interdenominational in spirit. The Missionary Training Institute, for example, was sponsored by the Christian and Missionary Alliance (not technically a denomination in its early days). Yet students from a wide variety of religious traditions attended the Institute. The founders of Gordon were Baptists, as were the later leaders and many of the trustees, but decidedly the school reached beyond Baptist students. Besides setting an example of interdenominationalism, the leaders of schools like Moody countered denominational divisions by insisting that true Bible study and earnest evangelization—that is, the real stuff of religious life—were unsectarian in their very nature. Furthermore, Bible school teaching focused upon methods and know-how, fostering a doctrinal neutrality, an agreement on means and goals that ignored theological differences.

But some of the most pervasive divisions in fundamentalism transcended denominational borders. With increasing intensity after 1930, a struggle went on between "separatists" and "moderates." Moderates tried to work within the established denominations, however dismayed they might feel about the liberalism they found there. Separatists insisted that the old denominations had succumbed to an apostasy too great to be amenable to reform, and counseled the formation of new, pure church bodies. Unfortunately for conservative evangelical unity, neither side hung back from bitter criticism of the other.[2] Through this internecine battling Bible school leaders usually tried to steer a middle course. When asked for their advice by troubled evangelicals trying to decide whether to leave churches and denominations they considered unfaithful, Bible school leaders usually counseled inquirers to stay with their old denominations, but at the same time they pleaded for tolerance for both "come-outers" and loyalists alike. They tried to rise above the clashes between moderates and separatists and to minimize the differences between these groups.[3]

Another important conflict running through conservative evangelicalism is hard to label; it involved differences in social origin, style, and degree of theological sophistication that can be traced back to the earliest stirrings of fundamentalism. On one side of this division stood fundamentalists with a zeal for education and a strong concern for the middle class virtues of respectability, punctuality, order, decorum, and rationality. They tended to be more doctrinally and theologically oriented. On the other side were those who described themselves as "Spirit-led" in an immediate and intense sense; they were more demonstrative, freer in their display of religious emotions, less impressed with middle class convention, and often employed more colloquial language then other fundamentalists. They tended to emphasize experience over theology, and frequently harbored a distrust of schooling, particularly higher education, as stultifying to the spirit and unnecessary to the achievement of evangelistic goals. When these people turned to doctrine they sometimes came up with novel and exotic forms of it, with a fine disregard for what others might regard as the orthodox position. Representatives of both of the above camps fell basically into the middle class, but those from the second group were apt to cluster in the lower end of that class.

This division—not always easy to pin down but nevertheless quite palpable—accounted for some of the substantial differences between conservative groups, for example, conservative Presbyterians on the one hand and pentecostals on the other hand. But the tension also divided individual fundamentalist groups, including pentecostal ones. The division was endemic to the Christian and Missionary Alliance, even though its leader, a former Presbyterian, came down on the side of the more sober and conventionally orthodox; recall that A. B. Simpson expelled pentecostals from the Alliance at the beginning of this century. And when tumultuous religious activities were reported in Maine he disavowed them: "We are glad to say that they are not part of the Alliance work, nor do our workers ever encourage an unhealthy state of religious excitement in which visions, trances, and marvelous manifestations are held up as special signs of God's blessing."[4] Perhaps Simpson succeeded in turning away the most extreme of his would-be followers, but even if he wanted to he was unable to discourage completely a wing of his group that chose a more intense and demonstrative piety and cared less about creating intellectual formulations of its faith.[5]

Bible schools have included representatives of both of these tendencies in fundamentalism; in fact, the receptivity of this institutional form to the "leadings of the spirit" helps explain why they caught on so well in groups otherwise hostile to the idea of schooling. But on balance—and increasingly as time went on—they strengthened and supported the first group. For in the end Bible school educators usually followed the course that promoted the stability and continuity of their institutions; they insisted upon rules and regulations to govern student and faculty activities; they disliked and avoided disruptive internal controversy, whether political or religious; they sought out reliable funding sources; they came down on the side of rationality; and they established at least minimal academic standards. They distrusted religious enthusiasms that threatened their ability to maintain institutional order and to uphold certain standards. Probably much of this cultural conservatism has derived from the inherent nature of Bible schools as educational institutions and organizing centers, regardless of what their founders or later leaders originally may have intended.[6]

The leaders of Moody Bible Institute, for instance, worked hard to check fundamentalist extremists, those they thought sounded too shrill or vehement, those too eager to condemn and turn their backs on other

conservative evangelicals, those who, if given their head, might have isolated fundamentalism decisively from the rest of American culture. This
was in spite of the fact—or perhaps because of it—that Moody was considered staunchly, even radically, fundamentalist. For instance, in opposition
to the extreme individualism, emotionalism, and anti-institutionalism of
some fundamentalists, Moody personnel were often outspoken in their
defense of reason, order, and authority. This attitude emerged in their
stance on pentecostalism, for instance. In an article on the pentecostal
movement, *Moody Monthly* editors cautioned that "Order and intelligence
is the way of God rather than the unusual and peculiar."[7] One of the
purposes of the Founder's Week Conference of 1922 was "To steady the
elect as against the extravagances and disorders of the Tongues Movement and professed faith healers."[8] Even though Moody people shared the
widespread fundamentalist ambivalence toward organization, they usually
ended up affirming its importance: "We believe in organization because
we believe in order and authority; . . ."[9]

In the interests of order, then, Moody leaders often thrust themselves
into the role of setting and upholding standards—theological, musical,
and even academic. Institute personnel acted as self-appointed guardians
of theological orthodoxy, not only vis-à-vis theological liberalism, but also
vis-à-vis the more flamboyant brands of fundamentalism. Institute leaders
steered clear of doctrines they saw as extremist or sensational and shunned
any intense religious emotionalism that threatened authority and order.
Besides avoiding involvement with pentecostalism, they criticized what
they regarded as excessive preoccupation with the practice of divine healing and frowned upon the more intricate and fanciful forms of dispensationalism.[10]

To be sure, individual members of the Institute community appear to
have held more receptive views on some of the above topics; at times,
for instance, zealots for such tenets as divine healing and "believer's baptism" infected the atmosphere, stirring up the students and perhaps some
of the faculty. But such "troublemakers" were kept within bounds. The
chronicler of James Gray's leadership at Moody Bible Institute suggested
that one of his strengths lay in his ability to dampen student upheavals
associated with such unrestrained enthusiasms.[11] Torrey also seems to have
come down hard on students who developed an appetite for unorthodox
religious groups: "He expected his students to keep clear of all cults in
which error was found."[12]

Institute leaders also prided themselves upon upholding standards
in evangelical music. This may appear paradoxical at first glance, since
the school's music department arose out of the success of the gospel
hymn developed by Dwight Moody's partner in revivalism, Ira Sankey. The
gospel song with its catchy rhythms and unashamed sentimentality—so
perilously close to the popular songs of the day—could barely claim respectability, let alone the imprimatur of the upholders of musical "stand-

ards." In 1929, nevertheless, the Institute introduced an "advanced" three-year Music Course to improve the quality of evangelical church music. In outlining the need for the new, extended music course, Gray explained that the early gospel song writers and performers—men such as Sankey, Bliss, and Towner—had been followed by "smaller men," who, "as is not unusual," made "that sometimes ridiculous" which "their predecessors made an art." "The Moody Bible Institute," he added primly, "has set its face against such extravagances."[13] Also in the interest of maintaining musical standards, students at the Institute after about 1915 went beyond the confines of evangelical music to study and perform the works of Bach and other composers of classical church music.

To a lesser extent, Institute educators stood for the preservation of academic standards. This concern conflicted to a certain degree with Dwight Moody's original mandate, that the Institute welcome all applicants with a common school education. Not everyone connected with the Institute made academic excellence a top priority, but one of its chief early leaders, James Gray, assuredly did. His biographer records that Gray was pained by the remarks of those who belittled the school's academic standing and the permissiveness of its admissions policy. For this reason, says the biographer, he was always careful to comport himself as an "educated" person in public, "and he cautioned the students to do the same."[14] A man proud of his own educational attainments and given to quoting poetry, he clearly felt restive about the liberality of the Institute's admissions requirements.[15] Early in his administration, he suggested making a high school education mandatory for entering students, and also requiring Institute students to take an English course. Initially he encountered a "storm of protest" from those who insisted that Moody remain accessible to all who desired to attend.[16] Eventually, however, he realized some of his objectives. By 1914, "proficiency in rhetoric and composition were made a requirement for graduation."[17] And selected programs began to require high school diplomas; when the three-year Religious Education Course began in 1924, secondary school graduation was declared a prerequisite.

By means of the standards set in this Religious Education Course, Moody leaders became instrumental in helping raise the sights of religious education teachers in other Bible schools. The director of this course, Clarence H. Benson, exerted much of his influence through the Evangelical Teacher Training Association, a group that grew out of a Chicago meeting he called in 1930, with the encouragement of Gray. Representatives from the Bible Institute of Los Angeles, Philadelphia Bible Institute, Toronto Bible Institute, and Northwestern College responded. The resulting organization, the ETTA, set itself the task of devising courses of study by means of which Bible school students intending to go into Sunday school work could be trained as master teachers and go on to teach and certify other teachers. Benson, as secretary of the ETTA, authored most of the material for training such Bible school students, and in doing so drew heavily on his experience teaching Sunday school teachers at Moody. He also incorporated Gray's synthetic Bible study technique into the ETTA material.[18]

Bible school membership in the ETTA grew steadily after its founding, numbering about fifty by 1938. The success of the ETTA, combined with Benson's dominant place in it, meant, in effect, that the Christian Education courses in most of the major Bible schools closely resembled that of Moody Bible Institute in content and level. Furthermore, through its influence in the ETTA, the Institute took part in an early form of accreditation of Bible schools. This came about because the ETTA established minimal standards for full membership: schools must be at least three years old, must enroll a minimum of sixty students, and must possess libraries of 1590 or more volumes.

Institute leaders of the first few decades also upheld standards of propriety and decorum. Torrey and Gray cultivated reputations as dignified and reserved men, and attempted to transmit to students their preference for this style. The shirt sleeves, Billy Sunday type of evangelism, at home with slang and colloquialism, did not come into fashion at Moody Bible Institute during their administrations. Torrey "wore a finely tailored Prince Albert coat with white short, starched collar and cuffs, and white bow tie. His shoes were polished. There was hardly a wrinkle in his clothing."[19] His speech was simple and unadorned: "He was at all times refined with an inherent dignity" and shunned "sensationalism" or the "cheap advertising method."[20] His thinking was deliberate: "He was seldom moved by any wave of emotion in arriving at his decisions. Rather he was swayed by the logical element of cold reason." His addresses and sermons were well-organized: "Orderly presentation marked the evangelist's discourses. The firstly, secondly, and thirdly continued with unabated regularity. The work of God allowed no confusion. It must be orderly. The creative act of God was orderly."[21]

James Gray easily matched Torrey's style in conservative dress and personal habit. Despite the fact that he was an evangelistic preacher, his conduct in the pulpit was sedate. A woman admirer told him that worship under his direction had always been "restful" and praised "the quiet, orderly, reverential way" he conducted services.[22] A reporter remarked of Gray that he "cultivated gentlemanliness as a fine art,"[23] and he insisted that students and faculty do the same. Male students were required to wear coats and ties in the dining room. During a July 1908 heat wave he admonished faculty: "I have observed members of the faculty during this warm weather sitting in their offices without coats or vest. I beg the practice may not grow upon us, because of its effect on the students who need our example of conventionality."[24]

For both Torrey and Gray, personal dignity included an attention to punctuality. They habitually castigated easygoing attitudes toward schedules and deadlines. Torrey was notorious for cutting off any speaker who exceeded his time limit, in the middle of a sentence if necessary.[25] In 1926 Gray complained about "tardiness at the table [in the dorms] when meals are announced, which I am informed has increased to a degree that rather seriously affects our morale . . . it is reported to me that officials and employees not infrequently make their appearance from twenty to thirty minutes late, causing comments by our guests as well as students."[26]

The essential cautiousness of Torrey, Gray, and other Moody leaders also manifested itself in a distaste for noisy clashes and splits. Though Moody leaders strove to maintain doctrinal standards in the conservative evangelical movement, in the interest of harmony they avoided alienating those groups with which they differed. Moody personnel attempted to speak judiciously and moderately when they surveyed the newest and most exotic manifestations of fundamentalism. They criticized but with tact and moderation. In an editorial note on Aimee Semple McPherson, the pentecostal leader, for instance, a *Moody Monthly* writer said that while "we" disagree with many of her teachings, "It is a pleasure indeed to add that" several "who have written us, speak of Mrs. McPherson's personality, her sincerity and modesty as beyond question."[27] Similarly, an editorial the following year firmly denied the claims of some pentecostals that C. G. Finney and D. L. Moody spoke in tongues, but also claimed to bear a "Christian love" for pentecostals and allowed that "godly people" had joined their ranks.[28]

In addition to avoiding polemics against those it considered well-intentioned but "in error," those associated with Moody often eschewed an exclusivist point of view. Though the Institute was clearly identified as premillennialism, a *Moody Monthly* editorial in 1922 demonstrated an unwillingness to equate fundamentalism and premillennialism for fear of driving out "some good and strong men" who "are not opponents of premillennialist, but for one reason or another are not counted in its ranks."[29]

Also in the interests of unity, Moody leaders celebrated the Institute's brand of Bible study as unsectarian and conducive to agreement and harmony. Those who studied the Bible with an open mind, as directed by Institute teachers, were bound to wind up as theological brothers and sisters: "Now while men are prone to debate theological statements it is significant that debate almost entirely ceases in consecutive Bible study," a 1922 *Moody Monthly* writer urged.[30] Another spokesman writing in 1933 stressed the theological unity bred by the Moody approach to the Bible: "there is not one major segment of truth taught us in this place which does not fully accord with the Word of God, and which we could not preach in any pulpit in the world."[31]

Yet another element in Moody's basically moderate stance was the desire of many of its spokespersons to avoid offending the leaders of the traditional denominations and to discourage the come-outer mentality common among fundamentalists. Because of its interdenominationalism, to be sure, the Institute's support of denominational prerogatives sometimes faltered. R. A. Torrey tended to discount the importance of church boundaries and differences, and when asked his church affiliation, was given to responding, "I am an 'Episcopresbygationalaptist.'"[32] He also remarked, "The old distinctions between Presbyterians and Methodists, between Baptists and Congregationalists, between Lutherans and Episcopalians . . . have all lost significance for me. To be more exact they never had any significance."[33] Furthermore, the Moody Memorial Church, which was associated with the Institute and attracted the loyalty of many students and employees, was interdenominational. MBI itself functioned somewhat like a denomination, and took the place of a denomination in the minds of some fundamentalists.[34] It is understandable, then, that denominational leaders distrusted the intentions of school leaders.

But eventually, anxious for the Institute to be a force for harmony rather than disruption in fundamentalist ranks, Institute leaders took pains to quiet the suspicion that they were hostile toward denominations. By 1916 editors of the school journal were struggling to combat what they called "the erroneous impression in some quarters that the Institute takes the members of the churches away and destroys their interest in their home church."[35] When Will H. Houghton assumed the presidency in 1934 he pointedly eschewed membership in the Moody Church and instead joined a local Baptist congregation.[36]

This conservative, moderating impulse came into play at the Bible Institute of Los Angeles as well. In the early teens, as mentioned earlier, one of Biola's founders, T. C. Horton, felt compelled to clamp down upon three teachers who were spreading Bullingerism, an ultra-dispensationalism. During the twenties Biola was again troubled by controversy, this time over pentecostals. Actually for several years, Biola's founders, though not themselves pentecostals, had showed tolerance of the phenomenon. Biola presses, which did not confine their operations simply to Biola publications, had been doing printing jobs for the pentecostal Angelus Temple in Los Angeles. In the mid-twenties, however, Biola came under increasing pressure from prominent fundamentalists elsewhere to define its position vis-à-vis pentecostalism, and at length The King's Business issued a statement which, while avoiding an attack, clearly positioned Biola in the moderate middle of fundamentalist ranks, at a safe distance from pentecostalism. From this time on Biola administrators seem to have discouraged the phenomenon among students and faculty. In 1930, for instance, a woman student was described in the faculty minutes as "an intense McPhersonite, . . . apparently seeking the truth." The faculty decided that one of their number should question her "regarding her views, and if the interview is unsatisfactory to ask her to meet with the Executive Committee [of the faculty]" which presumably would then make a decision if necessary on how to discipline her.[37]

Bible school leaders sometimes did not confine themselves to safeguarding their own schools; they kept a wary eye on other institutions in what W. B. Riley referred to as the "Bible School Defense Line." During the late twenties Riley was distressed to see what he considered the modernist viewpoint taken by the dean of Biola, John MacInnis, particularly in his newly published book, *Peter the Fisherman*. Riley was also disturbed by some of the texts used in Biola's Christian Education department. After unsuccessfully appealing to Biola's board of directors, to MacInnis himself, and to other Biola principals for redress of the situation, Riley went public with his complaints in the editorial columns of the periodical of the Northwestern Schools. Among the allies in his attack upon MacInnis, he claimed other Bible school leaders such as Gray and Torrey. For several months Biola trustees resisted the considerable pressure exerted by Riley and his allies for MacInnis' resignation, but in the end they succumbed. MacInnis and several faculty and trustees left the school, and Riley predicted with satisfaction that Biola, returned "to a solid Bible basis," would fulfill its mission as "a great school of the prophets on the Pacific Coast."[38]

Thus, certain normative beliefs were imposed at Bible schools like Biola and Moody, both from within and without, and a middle class conventionality was promoted. These activities did not always advance unity among conservative evangelicals, of course. When Bible school leaders took it upon themselves to determine who and what lay inside and outside the boundaries of orthodoxy—especially when, as sometimes happened, they did so ungently—they were open to the charge of exacerbating the considerable tensions in the movement. To this accusation they would have replied with some justice that, in the long run, by defining the center as against the extremes, they promoted a coherence and moderation in the fundamentalist movement that would have been impossible had evangelicals of all viewpoints been welcomed equally into the fellowship of their schools.

The Bible Schools as Headquarters for Fundamentalists

Another role played by the Bible schools was to serve as bases of operations for conservative evangelicals. Many of those who became Bible school leaders and teachers were in need of just such bases; they had left their denominations because of religious disagreements or discontents, or had embarked on independent evangelistic activities that their denominations would not or could not back. Henry Wilson, for instance, who taught at the Missionary Training Institute early in the twentieth century, had early in his career lost a curacy in Canada for answering a Salvation Army altar call. A colleague of his, Albert Funk, who had taught at the same school since its New York City days, had left the General Conference of the Mennonite Church because as a pastor he had dissented from his

denomination's hostility to revivalism. A third early teacher, George Pardington, had run afoul of the trustees of the Methodist church, who had
withheld his salary when he advocated adult baptism.[39] Evangelists and
missionaries such as these not infrequently found themselves without institutional affiliation or dependable means of support except for the Bible
school at which they taught. The schools provided a degree of stability;
they offered institutional affiliation, a community of sympathetic colleagues and unusually dedicated students, and sometimes a small income.

At the same time as they supplied evangelicals with a home base, the
Bible schools offered them another advantage—a flexibility that the institutions had inherited from their training school origins. Evangelists could
usually teach at a Bible school part-time if they wished and still manage
to carry on other important evangelistic activities concurrently; for example, often a Bible school instructor could take to the road part of the
year as an itinerant evangelist or Bible teacher. The respect with which
fundamentalism treated missionaries and evangelists justified—indeed
encouraged—those who preferred not to devote all their time to teaching
and working in one place. This circumstance would hardly have applied
at the typical college, where professors would normally have been discouraged from dividing their hours between the school and other pursuits,
so much to the apparent disadvantage of the school.

The Bible schools, then, provided a freedom and scope for evangelistic
enterprise not customarily associated with educational institutions. Since
their leaders had few preconceived notions of what a Bible school should
or should not attempt in the way of religious education, restless and ener-
getic evangelists did not need to confine themselves within classroom walls
when they associated themselves with Bible schools. Bible school educators
did not limit their attention to regularly matriculated students, if indeed
they even recognized such a neat category. They organized evening classes,
extension classes, correspondence study, radio Bible classes, Bible conferences, Bible camps, periodicals, movie programs, city missions, foreign
missions societies, evangelistic campaigns in prisons, and distribution of
Christian literature; the list was often limited only by the number of available personnel and the extent of financial resources. Since almost any
evangelical-educational activity legitimately fell within the purview of Bible
schools, fundamentalists based in these institutions found ample opportunity to use whatever entrepreneurial ingenuity, energy, and zeal they
possessed.

This description of the relative freedom with which fundamentalists
operated in Bible school settings must, however, be qualified slightly.
Institutions inevitably make demands upon their leaders and workers, limiting their other possible options, and, notwithstanding the fact that its
yoke was relatively light, the Bible school was no exception. Eventually
those connected with the schools often had to decide whether they identified themselves as Bible school educators first and evangelists second, or

vice versa. Not that they necessarily had to give up one role or the other, but priorities had to be established, since time and energy were limited. The case of James M. Gray of Moody Bible Institute seems to illustrate this point. For several years before he became a full-time employee of MBI, he traveled extensively as a Bible teacher, serving the Institute only for a few months in the summer. He had in fact resigned from a successful Boston pastorate in order to be free to conduct Bible classes and occasionally assist Dwight Moody with his evangelistic campaigns. He was lured to the Institute on a permanent basis by the expectation that he would be only one of three coequal administrators, each of whom would devote a third of the year to running the school. During the rest of the year they would be at liberty to travel as evangelists and Bible teachers. The other two leaders, he understood, would be Reuben A. Torrey and possibly C. I. Scofield. However, this arrangement foundered when Torrey, long drawn to full-time evangelistic work and disagreeing with Gray over administrative issues, departed from the Institute altogether in 1908. To make matters worse, A. P. Fitt, Moody's son-in-law, resigned as Executive Secretary of the Institute in the same year. To his chagrin, Gray was left alone filling the post as full-time dean. Judging from the length and success of his career at the Institute, he did not find the leadership of the school as onerous as he might have feared in 1908; on the contrary, he found the scope of MBI's activities sufficiently broad to challenge his ambitions as an evangelist and itinerant teacher. But the significant fact is that initially he was attracted to the idea of a limited, one-third time commitment to MBI, and also that the Institute was prepared to oblige him had circumstances turned out more favorably.[40]

Other conservatives settled with more apparent satisfaction than Gray right from the beginning into full-time roles as school administrators; Nathan Wood, head of the Gordon school, seems immediately to have seen his primary role as educator and his chief domain as the school, though he continued frequently to fill the pulpits of Baptist churches as a visiting minister. Some conservatives, on the other hand, deliberately steered clear altogether of the tensions inherent in trying to serve simultaneously as institutional administrator and traveling evangelist. A well-known Bible teacher, Harry A. Ironside, for instance, refused all offers of permanent posts at MBI and other Bible schools (though he consented to work for Moody's Extension Department).[41]

It is possible, though difficult to document, that some Bible school educators who found the scope of their activities constricted by the mounting demands and complexities of their institutions moved on to newer, less highly organized schools, where they may have retained more freedom of movement and perhaps a greater theater for their talents. Such may have been the case with Reuben A. Torrey, who headed Moody Bible Institute until 1908. Two years later Torrey became dean of the Bible Institute of Los Angeles, a newer and smaller school where, it seems, he had more freedom to implement his educational ideas and also carry on concurrent revivalistic activities. In fact, Torrey made it a condition of his going to Biola that a church be founded in connection with the school and that a 3,500-seat auditorium be provided where he could conduct his evangelism. An article in Biola's periodical, *The King's Business,* recognized Torrey's extra-academic objectives, explaining that the church and auditorium would "enable him to continue the evangelistic preaching mission to which he believed God had called him."[42]

The Bible Schools as Vehicles for Conservative Groups

Notwithstanding the size and influence of the undenominational schools such as Moody and the Bible Institute of Los Angeles, we should not ignore the numerous smaller schools for which denominational identity was extremely important. Among the groups that sponsored Bible schools—often more than one—were the Advent Christians, the Friends, the Evangelical Free Church, the Churches of Christ, the Mennonites, the Pilgrim Holiness Church, and the Assemblies of God. Generally, because these schools drew from a more limited pool of potential students and often from a more circumscribed geographical area as well, they remained smaller and less prominent than the interdenominational schools.

The Bible school form proved to be particularly congenial to these groups. Many of them were financially hard pressed and could afford only very meager appropriations for education. In some of these denominations the membership was skeptical about the merits of formal education, preferring that funds be spent for missions rather than for training the ministry or the laity. Bible schools fit in with these conditions; they represented at best a modest investment in education, and their reasonable cost was matched by the modesty of their educational pretensions. For those who balked at the denomination's support of formal education, this was formal education at its least formal and therefore least objectionable.

The Advent Christian Boston Bible School was in many ways typical of such denominational schools. Advent Christians were rural, relatively poor, and included a significant contingent who distrusted schooling as an impediment to true piety; thus, a Bible school (rather than a liberal arts college or a seminary) best suited their needs. Furthermore, they required a school of their own because they taught unique doctrines. Though they were premillennialists, unlike most other premillennialists of the late nineteenth century, they recognized ties to the Adventism of the earlier 1800s, and particularly to the writings of William Miller. Furthermore, in contradiction to other Adventists and indeed to the majority of other Protestants, who believed that sinners would suffer eternal damnation, Advent Christians espoused "conditionalism," that is, they held that the wicked would simply be annihilated and that only the saved would experience resurrection to eternal life. They called this doctrine condition-alism, because, they said, human beings received immortality from God only conditionally (i.e., only if they were saved).[43]

The school was founded in 1897 by leaders convinced that the denomi-nation needed some way to train its young people, particularly its ministers. Otherwise, they feared, the coming generation would attend the educa-tional institutions of other groups and be lost to the denomination. Getting the go-ahead for the school had not been easy; its advocates had had to contend with the hostility of many Advent Christians who, scornful of "minister factories," as they called them, believed that a pastor ought simply to receive the call to preach from God and needed no other prepa-ration. Such grassroots suspicion of formal education persisted through the school's first decades, and for this reason, its leaders worked especially hard to demonstrate its loyalty and utility to the denomination.

Thus, the school advanced assiduously the special viewpoints of the denomination: instructors taught conditionalism and also emphasized the study of history in accordance with the Advent Christian belief—contrary to that of dispensationalists—that biblical prophecy had already been par-tially fulfilled in history. Textbooks were largely confined to Advent Chris-tian authors. The 1913–14 catalog declared that "Such text books are used as best lend themselves to the doctrinal holdings of the denomina-tion."[44] Not only were students exposed to denominational beliefs in the classroom, but also most of the occasional lecturers they heard were Ad-vent Christian ministers. Students were encouraged and not infrequently required to take part in denominational activities. They attended the an-nual meetings of the major denominational agencies, such as the publish-ing and missionary societies; it was not unusual for classes to be canceled for such purposes. Students also participated in ministers' meetings. One morning in about 1910, for instance, "the students were permitted to attend the monthly ministers' meeting and hear the address of Rev. A. H. Ericsson, Lit. B. S., on 'The Supreme Purpose of the Miraculous in Christianity'; and take notes on the address."[45] They also seem to have been absent from school upon occasion in order to attend meetings of their own state conferences. Frequently students spoke at denominational functions, led worship, provided the music, or even waited on tables. Fi-nally, the school cultivated ties with individual Advent Christian churches. Students often preached in these churches during the school year and the summers, and then went on to serve them as pastors after they gradu-ated. Instructors in the school sometimes doubled as ministers for Boston area Advent Christian churches.

At its inception the Boston Bible School was probably as thoroughly a denominational school as one could have found. Yet with time it moved more and more into the wider Bible school-fundamentalist orbit, as Advent Christians realized that, whatever the uniqueness of some of their doctrinal teachings, they nevertheless shared much in common with other conservative evangelicals: their premillennialism (albeit their own version), their interest in holiness, revivalism, and evangelism, their biblicism, and their special concern with prophecy. Advent Christians also became convinced that all conservative evangelicals faced the same enemy, that is, the modernist proclivities of the age.[46] Even early on the school had used R. A. Torrey's text, *What the Bible Teaches,* despite the fact that the denomination dissented from Torrey's dispensationalist orientation. In fact, the decision to set up a Bible school in the first place already signaled an awareness of educational trends in conservative evangelicalism and a willingness to follow suit. With time the nascent identification with the wider conservative movement, already apparent in the beginning, became more pronounced; during the twenties the school developed close ties with Gordon (many of its graduates continued their education there) and its students and faculty cooperated in ecumenical evangelical organizations and efforts in the Boston area.

This movement from greater to lesser denominational exclusiveness was not unique to the Boston Bible School. Whatever the distinctive characteristics of a given Bible school, and whatever its apparent religious parochialism, the "pull" of the generalized Bible school form was strong, as was the influence of the wider fundamentalist movement. The tendency at Bible schools toward uniform curriculum and standard student lifestyles affected even the most isolated schools. In this sense even the denominational Bible schools, while they clearly served the particular interests of their sponsors, also acted as unifiers of conservative evangelicalism. Ecumenicity, it seemed, was built into the very structure and purpose of Bible schools.

Marketing the Gospel

Bible schools contributed also to the prevailing style of fundamentalism. Of course, one treads on slippery ground making such an assertion, first because it is hazardous to define a fundamentalist "style" amidst so much variety, and second because it is difficult to determine the direction of the flow of influence—whether from the Bible schools to the movement or vice versa, or—most likely—back and forth.

This having been said, it seems fair to describe a prominent part of fundamentalism as having a flair for marketing and advertising. Many evangelicals demonstrated a genius for publicizing what they deemed important for people to know, a confident go-getter attitude that became especially apparent during the twenties and later. This aspect of fundamentalism has its ironies, since fundamentalists often deplored what they considered the spirit of the twenties (or the sixties or eighties): its materialism, its concentration upon the dollar, its permissive morality, its crime, and its religious laxity, among other things. But at the same time they often shared the twenties spirit of expansiveness, confidence, optimism, boosterism, hyperbole, and admiration for efficiency.

As in so many other matters concerning Bible schools, Moody Bible Institute presents itself as an example. It is probably no coincidence that the school was founded by a salesman extraordinaire. The commercial and achievement-oriented turn of mind was rife in the literature of the Institute. The appropriately named E. O. Sellers, a faculty member, had in 1911 compared the techniques of personal evangelism to the "personal solicitation" of the insurance man or politician.[47] Among the "methods of Christian work" in the class of that title given in that year was "advertising."[48] A writer in a 1922 *Moody Monthly* exhorted, "The disciple of Christ is to be an expert merchant in the commodity of time. He is always engaged in 'buying up opportunity.' . . . His vigilance must never sleep and he must never be away from the market. Every moment must be bought up for the King, and used in the service of His Kingdom."[49] A 1922 ad for the Correspondence Department promised, "Study of the Bible Gives Boldness and Success."[50] Finally, an alumnus was quoted in 1929 as arguing, "Every Christian should be a salesman—sell the gospel!"[51]

Institute leaders rarely missed an opportunity to promote the school and its evangelistic mission. As early as 1908 James Gray wrote to the business manager: "You will recall that two years ago . . . you and I planned a system of advertising the Institute to cover regularly all the newspapers of the country. It is to that that I attribute in part the marked increase in our student roster subsequently, and if it has been discontinued I should like to take it up again."[52] When young people's religious groups met for conventions and conferences in Chicago, the Institute offered them a free bus trip to the school and a tour of the campus.[53] At state and international expositions the administration customarily set up exhibits touting the school's activities and achievements.[54] Finally, the extension department was responsible for arranging promotional "Moody Bible Institute Weeks" in churches. The program for these events typically combined Bible study and "a presentation of the place and work of the Moody Bible Institute."[55]

Over the years the Institute built up an extensive mailing list consisting of anyone who had ever expressed the slightest interest in Institute programs. Response to advertisements for the correspondence courses constituted a prime source for names. The Institute typically placed "Bible tests" in magazines and journals (e.g., *The Prairie Farmer*). The follow-up to this test, which regularly exposed the ignorance of the test taker, was information on the Institute correspondence courses designed to correct the deficiency. Even when the Institute did not receive an immediate request for a course, it usually kept sending school literature anyway.[56]

Prospective contributors were assiduously cultivated. While teaching the Bible and conducting services in Detroit, Gray met two women, one of whom expressed tentative interest in paying for a scholarship. Before he left for home, Gray carefully provided for a follow-up, writing another Institute administrator: "My suggestion is, that you put both on the free list of the Tie [the name for the publication that later became the *Moody Monthly*] + make a memo, somewhere either to address them yourself later, or to have me do it."[57]

One result of the intensive attempt to sell the gospel (and the Institute) was that the school reinforced the growth of certain ingredients in fundamentalist speech and writing—the advertising slogan, the commercial metaphor, the harping on success and measurable achievement, and the pride in statistics. Admittedly Moody was far from the only source of this element; one has to look to the small American businessman, the upwardly mobile petite bourgeoisie, whose language this was. They were attracted to fundamentalism in great numbers and brought with them their characteristic preoccupation with tangible benefits, efficiency, and numbers. Moody Institute's particular role in fostering the commercial turn of mind came through its influence upon its students and upon other Bible school administrators, who emulated its sales techniques and style.

Certainly the selling-the-gospel approach was common in other Bible schools. It was implicit in the eagerness with which school leaders embraced radio, mass rallies, periodicals, and traveling musical "ambassadors"—anything that would push the message and the messengers. The marketing theme was striking in a thirties acquisition of the Bible Institute of Los Angeles; on its roof towered two seven-foot red neon signs, visible over much of Los Angeles, that advertised, "Jesus Saves."[58] Basically the same message, in those same or similar words, would echo and re-echo in evangelical advertising of this century: on other neon signs, on billboards, on television screens, on leaflets, on bumper stickers and banners, on badges and pens, and in mass mailings. And Bible school teachers, students, and graduates would play a prominent role in creating and staffing this strenuous promotional campaign for the Kingdom.

XI

THE BIBLE SCHOOLS AND
AMERICAN EDUCATION

Outside observers have generally regarded Bible schools as maverick institutions located on the fringes of the American educational scene. They
have found them difficult to classify and difficult to understand both in
themselves and in relation to other developments in education. But these
problems stem more from the paucity of relevant studies of Bible schools
and from the distaste that many secular educators feel for institutions
associated with religious fundamentalism than from the nature of the
institutions themselves. The most cursory review of the history of the
schools leads quickly to the conclusion that the Bible schools fit quite neatly
into many of the major themes of American educational history. Some
of the evidence for this assertion has already been suggested. Whatever
their other—and sometimes conflicting—educational goals, Bible school
leaders were sensitive to rising academic standards and concern for accreditation; in other words, they were attentive to educational norms. Moreover, insofar as Bible schools were practical, vocational institutions, they
followed prevailing educational fashion. In the late nineteenth and early
twentieth centuries, American educational reformers raised their voices
against the teaching of abstract theory, insisting that learning be closely
related to experience and practice. In its most sophisticated form, such
thinking emerged in the pragmatism of John Dewey, who defined education instrumentally—albeit broadly—as "the reconstruction or reorganiza-
tion of experience which adds to the meaning of experience and which
increases ability to direct the course of subsequent experience."[1] His philosophy discouraged an approach to teaching and learning that remained
exclusively intellectual and oriented to information gathering.

The widespread advocacy of practical education led to reforms and
innovations in secondary schools and colleges. The first high schools for
manual training appeared in the 1880s and 90s, at the same time as the
pioneer Bible training schools. The traditional forms of education for
the professions of medicine, law, and the ministry underwent reforms
geared to produce better practitioners by giving students more experience.
New or reorganized medical schools that devoted more attention to the

practice of medicine through the introduction of clinical education attracted universal admiration.[2] In seminaries which had previously concentrated almost exclusively upon theology and biblical languages, the "practical fields"—religious education, practical theology, and psychology—soon became well established, and field education took on new importance as a source of experience and learning rather than merely of student income. New types of professional and semi-professional schools, also oriented to practice, came into being: normal schools, kindergarten training schools, teachers' colleges, engineering schools, schools of social work, and graduate schools of business. Schools for secretaries, accountants, business people, salesmen, and nurses—many, like Bible schools, at indeterminate academic levels—made their first appearances in force around the turn of the century. Bible schools deserve at long last to take their places in this catalog of practical and vocationally oriented institutions.

The Bible schools had much in common with all the institutions mentioned above, but perhaps they most strikingly resembled the normal schools. The lines between the early representatives of the two types of school sometimes in fact blurred; at least one Bible school began as the "Christian Normal Institute," and retained that name for decades (see the chart in chapter 5). Furthermore, a major function of the Bible schools coincided with that of the normal schools: to train teachers. In the case of Bible schools, to be sure, the goal was to produce a more narrowly defined kind of instructor: Bible, Sunday school, and Christian school teachers. Nevertheless, pedagogy was an important concern of the Bible schools as well as of the normal schools.

The most obvious similarity between Bible schools and the early normal schools lay in the consistent emphasis both placed upon the practical experience that accompanied the classroom learning. Even in the classroom itself, skills and methods received a great deal of attention from educators of both institutions. Some subject matter, such as manual training and pedagogy, overlapped between the two schools.

This is not to take the comparison as far as it can go, however; Bible and normal schools shared their practical work requirement and their preoccupation with methods classes with a great many other educational institutions of the time. Also striking is a comparison of the typical student bodies in the Bible schools and early normal schools. Both enrolled students of modest educational backgrounds, students of "meager attainments," as it was sometimes put. Generally speaking, both taught their students on a secondary rather than post-secondary level. Both posted lenient entrance requirements, usually designating a common school education as the prerequisite (and sometimes accepting students with only the merest rudiments). Consequently, both kinds of schools customarily needed to provide a minimum of very basic classes in subjects such as reading, composition, arithmetic, history, and even spelling and penmanship. Though educators in both institutions frequently tried to raise standards, in doing so they had to add preparatory departments to accommodate weak students.

In addition to modest educational backgrounds, Bible and normal school students shared unexceptional social origins. They came from the middle or lower middle classes. Most had grown up on farms or in small country towns, and therefore lacked the sophistication of their urban peers. Upper middle class people who had received an education at a prestigious high school or liberal arts college tended to look down upon normal school students and later upon Bible school students, perhaps because such students were chronically short of funds and needed to work at a wide variety of jobs in order to make up their financial deficits. Furthermore, judged by academic standards, the institutions they attended were not quite respectable. (Because tuition was free, the student at a state normal school was often perceived as being on the public dole.) Yet, despite the fact that neither Bible nor normal schools could by any stretch of the imagination be considered elite, students used both types of education to achieve upward social and economic mobility.

Both normal and Bible schools were almost always coeducational. (The normal school usually had a preponderance of women; often the Bible school did also.) Considering the level of education they were receiving, Bible and normal students were relatively mature. Most had reached their early twenties at least and had already had work experience of some kind.

Early normal school students pursued their studies in a religious atmosphere not unlike that which later enveloped Bible school students. Those who attended Oswego Normal School soon after the middle of the nineteenth century went to chapel daily, and participated in frequent prayer meetings and Bible readings. During the 1870s both the Illinois State Normal University and the town in which it was located became caught up in religious revival, and "work was disrupted for a month." Not surprising given the emphasis upon students' spiritual condition, normal school graduates became not only public school teachers but also evangelists and missionaries.[3]

The first generations of normal school students were tightly circumscribed in their personal lives, as were their later counterparts at Bible schools. Prohibitions against dancing and theater attendance, as well as against the more obvious vices, were common. Until 1908 no dancing was tolerated at Illinois State University; Oswego students received temperance instruction.[4] Usually men and women students were segregated; the few occasions upon which they mingled were carefully supervised.

There was one major difference between normal and Bible schools, and it is as instructive as the similarities. Though the liberal arts college served as an example and influence for both Bible schools and normal schools, its impact upon the normal school took place earlier and more powerfully; normal schools adopted collegiate elements—literary societies, liberal arts subjects, and other marks of "general culture" as rapidly as possible. In part the swift march of the normal schools in the direction of the liberal arts colleges was simply a function of their earlier appearance on the educational scene. (The first normal school dated from 1839, compared with 1882 for the earliest known Bible training school.) But additional factors explain the speed with which normal schools adopted the liberal arts. Most important, the schools received much more scrutiny from educators, figuring in any number of private and government surveys from the turn of the century onward. At the same time, in contrast, such educators and surveyors virtually ignored Bible schools. Consequently, normal school educators came under great external pressure—or encouragement—to raise standards, introduce the liberal arts, and strive for accreditation as colleges. And normal school educators welcomed the liberal arts with less ambivalence. Whatever their misgivings about injecting the liberal arts into a "professional" program, normal school educators, increasingly secular minded, did not usually worry that introducing the liberal arts would replace religious concerns in their curricula, a fear that has haunted their Bible school counterparts up to the present. Normal school educators were quite content to follow the lead of the liberal arts colleges and the universities into the modern age, and they usually commanded more funds to do so. Thus, the way was much smoother for their institutions to maneuver into the middle of the educational mainstream. Bible school educators would eventually move in that direction, but for them change would come much more slowly and painfully.[5]

The Bible Schools as Popular Educators

If a large number of Americans were to adhere to the "faith once delivered to the saints," if fundamentalism was to survive and even flourish as a popular movement, it was incumbent upon conservative Protestant leaders to educate widely and effectively. Bible school educators led in this enormous task; as zealously and successfully as any pedagogues of their time, in fact, they promoted popular education.

Their concern with popular education was far from unique; they shared this enthusiasm with many of their secular counterparts. In fact, American educators since the early days of the Republic had consistently attempted to educate ever growing numbers, and just as assiduously learners had striven to increase their opportunities to learn. Educators in the late nineteenth century continued these efforts, inventing new devices or reviving old ones to reach students beyond their regular classrooms; they turned to study by mail, extension lectures, summer schools and institutes, university presses, and evening classes.[6] New schools sprang up to train people in fields for which preparation had not previously been available: schools for secretaries, nurses, mechanics, and salesmen. Junior colleges were created for those who aspired to more than a high school education but less than a full four-year college course. What was unique about Bible school efforts on behalf of popular education, besides the nature of their message, was simply the aggressiveness and resourcefulness with which they pursued them.

Bible school educators were self-conscious about their intentions as popular educators. The editors of the *Moody Bible Institute Monthly,* for instance, argued that theological seminaries served "a privileged few only," whereas "with the rise of the Bible schools, the door of opportunity was thrown open to thousands."[7] In their enthusiasm for popular education, Bible school educators were influenced by the familiar arguments for an informed and virtuous citizenry that were heard on all sides. But their zeal for instructing the widest possible public was also shaped by several special circumstances.

First, most Bible school educators held that evangelism in its best sense meant that absolutely everyone—no matter how poor, how despised, how wicked, how untutored, or how unskilled in the use of English—was an appropriate candidate for proselytization. The more widely a Bible school threw its educational net, then, the truer the quality of its evangelism.

Second, in the thinking of Bible school educators, evangelism had come of late to require education as an ally; in fact, the word "evangelism" had grown to mean much the same thing as "education." An editorial note in the *Moody Monthly* asserted that the most effective evangelists were really teachers. This had been less true, the editor admitted, when, in the early nineteenth century, most of the adult population in the United States had routinely absorbed the basic teachings of Protestant Christianity as children. At that time the evangelist simply needed to remind an adult audience of what they had already learned, and perhaps chide them for backsliding. But nowadays, given the widespread ignorance or rejection of things spiritual, the writer continued, evangelists must be skillful and persuasive teachers "as well as exhorters."[8]

Third, fundamentalist educators assumed that religious knowledge was easy to comprehend and disseminate if only it were clearly presented. Spiritual matters were not arcane, as some interpreters would suggest; when there was confusion or mystery, the fault lay in the way Christianity was explained, not in the material itself. A *Moody Monthly* editor castigated the "pedantic snobbishness" habitually practiced in "the spiritual realm of knowledge," and went on to claim that

> Books, allusion and phraseology of which can be understood only by the highly educated, are undesirable when a little pains born of Christian humility would bring them within the range of a more general mental capacity. The same is true of biblical interpretation, which despises the ancient dic-

tum, "When the plain sense makes good sense, seek no other sense," and preaching which goes over the people's heads. These are things of which "common people," such as those who heard Christ gladly (Mark 12:37), have just cause to complain in our day.[9]

As a corollary, Bible school educators assumed that earnest study conducted in a commonsense manner would lead ordinary people to interpret Scripture similarly—and of course correctly.

Fourth, fundamentalists believed, sometimes to a naive degree, in the power of ideas to affect and influence. A *Moody Monthly* editor claimed, "the philosophy taught in our universities trickles down into the realm of practical life and conduct."[10] This belief, indeed, explains why fundamentalists worried so much about what was being taught in the universities and seminaries outside their control. In the Bible school understanding of pedagogy, students who were taught "bad" ideas learned "bad" ideas and therefore behaved badly; those who were taught "good" ideas learned "good" ideas and conducted themselves virtuously; it was as simple as that. Often Bible school educators forgot that instruction sometimes leads to results surprisingly different from those intended by the instructor. Perhaps too they had an exaggerated idea of how impressionable students were. Whatever the reason, the result of their tremendous faith in the potency of ideas was a firm conviction of the importance of imparting instruction to the largest number possible.

Fifth, and perhaps most important of all, Bible school educators inherited the task of teaching the Bible to a popular audience. To understand how this happened, it is necessary to review briefly the history of popular Bible study in late nineteenth century America.

Starting around 1870, American Protestants had undergone an intensification of their perennial interest in the Bible. Initially, the rise of the higher criticism was both a symptom of and a contributor to this renewed interest; so also was the enthusiasm for dispensationalism, the popularity of Bible conferences, the organization of chautauquas (following the original Chautauqua in 1871), in which Bible study figured prominently, and the eminence of Bible teachers such as William Rainey Harper. Harper, who later became the first president of the University of Chicago, had managed to straddle the worlds of biblical scholarship on the one hand and popular, reverent fascination with the English Bible on the other hand. As a biblical scholar he contributed to the prestigious *International Critical Commentary* and launched many a scholarly career; as a teacher he popularized instruction in Hebrew, conducted huge classes in the English Bible, organized a Bible correspondence course, and edited a magazine of popular Bible study. Harper asked rhetorically in "The University and Democracy,"

Has not the day come when scholarship and the results of scholarly work shall no longer be kept apart and away from the masses? There are scholars

who . . . feel that they are casting pearls before swine, if they make a statement which may be understood by others than those working in their own
specialty. Is not this idea becoming antiquated? Is the popular presentation
of scientific truth at all inconsistent with a real appreciation of that truth?[11]

The importation of the higher criticism from Europe and England was
shortly followed, however, by the formation of guilds of biblical scholars,
whose chief reference point was the university graduate school and whose
audience was increasingly limited to their academic peers. After populariz-
er-scholars like Harper had passed from the scene, the public hunger
for Bible study found fewer sources for satisfaction. Therefore, after about
1910, an increasing number of Protestants who continued to regard the
Bible as the very word of God and who sought instruction geared to
the lay person's level, turned to the emerging fundamentalist movement.
They studied the Bible in local Bible classes, by themselves with manuals,
in Bible conferences, and of course in Bible schools.[12]

The attempts of Bible school leaders to open learning to a wider public
had two implications for their institutions: first, a more inclusive attitude
toward the admission of "regular" students to the school classrooms, particularly during the daytime, and second, a concerted drive to reach those
who could not be present within the school, but who could be taught
by means of the mail, the media, or the school's itinerant faculty.

In determining whom to admit, Bible school educators were often more
permissive than their counterparts at colleges or theological seminaries.
Bible school leaders typically made greater allowances for students with
weak educational backgrounds.[13] They also assumed that many of their
students would not command much money and so kept expenses to a
minimum, often charging no tuition and providing ways students could
make up their financial deficits. Some Bible schools scheduled a preponderance of evening classes for students who had jobs or other obligations
during the day. In 1935, for instance, the Bible Institute of Pennsylvania
enrolled only forty-three day students, but had 638 night students.[14] Unlike
many theological seminaries and colleges, Bible schools universally accepted women. And finally, they welcomed older students who had found
their vocations late in life.

When they looked beyond school walls for potential clientele, Bible
school leaders resorted to a number of instructional vehicles. Few schools
used them all, except possibly the giant of evangelical outreach, Moody
Bible Institute, but most schools employed at least a few measures designed
to reach students outside their classrooms. They organized Bible conferences all over the United States, and in all seasons. The Philadelphia
School of the Bible, for instance, sponsored an annual Bible conference
in Philadelphia, and other Bible conferences in the vicinity. Christian
presses owned and operated by the schools printed and disseminated moderately priced religious literature aimed at popular audiences. Prominent

among the publications of these presses were manuals, especially on the Bible, designed to promote self-study. Many schools sponsored extension Bible classes, sometimes at considerable distances; others hosted camps and camp meetings for young people. Some schools produced magazines and journals which, far from concentrating only on school affairs, brought Bible study and information on missions to the widest possible audiences.[15] The *Moody Monthly* was probably the organizing tool for groups like the "Bible Mastery Campaign"; farflung subscribers to this "campaign," inspired by James Gray's Bible synthesis technique, agreed to read a designated book of the Bible through daily for a month.[16]

Through correspondence courses, students in remote areas were enabled to study the Bible or learn to do personal work.[17] In populous locales, where a number of correspondence students might be taking the same course, they sometimes studied and discussed the subject matter together. Some Bible schools reached substantial audiences, including the unchurched, through radio; the fortunate few schools had stations of their own; others arranged to broadcast over a local station. Through attractive films, schools taught hundreds of audiences about the wonderful work of God the creator. Musical groups—choirs, quartets, and other vocal groups—participated in the evangelical and educational campaigns.

Finally, one cannot ignore the extensive educational effort carried on by regular Bible schools students as they went about their practical work assignments. They themselves were learners, but in the process they also taught others. They conducted Sunday school classes, Bible classes, manual training classes, and English classes. But they also educated in a broader sense when they evangelized in hospitals, prisons, and on street corners.

Thus, just as Protestantism was apparently contracting to occupy a smaller role in American life of the secular and pluralistic twentieth century, fundamentalist evangelical and educational efforts emerged on the scene, vigorous and comprehensive. Through radio, print, film, and eventually television, fundamentalists reached wider numbers than had any Protestant teachers before them. How did they manage to accomplish this when by all reports the cultural tides seemed to be flowing in the opposite direction? Their success calls into question assumptions about how deeply into the American populace that tide of secular and critical attitudes actually reached.

Bible schools have survived longer than their detractors would have judged possible, and certainly they have occupied the earthly landscape for more time than their premillennialist promoters hoped would be necessary. A large part of the strength and endurance of this educational movement, it is clear, is derived from the fundamentalist-evangelical tradition itself, in which a powerful evangelistic thrust has inspired particularly vigorous educational efforts. Whatever their initial misgivings about modernity and "newfangled" inventions, evangelists in the tradition have shown a willingness, even an eagerness, to make use of innovative communications technologies: radio, film, television, and in recent years, communications satellites and computers. They have pressed into service—and exploited fully—any tools that enabled them to reach larger numbers of potential converts. In recognizing the possibilities in such tools, Bible school educators—notably those at Moody—have often led the way.

Evangelists linked to the fundamentalist tradition have been helped by an effective rhetoric that is readily appropriated and disseminated and that has carried particularly well over the mass media. They have also benefited from a relatively uncomplicated theology; the "five points" which supposedly summed up fundamentalist doctrine constituted an extreme reduction, but the persistent notion of "five points" is symptomatic of the tendency of fundamentalists to summarize their theological positions in compact formula—not in five points, perhaps, but in twelve, or twenty. The penchant for packaging ideas by means of methods and manuals, making them manageable and easy to remember, has also furthered educational efforts. All in all the movement's educators have manifested an extraordinary confidence in the possibility of teaching Christian truth and practice to ordinary people without undue expenditure of time and money. Again, Bible school educators have been instrumental both in taking advantage of these features of conservative evangelicalism and in augmenting their use in the movement.

Another explanation for the strength of Bible schools lies in the institutions themselves. Uninhibited by the usual educational conventions, early Bible school founders started out by attracting lay people, including large numbers of women, who had not before enjoyed access to formal theological or religious education, and provided them with an inexpensive and flexible period of training. The founders and their successors also raised their sights to prospective students beyond their school walls. Thanks to their efforts, larger numbers of lay people than ever before received religious training; afterward they amply repaid the resources expended on them by contributing their energy, vitality, and skills to the movement.

Furthermore, Bible schools have benefited from the fact that they have offered practical education in pragmatic America. Not only have they provided training for Christian vocations, but in the process, as a byproduct, they have placed graduates in a stronger position to enter secular vocations such as business or public school teaching.

In the past few years circumstances not of their own making have reinforced the efforts of Bible school and other evangelical educators. Many Americans outside the evangelical orbit have been rendered more receptive to their message as they have come to concur in some of the negative judgments of modernity, at least in broad outline. These citizens join evangelicals in criticizing materialism, selfishness, scientism, and narcissism; lax mores in the public and private spheres; and large, bureaucratized, and unresponsive institutions. Like evangelicals, they miss a sense of stability and of ties to the past; they may even deplore the "decline" of the religious imagination and the ability to believe. Ironically, even though evangelicals dissented from the activities and axioms of protesters in the sixties (they were decidedly unwilling to see students in evangelical schools protesting in the streets), that decade may have rendered the evangelical point of view more acceptable. As a legacy of that period, many non-evangelicals turned to pessimistic and even apocalyptic assessments of the future. Moreover, the revivalistic style of American Protestantism took on new meaning to activists of the 1960s—even when they were unaware of its origins—first in the civil rights movement and later in the protests over Vietnam. When thousands gathered at the Washington Monument, sang "We Shall Overcome" and "Give Peace a Chance," thrilled to the exhortations of exciting speakers, and yearned for the conversion of the rest of the United States, they were staging a variation on a very old American style.

If the evangelical viewpoint has become more acceptable of late, so has evangelical education, when judged by conventional standards. The "third stage" of academic respectability outlined in chapter 6 is well advanced and is shared by the increasing numbers of evangelical colleges and seminaries that have qualified for standard accreditation and federal student loans. Many Bible schools, including the oldest and largest, now subscribe to their own accrediting agency, the American Association of Bible Colleges, a creation of the 1940s. Urged on by this Association and by the pressure of prevailing educational norms generally, some Bible school educators have raised their academic standards and increased their liberal arts offerings, making their institutions almost indistinguishable from Christian colleges.

It remains to be seen what directions evangelical education will take from here, but most likely the course will be charted in part by leaders whose pedagogical and religious views have been shaped by their experience as students and teachers in the Bible school movement. The history of Bible school education and the continuing prominence of the Bible schools in evangelical Protestantism would tend to suggest that evangelical educators might continue to focus upon transmitting methods for accomplishing specific tasks and upon inculcating unambiguous statements of "the truth," downplaying humanistic learning in the process. For the foreseeable future, it would seem, evangelical educators will continue to aim at a mass audience, and in their hands the Bible will continue to be a book of prophecy and a "roadmap" of faith and practice.[18] On the other hand, the gradual introduction of the liberal arts into Bible schools and the increasing prominence of Christian liberal arts colleges and seminaries will undoubtedly modify the traditional directions of evangelical education, set originally by the leaders of Bible schools, in yet undetermined ways.

APPENDIX

Defining Fundamentalism

Few terms in American religious history are more difficult to define than Protestant fundamentalism. Part of the problem is that until recently so few historians or sociologists attempted to address the task. Over the past sixty years efforts have been sporadic at best. Furthermore, due to the lack of sustained historical interest, the sources for study have remained scattered or, worse, have disappeared. Most important, almost all the writers who have tried to characterize the movement have been partisans on one side or the other of the "modernist-fundamentalist" conflict, and as partisans, they have tended to bring a limited vision to their subject. But even when the problem of defining fundamentalism has received sustained and thoughtful attention—as recently—there have been no easy answers.

The line of "classical" attempts to delineate fundamentalism began with H. Richard Niebuhr, whose definition had two main aspects: first, he described the phenomenon as a struggle for political power, and focused particularly on conservative Protestant attempts to outlaw the teaching of evolution. Consequently, he viewed the Scopes Trial of 1925, which tested legislation banning the teaching of evolution in Tennessee schools, as a paradigmatic conflict. Probably because most of these political struggles took place in the South and Border states, and hardly at all in the Northeast or Middle Atlantic regions, Niebuhr portrayed fundamentalism as a regional product, clustered in the South and adjoining states. Second, he interpreted fundamentalism as a rural protest against urbanism and industrialization. In his portrayal, fundamentalists appeared as ill-educated farmers who feared the encroachments of a changing world. Until the last decade or two the majority of writers who dealt with fundamentalism have followed Niebuhr's conceptual lead, at least in part. They have viewed fundamentalists as backward looking folk, unimportant actors on the margins of American history, fighting essentially futile and rearguard battles.[1]

Stewart G. Cole (1931) and Norman F. Furniss (1954) understood fundamentalists to be members of the conservative side in the struggle for control of Protestant denominations, and they traced with particular interest the battles during the twenties for leadership of foreign missions boards and seminary education. Their theological definitions of fundamentalism were limited to a listing of the so-called "five points," which in their view summarized the movement's doctrinal position: the inerrancy of scripture, the virgin birth, the substitutionary atonement, the bodily resurrection, and the second coming.[2]

The first important attempt to take a new look at fundamentalism came in 1970, with Ernest Sandeen's publication of *The Roots of Fundamentalism,* and also in his articles and other shorter works.[3] Sandeen offered a primarily theological definition of fundamentalism; he saw it as a grouping of conservative Christians, mostly from Calvinist backgrounds—Baptists and Presbyterians—whose theological "roots" consisted of two parts: a premillenialism which Sandeen traced to British and American millenarianism of the early nineteenth century, and a doctrine of biblical inerrancy that he ascribed to the tradition of Princeton Seminary. Not only was Sandeen one of the first historians to take the theology of fundamentalism seriously; he was also the first to explore carefully the network of relations that existed among early fundamentalists, pointing out the high degree of organization that manifested itself in the movement's Bible schools, conferences, periodicals, and missionary societies.

Though Sandeen's work has won universal respect from students of fundamentalism, his views have not gone unchallenged. Most critics have focused upon what they saw as the narrowness of his definition. George M. Marsden, for example, objected to Sandeen's identification of millenarianism as the one "root" (except for the Princeton theology) of fundamentalism. He suggested other roots: certain enduring elements of nineteenth century evangelicalism, the shock from the rapid decline of what had been a solidly Protestant culture, and a continuing current of anti-intellectualism.[4]

LeRoy Moore questioned whether a theological understanding such as Sandeen's is sufficient to account for the political events of the twenties.[5] Many people, he pointed out, associated themselves with what Moore referred to as the "fundamentalistic party" who did not fit Sandeen's theological definition. William Jennings Bryan, the most famous national figure associated in the popular mind with fundamentalism, and a prominent actor in the Scopes Trial, never embraced the doctrine of premillennialism.

In response to these criticisms, Sandeen claimed that the additional "roots" suggested by Marsden were merely "characteristics"—not *roots*—of millenarians, shared with other descendants of nineteenth century Protestantism. He also argued that the colorful decade of the twenties, which has received so much attention from students of fundamentalism, was not as crucial in its history as has been supposed. The acrimony, defensiveness, and aggressiveness displayed by fundamentalists during this decade, and often treated as distinctive attributes of the movement, he observed, were equally characteristic of some non-fundamentalists of the twenties.[6]

George M. Marsden has done more than respond to Sandeen; he has come up with a second major work of defining and describing fundamentalism. In his *Fundamentalism and American Culture,* he has richly amplified his contention that fundamentalism consisted of more major ingredients than millenarianism and the doctrine of scriptural inerrancy.[7] He has paid attention to the many continuities between fundamentalism and the great body of nineteenth century American Protestant evangelicalism. Furthermore, he has done valuable work on the place of holiness in the movement, an aspect largely ignored by Sandeen.[8] If Marsden could be said to have a brief definition of fundamentalism it is as follows:

> During this period of its national prominence in the 1920s, fundamentalism . . . was militantly anti-modernist Protestant evangelicalism. Fundamentalists were evangelical Christians, close to the traditions of the dominant revivalist establishment of the nineteenth century, who in the twentieth century militantly opposed both modernism in theology and the cultural changes that modernism endorsed. Militant opposition to modernism was what most clearly set off fundamentalism from a number of closely related traditions, such as evangelicalism, revivalism, pietism, the holiness movements, millenarianism, Reformed confessionalism, Baptist traditionalism, and other denominational orthodoxies.[9]

In my thinking about fundamentalism I follow many of the leads set out by Marsden; like him I would argue the need for a wideranging definition containing not only theological and religious dimensions but also cultural, educational, social, political, economic, and psychological ones. Briefly speaking, I would describe fundamentalists as those twentieth century Protestants who have considered certain religious experiences to be central and essential: a radical conversion and often a second spiritual crisis, referred to as sanctification or "entering into holiness," depending on the tradition of the speaker or writer. For some fundamentalists desirable spiritual experiences have included that of speaking in tongues. Theologically speaking, fundamentalists have believed the Bible to be inerrant and divinely inspired, have held to the substitutionary atonement, the virgin birth, the divinity of Christ, and the existence of miracles. Most fundamentalists have been premillennialists, that is, they have believed that Jesus Christ would return at any moment to rule over an earthly kingdom in Jerusalem. They have revered Scripture with great intensity; to be sure, the majority of American Protestants have been Bible-centered, but fundamentalists have been especially so, particularly in the context of this century. They have also been evangelists par excellence; in the last sixty years or so they have been conspicuous leaders in foreign and home missionary efforts.

Generally fundamentalists have also subscribed to a strict personal moralism and have tended to be opposed to—or have ignored—those important currents in American culture that involve relativism, historicism, and the scientific method. To varying degrees they have seen themselves as over and against the culture in which they found themselves. Finally, fundamentalists have been associated with certain classes of institutions and activities—the Bible schools, Bible conferences, and revivalism, for instance. And they have come to be identified with particular organizations, such as *The Sunday School Times,* Fleming H. Revell Publishing Company, the China Inland Mission, Youth for Christ; the organizations shift somewhat, depending upon what decades one is talking about. Readers familiar with the literature will notice that I include more varieties of people in my notion of fundamentalism than Sandeen or even Marsden. Whereas both of these writers limit fundamentalism to those Protestants with Calvinist backgrounds— Baptists, Presbyterians, Congregationalists, and associated groups—I include those with Wesleyan or Methodist backgrounds as well. I fail to be convinced that we should confine fundamentalism to those with Calvinist Reformed backgrounds and wonder if historians are perpetuating a tendency, exhibited elsewhere in American religious history, for concentrating on Calvinist groups to the exclusion of others. For example, I would certainly be inclined to describe Advent Christians, who conducted the Boston Bible School, as fundamentalists. They voiced much the same critique of modernity; they were premillennialists and subscribed to biblical inerrancy. Yet they deviated from the narrowly defined fundamentalist pattern in that they were methodistic in polity and many of their adherents came from Methodist backgrounds. I would also admit another group of Bible school founders, pentecostals, into the company of fundamentalists, even though many of them hailed from Methodist traditions, and, until later on, did not have much contact with other conservative evangelicals. The same sorts of arguments could be made for the Christian and Missionary Alliance; the group's founder, A. B. Simpson, started out his ministry as a Presbyterian, but many of his followers had Wesleyan roots and the Missionary Training Institute was considered to be a safe place for Wesleyan holiness people to send their children. It seems to me that there was so much crossing of denominational borders, so much flux, so much coming and going, that the lines between conservative evangelical groups tend to blur. It sometimes becomes difficult to know, for example, whether to label a conservative group as basically Wesleyan or Baptist in background.

Another way in which I differ from Marsden is that I do not put as much emphasis on fundamentalists' opposition to modernity and liberal Protestantism as he does in defining the phenomenon. The element, to be sure, was there, but it was not as central, I think, as Marsden makes it. I am not certain about how much emphasis *should* be put on the factor of opposition; however, Marsden, I would argue (with Sandeen), is too much influenced by the twenties, when opposition was at its most vehement and vituperative and when the scene was dominated by flamboyant and outspoken figures such as W. B. Riley, Frank Norris, Billy Sunday, and R. A. Torrey. Other leaders—James M. Gray at Moody Bible Institute and G. Campbell Morgan, for instance—were much gentler in their rhetoric. Yet no one would deny that Gray, as head of Moody Bible Institute, was a significant fundamentalist leader. The attitudes and approaches of moderate leaders like him deserve closer attention than they have received in the past.

The notion of opposition to modernism seems particularly problematic when it is preceded by the adjective "militant". Obviously few fundamentalists toted arms (one exception being J. Frank Norris, who shot a man to death in his office); usually, of course, the adjective "militant" is applied to their statements and attitudes rather than to their activities. What sorts of fundamentalist phrases, then, qualify as "militant"? (The answer to this question may in fact be a worthy subject for future exploration.) And when we are talking about fundamentalists below the level of the national leadership, how much warlike rhetoric did they really indulge in?

Probably my conception of fundamentalism is affected by the fact that my primary focus has been upon Bible schools. Certain consequences may follow from this circumstance. First, the decade of the twenties, which looms so large in much work on fundamentalism, does not have particular importance to me. Rather, the years of the founding of the earliest Bible schools—1882–1915—hold at least equal interest. But, ironically, during those years there was no fundamentalist movement in any formal or public sense. Strictly speaking, there was no such thing as "fundamentalism" at the time some of the foremost future standard bearers of the movement—the Bible schools—were coming into being. Hence, I am often more interested in "fundamentalistic" elements of thought and experience than in fundamentalism considered as a formal movement. Second, because this study focuses upon Bible schools, its definition of fundamentalism perforce stresses the moderate and less politically oriented strains of the movement, strains which were often urban and frequently Northern or Midwestern. Thus, I am least concerned with what Bruce Shelley called the "militant" style of fundamentalism particularly identified with the twenties. This brand of fundamentalism has issued in ultra-conservative politics, and has been prevalent in the South, Border States, and Far West. Though this is obviously a subject worthy of further study, as was amply demonstrated by Richard Hofstadter in his essay, "Pseudo Conservatism Revisited—1965," the militant and combative political style in its extreme form has least influenced fundamentalist education, and therefore figures less prominently in this study.[10]

Though as the above discussion suggests, the problem of defining fundamentalism has received much more attention in the past few years—sometimes to the point of exhaustion—there are certain issues that I think we have failed to address completely:

(1) What elements do historians consider most crucial in defining fundamentalism? Theological and doctrinal? Behavioral? Institutional—i.e., who has ties to which significant institutions and agencies? Even if we agree to emphasize one or another of these general criteria, the question is still not settled. If we stress a theological definition, for instance, then which doctrines should be uppermost? Premillennialism? Belief in biblical inerrancy? True, I argued earlier for a definition with many dimensions, but one must still ask whether certain criteria should be more important than others in determining whether a group or individual is or is not fundamentalist.

(2) Perhaps because we have failed to settle the issues in (1), have we historians followed too uncritically the lead of the historical actors themselves in classifying fundamentalists and nonfundamentalists? For example, W. B. Riley, Moody Bible Institute leaders, and others refused to admit pentecostals to the informal funda-

mentalist fellowship. But at least some pentecostals considered themselves fundamentalists. Then to whom (if anyone) do we listen? Obviously to date we have
heeded Riley and the others. Why were they really objecting to association with
pentecostals—on theological grounds or on socioeconomic and racial grounds
(many pentecostals were black and most pentecostals were relatively poor). Riley
and company would, of course, have cited doctrinal differences that separated
them from pentecostals, but I doubt we should uncritically take their word for
it.

To cite an even more glaring example, Gresham Machen spurned the title "fundamentalist" for himself, yet many fundamentalists would have been loathe to
let him depart from what they conceived of as the fundamentalist fold. Certainly
few took him at his word; he was universally dubbed a fundamentalist.

Even if we do take the word of the groups or individuals themselves, whom
do we listen to—the Indians or the chiefs? For example, would ordinary Christian
Reformed people—those who listened to WMBI and expected the second coming—
have been more willing to style themselves fundamentalists than the leadership?
I am not sure, but these are important questions to ask. The same sorts of queries
might be made about Southern Baptists. In other words, we get embroiled in
contradictions and confusions if we follow the labeling practices of the principals
themselves. When all is said and done, I am not convinced that a definition of
fundamentalism need be hard and fast; must we be able to say definitely who
was a fundamentalist and who was not? I would be inclined to set the following
rule as my guideline: if *most* "fundamentalistic" characteristics—that is, most elements of the definition outlined in chapters 1 to 3—seem to fit particular individuals or groups, then we ought to feel free to include them in the ranks of
fundamentalists.

Perhaps given the definitional difficulties outlined above, the wisest course would
be to forswear the use of "fundamentalist" and "fundamentalism" altogether. This
option becomes especially attractive when one realizes that the terms not only
introduce problems of definition but also function as powerful symbols. The labels
have been wielded by friend and foe alike in highly emotional contexts. Presently
the more moderate descendants of the older fundamentalists view the label as
a term of opprobrium, preferring to be called "evangelicals," or "neo-evangelicals."
Even in the early twentieth century, as suggested above, not all conservative Christians consented to being called "fundamentalists." Machen, mentioned above, preferred to refer to himself and others of like persuasion as "Christians," as opposed
to others who were, he claimed, "liberals" or "modernists," and not Christians
at all.

Troublesome as the name "fundamentalist" is, however, alternatives all suffer
from crippling drawbacks. "Conservative" is a vague word when applied to a Protestant, not helpful unless it is used in a precise context. "Orthodox" is also an
imprecise adjective unless, again, the context makes it clear and we can agree
on what constitutes orthodoxy in that particular case. To some the most obvious
substitute for "fundamentalist" might be "evangelical," but in the nineteenth century and well into the twentieth, most Protestants thought of themselves as evangelicals, with the exception of some Unitarians, Universalists, Lutherans, and
Episcopalians. Thus, to refer to fundamentalists as if they were the *only* evangelicals
of the early twentieth century would be to make a perhaps unflattering and possibly
unwarranted judgment about the other Protestant churches. For better or worse,
it seems, we are saddled with the word "fundamentalism"; and, employed in its
historical context and with all possible neutrality, it will probably best serve the
purpose.

But at least one difficult problem in nomenclature persists. The noun "fundamental" in the sense of the "fundamentals of the faith" came into use only in

the second decade of the twentieth century, with the publication of *The Fundamentals*. And the designation of the word "fundamentalist" for Christians who adhered to the "fundamentals" did not become usual until the twenties.[11] Still, despite the lateness of the appearance of these terms, most of the characteristics of fundamentalists and fundamentalism—except the outspokenness and vituperation of their opposition to modernism—existed long before these decades. Yet, I am not comfortable applying the term "fundamentalism" to the wide variety of phenomena that appeared before 1910; I have even more difficulty identifying certain Protestants of the late 1880s and 90s as "fundamentalists." Rather, I think of them as the immediate *forerunners* of the people widely known as fundamentalists. Often I will resort to using the term "conservative evangelical" in describing members of the generation or two before the fundamentalists proper emerged. At times, however, nothing will work satisfactorily; the writer begs the reader's indulgence as she stumbles through this poorly charted territory.

NOTES

Preface

1. *The Christian Workers Magazine* 11 (September 18, 1910): 138. The Moody Bible Institute of Chicago, *Fortieth Annual Catalogue, 1927–28*, p. 14.

2. Quoted in Gene A. Getz, *MBI: The Story of Moody Bible Institute* (Chicago: Moody Press, 1969), p. 96.

Introduction

1. See appendix for an extended discussion of the term "fundamentalism."

2. Kenneth Briggs, "Evangelical Colleges Reborn" *New York Times Magazine,* December 14, 1980, pp. 140–54.

3. There are presently some 200 Bible schools, not including evening classes sponsored by individual churches. Bible schools accredited by the American Association of Bible Colleges enroll a little over 30,000 students. This does not account for the many unaccredited schools, which amount to well over half of the estimated total of 200. Nor does it include correspondence students, of which Moody Bible Institute, for instance, had about 79,000 in 1974. Kenneth Gangel, "The Bible College: Past, Present and Future," *Christianity Today* 24 (November 7, 1980): 1324–25; "Rock of Ages at the Edge of Old Town," *Midwest*, January 27, 1974, p. 4. See chart in chapter 5 for a listing of the early Bible schools and the dates of their foundings.

4. For a brief but helpful attempt at explanation see Donald Tinder, "Why the Evangelical Upswing?" *Christianity Today* 22 (October 21, 1977): 10–12.

5. For the Bible and prophetic conference see Ernest R. Sandeen, *The Roots of Fundamentalism: British and American Millenarianism, 1800–1930* (Chicago: University of Chicago Press, 1970), pp. 132–61.

6. Frank E. Gaebelein, "The Story of the Scofield Reference Bible, 1909–1959" (New York: Oxford University Press, 1959), pamphlet.

7. Lyman Stewart explained why he financed *The Fundamentals:* "I was impressed with the thought that a great many good, honest men were teaching error because they have never been properly instructed, many of them being limited in their reading to church literature, which, in many cases, is prejudiced." Quoted in James O. Henry, "Black Oil and Souls to Win," *BIOLA Broadcaster* 3 (December 1973): 13.

8. "Don't draw on your imagination for facts; preach what you learn from the Bible. . . . Don't use big words for show; make the weakest understand you. . . . Don't be haughty; be a man of the people." Ashley S. Johnson, founder of the Johnson Bible College, quoted in Robert E. Black, *The Story of Johnson Bible College* (Kimberlin Heights, Tenn.: Tennessee Valley Printing Co., 1951), pp. 22–23.

9. E.g., J. C. Massee, Tremont Temple Baptist Church, Boston; A. Z. Conrad, Park Street Church, Boston; John Roach Straton, Calvary Baptist Church, New York City; Isaac M. Haldeman, First Baptist Church, New York City; Clarence E. Macartney, Arch Street Presbyterian Church, Philadelphia, and later the First Presbyterian Church, Pittsburgh; A. C. Dixon, Paul Rader, and P. W. Philpott

at Moody Memorial Church, Chicago; William Bell Riley, First Baptist Church, Minneapolis; J. Frank Norris, First Baptist Church, Ft. Worth, Texas; and Reuben A. Torrey, Church of the Open Door, Los Angeles.

10. Gangel, "The Bible College," p. 1325. It is impossible to get figures on how many students attend unaccredited Bible schools of various types.

11. Sandeen, *The Roots of Fundamentalism*, pp. 183, 242.

12. See, e.g., Everett C. Hughes et al., *Education for the Professions of Medicine, Law, Theology, and Social Welfare* (New York: McGraw-Hill, 1973), which includes slightly over a page on Bible schools; and C. Robert Pace, *Education and Evangelism: A Profile of Protestant Colleges* (New York: McGraw-Hill, 1972). See also the "Report of the Danforth Commission": Manning M. Patillo, Jr. and Donald M. Mackenzie, *Church-Sponsored Education in the United States* (Washington, D.C.: American Council on Education, 1966), p. 16. It says only, "About 250 Bible colleges and institutes have begun operation in the United States and Canada, half of them since World War II. The latter institutions do not come within the purview of our study, but they deserve to be mentioned as a growing segment of education at the collegiate level." Exceptions to the general omission of Bible schools from surveys and histories of higher education are William C. Ringenberg, *The Christian College: A History of Protestant Higher Education in America* (Grand Rapids, Mich.: William B. Eerdmans, 1984) (see especially pp. 157–173); and Lawrence A. Cremin, *American Education: The Metropolitan Experience, 1876–1980* (New York: Harper & Row, 1988).

1. Enthusiasms

1. For a fine discussion of this point, see Donald George Tinder, "Fundamentalist Baptists in the Northern and Western United States, 1920–1950" (Ph.D. dissertation, Yale University, 1969), pp. 35–43. The Straton quote is from Tinder, p. 38.

2. Douglas Sloan, "Harmony, Chaos, and Consensus: The American College," *Teachers College Record* 73 (1971–72): 221–51.

3. *The Christian Workers Magazine* 11 (October 1910): 124, 125.

4. E.g., see evangelist George Pentecost's suggestions that students buy Bibles with large enough margins so that they could record their reactions while reading the scriptures. P. C. Headley, *George F. Pentecost: Life, Labors, and Bible Studies* (Boston: James H. Earle, Publishers, 1880), pp. 192–93. C. I. Scofield produced his famous Scofield Reference Bible by organizing marginal notes he had written over the course of years of Bible study and Bible teaching. See Charles G. Trumbull, *The Life Story of C. I. Scofield* (New York: Oxford University Press, 1920), p. 63.

5. Edmund Gosse, *Father and Son: Biographical Recollections* (New York: Charles Scribner's Sons, 1908), pp. 72–73.

6. For the history of the Methodist stream of the holiness movement, see George E. Failing, "Developments in Holiness Theology After Wesley," in Kenneth Geiger, ed., *Insights into Holiness: Discussions of holiness by fifteen leading scholars of the Wesleyan persuasion* (Kansas City, Mo.: Beacon Hill Press, 1962), pp. 11–31; John L. Peters, *Christian Perfection and American Methodism* (Nashville: Abingdon Press, 1956); Bruce Shelley, "Sources of Pietistic Fundamentalism," *Fides et Historia* 5 (Spring 1973): 68–70; and Timothy L. Smith, *Called unto Holiness: The Story of the Nazarenes: The Formative Years* (Kansas City, Mo.: Nazarene Publishing House, 1962). For Keswick history, both British and American, see Charles F. Harford, *The Keswick Convention: Its Message, Its Method and Its Men* (London: Marshall Bros., Keswick House, 1907); Philip E. Howard, *Charles Gallaudet Trumbull: Apostle of*

the Victorious Life (Philadelphia: The Sunday School Times Co., 1944); A. T. Pierson, *The Story of Keswick and Its Beginnings* (London: Marshall Brothers, 1897), and J. C. Pollock, *The Keswick Story: The Authorized History of the Keswick Convention* (London: Hodder and Stoughton, 1964).

7. For a discussion of the differences and similarities between the Wesleyan and Keswick traditions of holiness, see Everett L. Cattell, "An Appraisal of the Keswick and Wesleyan Contemporary Positions," in Geiger, *Insights into Holiness*, pp. 263–80.

8. A. T. Pierson, "The Message: Its Practical Application," in Harford, *The Keswick Convention*, pp. 92, 93.

9. A. B. Simpson, "The Separated Life," *Alliance Weekly* 66 (June 27, 1931): 312.

10. "Hindrances to Healing," *Christian Alliance and Missionary Weekly* (January 30, 1891): 66.

11. Kenneth Mackenzie, "My Memories of Dr. Simpson" (Part I), *Alliance Weekly* 72 (May 22, 1937): 324.

12. *Christian and Missionary Alliance* 18 (April 30, 1897): 410.

13. Mary Ella Bowie, *Alabaster and Spikenard: The Life of Dr. Iva Durham Vennard* (Chicago: Chicago Evangelistic Institute, 1947), p. 53.

14. *The Autobiography of George Muller* (Springdale, Pa.: Whitaker House, 1984) and A. T. Pierson, *George Muller of Bristol and His Witness to a Prayer-Hearing God* (New York: Baker and Taylor Company, 1899). So pervasive has been the fascination with the life of George Muller that the Moody Bible Institute library, for instance, has a whole shelf of books on him.

15. Dr. and Mrs. Howard Taylor, *J. Hudson Taylor: A Biography* (Chicago: Moody Press, 1965). The objectives of Taylor and his emulators were described as follows: "Complete dependence upon God for means of support. Money is never asked for, though the story is told freely. There are no 'drives,' no special methods, but unfailingly money has come. . . . Expenses here at home are kept at the lowest level. There is no complicated organization, no elaborate offices, no high-priced executives, and no debt for money borrowed at any time. The whole plan appears to us as most like the evangelizing in the early days of the church than of any effort we know. We can all learn to our profit to depend more on the Lord and less on human persons and methods." *The Presbyterian*, quoted in *Moody Bible Institute Monthly* 32 (April 1932): 397.

16. "Leaves from the Diary of a City Missionary," *Christian Alliance* 1 (March 1888): 43.

17. Bowie, *Life of Iva Durham Vennard*.

18. Charles H. Brackett, "The History of Azusa College and the Friends" (M.A. thesis, University of Southern California, 1967), p. 55.

19. J. Melvin Miller, "The Torch Held High: A History of Pacific Bible College of Azusa, California" (M.A. thesis, Pacific Bible College, 1957), p. 6. After leaving the school Abel spent his life as a foreign missionary.

20. Charles Stelzle, *A Son of the Bowery* (New York: George H. Doran Company, 1926), p. 56.

21. Donald Meyer, *The Positive Thinkers: A Study of the American Quest for Health, Wealth and Personal Power from Mary Baker Eddy to Norman Vincent Peale* (New York: Doubleday and Co., 1965), pp. 20–31.

22. Interestingly, though his followers suffered from organic diseases such as cancer and tuberculosis—and claimed relief from them—many also complained of illnesses that often lend themselves to psychosomatic explanations: bad stomachs, headaches, neurasthenia. They were also troubled by such minor ailments as toothaches, "La Grippe," coughs, bad throats, fever, dog bites, and "disabled wrists," many of which heal by themselves in time.

23. Obituary of Annie McFedries, *Alliance Weekly* 67 (November 12, 1932): 731.

24. Stephen Gottschalk, *The Emergence of Christian Science in American Religious Life* (Berkeley, Los Angeles, London: University of California Press, 1973), p. 234.

25. *Christian and Missionary Alliance* 24 (March 24, 1900): 180.

26. John H. Cable, *A History of the Missionary Training Institute: The Pioneer Bible School of America* (Harrisburg, Pa.: Christian Publications, 1933), p. 31. For the phenomenon of divine healing and mind cure see also Raymond J. Cunningham, "From Holiness to Healing: The Faith Cure in America, 1872–1892," *Church History* 43 (December, 1974): 499–513; Dennis Voskuil, *Mountains into Goldmines: Robert Schuller and the Gospel of Success* (Grand Rapids, Mich.: Eerdmans, 1983), chapter 7; David Edwin Harrell, Jr. *All Things Are Possible: The Healing and Charismatic Revivals in Modern America* (Bloomington: Indiana University Press, 1975).

27. For this phrase and the source of this concept see 1 Thess. 4:16–17: "For the Lord himself shall descend from heaven with a shout, with the voice of the archangel, and with the trump of God: and the dead in Christ shall rise first: Then we which are alive and remain shall be caught up together with them in the clouds, to meet the Lord in the air: and so shall we ever be with the Lord."

28. Kenneth Mackenzie, "My Memories of Dr. Simpson" (Part IV), *Alliance Weekly* 72 (August 7, 1937): 500.

29. Premillennialism contrasted with the postmillennialism of other American Protestants who thought Jesus Christ would appear only after a thousand year period of peace and prosperity, thus putting the second coming at a considerable remove from the present. Postmillennialists often pictured the millennium as a harmonious period of enlightened political and social life, inspired, to be sure, by the spirit of Christ but not actually established or presided over by him. It is probably true to say, however, that most ordinary Protestant lay people of the nineteenth century had not given eschatology enough thought to be either premillennialists or postmillennialists. Both viewpoints were indicative of increasing religious activity and interest and both were on the rise in the late nineteenth and early twentieth centuries.

30. For some European movements, see Norman R. C. Cohn, *The Pursuit of the Millennium: Revolutionary Messianism in Medieval and Reformation Europe and Its Bearing on Modern Totalitarian Movements* (London: Secker and Warburg, 1957).

31. William E. Blackstone, *Jesus Is Coming* (Chicago, New York, Toronto: Fleming H. Revell Co., 1908), p. 97.

32. Cornelius Woelfkin, "The Religious Appeal of Premillennialism," *Journal of Religion* 1 (1921): 260. W. E. Blackstone, in the widely read *Jesus Is Coming*, explained the excitement with this analogy:

> As followers of Christ we are compared to soldiers, fighting the fight of faith . . . and perhaps no better illustration could be given us of watching, than that of picket duty in the army.
> Old soldiers know that out on the skirmish line it is full of life and excitement, because they are watching for something immediately possible. But in camp it is a dull, soulless drudgery, because they are expecting nothing until the outer pickets, perhaps five or six miles away, are driven in. . . .
> Pre-millennialists believe that He may come at any moment, and that we should ever be found watching and waiting, with our loins girded about, and our lights burning, and ourselves like men that wait for their Lord. Pp. 64, 65.

33. Thomas F. Henstock, "A History and Interpretation of the Curriculum of Central Bible Institute" (M.A. thesis, Central Bible Institute, 1964), p. 12.

34. Walter J. Hollenweger, *The Pentecostals: The Charismatic Movement in the Churches* (Minneapolis, Minn.: Augsburg Publishing House, 1972); Vinson Synan,

The Holiness Pentecostal Movement in the United States (Grand Rapids, Mich.: Eerdmans, 1971). See also David W. Fauper, "A Brief Bibliography of Pentecostal Literature" (Typed, in Union Theological Seminary Library, New York).

35. Pentecostal education is almost a totally unexplored area of study and would require an ambitious researcher, because the historical sources are so widely scattered. To investigate black pentecostal education would present even greater challenges and would no doubt involve oral history.

2. Systems

1. Quoted in Donald George Tinder, "Fundamentalist Baptists in the Northern and Western United States, 1920–1950" (Ph.D. dissertation, Yale University, 1969), p. 42; originally from *Baptist Beacon*, May 1924, p. 4. In addition to valuing theological permanence for its own sake, Riley was of course also pointedly countering the liberal Protestant preference for a theology that changed over time to adapt to its culture.

2. *Catalogue and Prospectus of the Gordon Missionary Training School*, Seventh Year, 1896.

3. Edmund Gosse, *Father and Son: Biographical Recollections* (New York: Charles Scribner's Sons, 1908). For the Plymouth Brethren see Ernest R. Sandeen, *Roots of Fundamentalism* (Chicago: University of Chicago Press, 1970), pp. 59–102.

4. E.g., Cameron Townsend, founder of the Wycliffe Bible Translators and in the twenties a missionary to Guatemala, when asked about his theological background, replied, "I didn't finish college and never went to Bible school. Maybe I'll finish my education sometime. But here I seldom see a book on theology or church history. I spend my devotional time studying the Bible and Scofield's Notes." James and Marti Hefley, *Uncle Cam: The Story of William Cameron Townsend, Founder of the Wycliffe Bible Translators and the Summer Institute of Linguistics* (Waco, Texas: Word Books, 1974), p. 59.

5. C. I. Scofield outlined the seven dispensations in this fashion (his exposition is abbreviated here):

> 1.) Man Innocent (Gen. 2:7 to Expulsion from the Garden). Natural man, represented by Adam, was not content with God's gift of innocence, and the result of divine judgment upon him was the loss of Eden. 2.) Man under Conscience. "By the Fall, Adam and Eve acquired and transmitted to the race, the knowledge of good and evil. This gave conscience a basis for right judgment, and hence the race came under this measure of responsibility—to do good and eschew evil." Human beings failed to obey their consciences, Scofield continued, with the result that the second dispensation ended in the judgment of the flood. 3.) Man in Authority over the Earth. Eight persons were saved from the flood, to whom God "gave the purified earth with ample power to govern it." But "the Dispensation of Human Government resulted . . . in the impious attempt to become independent of God and closed in judgment—the Confusion of Tongues" (the Tower of Babel). 4.) Man under Promise. "Out of the dispersed descendants of the builders of Babel God now calls one man, Abram, with whom He enters into covenant. Some of the promises to Abram and his descendants were purely gracious and unconditional. These either have been, or will yet be, literally fulfilled. Other promises were conditional upon the faithfulness and obedience of the Israelites." The failure of Israel to live up to its part of the covenant resulted in another judgment, the bondage in Israel. 5.) Man under Law. God led his chosen people out of Egypt and gave them the "covenant of Law" in the wilderness. Again, they failed to live up to their word, despite repeated warnings, and were driven into exile. "A feeble

remnant returned under Ezra and Nehemiah, of which, in due time, Christ came: . . . Him both Jews and Gentiles conspired to crucify," again demonstrating human perfidy. 6.) Man under Grace. This dispensation, the present one, was initiated by Christ's "sacrificial death" and was characterized by God's gift of pure grace. "Salvation, perfect and eternal, is now freely offered to Jew and Gentile upon the one condition of faith." Predictably, response to even this gift has been "an unbelieving world and an apostate Church." The next event, Scofield expected from his reading of Scripture, would be "the descent of the Lord from Heaven, when sleeping saints will be raised and, together with believers then living, caught up 'to meet the Lord in the air: and so shall we ever be with the Lord.' 1 Thess. 4:16, 17." With the faithful ones safely out of harm's way, "the great tribulation" would engulf the earth. Following this, the Lord would return to earth, accompanied by his "saints," who had previously been "caught up." 7.) Man Under the Personal Reign of Christ (the Millennium). Christ, returning bodily to the actual Jerusalem, would rule over the "restored Israel" for a thousand years, the golden age. However, "when Satan is 'loosed a little season' he finds the natural heart as prone to evil as ever, and easily gathers the nations to battle against the Lord and His saints, and this dispensation closes, like all the others, in judgment. The 'great white throne' is set, the wicked dead are raised and finally judged, and then come 'the new heaven and a new earth'—eternity begun."

Rightly Dividing the Word of Truth (New York, Chicago, Toronto: Fleming H. Revell Co., n.d.), pp. 13–19. Scofield's scriptural quotations in section seven come from Revelation.

6. A few years ago, on a flight to Chicago, I sat next to an accountant from Wisconsin who spent the trip intently revising numerous closely written pages in a notebook he balanced on his knee. He and a fellow layman in his independent Baptist congregation, it turned out, were waging a friendly theological battle, each turning out many pages of arguments supporting his position against that of the other. The point in contention was whether "the rapture" would happen before or after the Great Tribulation. One disputant was an earnest pre-tribulationist, the other an equally fervent post-tribulationist. This encounter taught a couple of lessons, first, that details in the dispensationalist scheme are hardly viewed by dispensationalists as merely of academic interest and second, that lay people in the evangelical churches of the present involve themselves in theological matters with great energy, and in the process carry on a remarkable activity of self-education. The question of whether the rapture will come before or after the tribulation—or during it—is the main focus of Hal Lindsay's best seller, *The Rapture* (New York: Bantam Books, 1983).

7. Note that even today an evangelical leader such as Jerry Falwell is a firm supporter of the state of Israel.

8. Katherine Alberta Brennan, "Mrs. A. B. Simpson, The Wife or Love Stands" (pamphlet, n.d.), p. 25. Nyack College Library, Nyack, New York.

9. Scofield, *Rightly Dividing the Word of Truth*, pp. 10–12.

10. D. M. Panton, "Bullingerism," *Moody Bible Institute Monthly* 33 (December 1932): 254.

11. Scofield, *Rightly Dividing the Word of Truth*, p. 2.

12. Dispensationalist doctrine produced some exotic flowers. One was called Bullingerism, after an Anglican clergyman (d. 1913) who held that only Paul's writings—those composed after his imprisonment depicted in Acts 28—were "binding" upon the church. This meant that the Lord's Supper, baptism, and the Sermon on the Mount were considered "purely Jewish"—intended only for Jews, not Christians. A writer in the *Moody Monthly* described Bullingerism as "A system which

cuts out all the injunctions involving the Church's responsibilities, and the passages exposing our spiritual poverty, retaining almost solely, the passages of grace and privilege." In the early 1930s Bullingerism was reportedly on the rise among Midwestern fundamentalists. See "Dispensationalism Running Wild" (editorial), *Moody Bible Institute Monthly* 33 (February 1933) 253–54; Panton, "Bullingerism," pp. 254–55.

13. Interview with Samuel H. Sutherland, July 25, 1982.

14. Observing evangelicals in the present, James Davison Hunter shrewdly notes what he calls the "increasing methodization and standardization of spirituality" evident in the abundant mention of "principles," "rules," "steps," "guidelines," "laws," "codes," and the like in the literature of the movement. However, Hunter treats this methodization as a recent development, whereas I would argue that it has been present from the beginning. James Davison Hunter, *American Evangelicalism: Conservative Religion and the Quandary of Modernity* (New Brunswick: Rutgers University Press, 1983), p. 74.

15. Gene A. Getz, *MBI: The Story of Moody Bible Institute* (Chicago: Moody Press, 1969), p. 232.

16. J. C. Pollock, *The Keswick Story: The Authorized History of the Keswick Convention* (London: Hodder and Stoughton, 1964), p. 118.

17. Pollock, *Keswick Story,* p. 162.

18. Renald Showers, "A History of Philadelphia College of the Bible" (Th.M. thesis, Dallas Theological Seminary and Graduate School of Theology, 1962), p. 109.

19. William Cobb, "The West Point of Fundamentalism," *American Mercury* 16 (1929): 105.

20. This is truer of some fundamentalist groups than others. For instance, pentecostals, generally lower class than other fundamentalists, tended to turn earlier in the twentieth century to more informal and colloquial language, even in their dealings with the deity. It was this tendency to which the fundamentalist (but definitely nonpentecostal) leader, A. C. Gaebelein, was alluding when he complained that Christians involved in "the tongues movement," as he called it, addressed Jesus without appending the title, "Lord." This practice displayed too much familiarity, he sternly chided. A. C. Gaebelein, "Christianity vs. Modern Cults," *Moody Bible Institute Monthly* 22 (March 1922): 861.

21. The Yale-educated R. A. Torrey stayed away from Latinate forms when he scolded *Moody Bible Institute Monthly* readers: "A lot of you folks are as full of knowledge as an egg is of meat, but you do not have enough zeal to ever talk to anybody of Christ while there are others here of the tinpail brigade, humble, hard-working men and women, who do not know as much in a month as you do in a day, but who are brimful of zeal every day of their lives." R. A. Torrey, "What The Moody Bible Institute Has Stood For During the Twenty-Five Years of Its History and What It Still Stands for Today," *The Christian Workers Magazine* 16 (February 1916): 444. Billy Sunday, a major contributor to this brand of speech, often verged upon the vulgar in the interests of capturing his audience: "Many a preacher reminds me of a nursing bottle, and there are two or three hundred rubber tubes, with nipples on the end, running into the mouths of two hundred or three hundred or four hundred great big old babies with whiskers and breeches on, and hair pins stuck in their heads and rats in their hair, sitting there, and they suck and draw from their preacher." Karen Gullen, ed. *Billy Sunday Speaks* (New York: Chelsea House Publishers, 1970), p. 14. Of course, the analogy between spiritual sustenance and milk is traditional, but not in this rhetorical form! Other examples of "folksiness": "he wasn't going in the backdoor of Babylon to get it"; "money was as scarce as mosquitoes in January"; "semi-jazz, rattle-trap dishwa-

ter music." Robert H. Reardon, *Early Morning Light* (Anderson, Indiana: Warner Press, 1979), p. 56; Gullen, *Sunday Speaks,* pp. 208, 124. For nostalgia see this vintage Sunday: "Shall I ever forget the home of my childhood? Yes; when the flowers forget the sun that kissed and warmed them. Yes; when the mountain peaks are incinerated into ashes. Yes; when love dies out in the human heart. Yes; when the desert sands grow cold." Gullen, *Sunday Speaks,* p. 211.

3. Fundamentalists in Society

1. Fortunately we now have demographic studies that contribute to an economic, social, and political portrait of conservative evangelicals in the present. See, e.g., James Davison Hunter, *American Evangelicalism: Conservative Religion and the Quandary of Modernity* (New Brunswick, N.J.: Rutgers University Press, 1983).

2. Richard Ellsworth Day, *Breakfast Table Autocrat* (Chicago: Moody Press, 1946) (H. P. Crowell); Gordon P. Gardiner, *Champion of the Kingdom: The Story of Philip Mauro* (Brooklyn, N.Y.: Bread of Life, 1961); R. G. LeTourneau, *Mover of Men and Mountains: The Autobiography of R. G. LeTourneau* (Chicago: Moody Press, 1967); "The Stewarts as Christian Stewards, the Story of Milton and Lyman Stewart," *Missionary Review of the World* 47 (August 1924): 595–602. The sources of conservative Protestant funding constitute a particularly unexplored area.

3. *Christian Alliance* 1 (June 1888): 86.

4. *Christian and Missionary Weekly* 6 (January 16, 1891): 33.

5. E.g., *Moody Bible Institute Monthly* 27 (September 1926).

6. Christina E. Lang, "My Call to India," *World's Crisis,* October 18, 1922.

7. Robert Elwood Wenger, "Social Thought in American Fundamentalism, 1918–1933" (Ph.D. dissertation, University of Nebraska, 1973), pp. 57–75. Bureau of the Census, *Religious Bodies: 1926* (Vol. II) (Washington, D.C.: Government Printing Office, 1929), p. 308. The urban-rural distribution of fundamentalists appears to depend somewhat upon what group one is talking about. Advent Christians, for instance, came mostly from rural areas of New England. Looking at data from the present, James Davison Hunter finds that 43.7% of evangelicals live in rural areas, 19.3% in towns with populations of 2,500 to 49,999. However, the equivalent figures for liberal Protestants are 33.6 rural and 18.3% small town. Apparently evangelicals in the present are more rural and small town than other Protestants, but not markedly so. Hunter, *American Evangelicalism,* p. 52.

8. Wenger, "Social Thought," pp. 294–312.

9. William E. Blackstone, *Jesus Is Coming* (Chicago: Fleming H. Revell, 1908), p. 112.

10. C. Allyn Russell, *Voices of American Fundamentalism: Seven Biographical Studies* (Philadelphia: Westminster Press, 1976), p. 148. Even in the present, James Davison Hunter finds it difficult to generalize about the political leanings, Republican or Democrat, of Protestant evangelicals; often their political views seem to be affected as much by other variables—social status, education, and age—as by their religious identification.

11. *Christian Alliance and Missionary Weekly* 11 (October 20, 1893): 244.

12. T. J. Jackson Lears, *No Place of Grace: Antimodernism and the Transformation of American Culture, 1880–1920* (New York: Pantheon Books, 1981).

13. William M. Halsey, *The Survival of American Innocence: Catholicism in an Era of Disillusionment, 1920–1940* (South Bend, In.: University of Notre Dame Press, 1980); Mel Piehl, *Breaking Bread: The Catholic Worker and the Origin of Catholic Radicalism in America* (Philadelphia: Temple University Press, 1982).

14. David Eubanks, "An Historical Account of the Development of Johnson Bible College" (M.A. thesis, Johnson Bible College, 1958), p. 58.

15. Granville Hicks, "A Spokesman for the Fundamentalists, an Interview with Hilyer Hawthorne Straton," *The Baptist* 8 (April 2, 1927): 440.

16. Starting with this assumption that fundamentalists were self-consciously dissenting from their culture, it could be argued that many Southern Protestants, including Southern Baptists, did not exhibit a salient "fundamentalist" characteristic until after about 1920, or even 1930. Since most of the South was theologically and culturally conservative, there was nothing for Southern Protestants to stand "over and against," except in the abstract and at a distance. Furthermore, I would not describe black Protestants as fundamentalists during any period, even though many of them have held to typical "fundamentalist" doctrines and experiences. In the main, blacks have not dissented from the mainline culture (usually they have not had the choice); they have simply been isolated from it, not by religious questions, but by overriding issues of race and poverty. Admittedly, the lines of definition become blurred in these areas, and it is possible to argue both sides of these issues.

17. E.g., James Oliver Buswell, Jr., "Reflections on My 'Liberal' Education—I," *The Bible To-Day* (February 1924): 485. "I am sure of one thing, that my retaining my faith in the inerrancy of the Bible is not due to my having accepted what I was taught without thinking."

18. Joseph Taylor, "Is Prohibition to Blame?" *Moody Bible Institute Monthly* 33 (September 1932): 14.

19. "True science, which is true knowledge of the universe or the facts of nature, cannot contradict the Bible, because God would then be contradicting Himself." *Moody Bible Institute Monthly* 27 (October 1926): 52.

20. Taylor, "Is Prohibition to Blame?" Fundamentalists were not the only ones to express this attitude in the twentieth century: Jacques Maritain, a Catholic, wrote in *Art and Poetry* (1943), "To love only to seek—on the condition of never finding—to want only disquietude, that is to hate truth." Quoted in Halsey, *The Survival of American Innocence*, p. 17.

21. Among the clearly conservative or fundamentalist colleges were Taylor University, Upland, Ind. (founded 1846); Houghton College, Houghton, N.Y. (1883); Asbury College, Wilmore, Ky. (1890); Eastern Nazarene College, Wollaston, Mass. (1900); Olivet Nazarene College, Kankakee, Ill. (1907); Marion College, Marion, Ind. (1920); Bob Jones University, now in Greenville, S.C. (1927).

22. Grant Wacker compares liberal and conservative evangelicals of the late nineteenth and early twentieth centuries, arguing that both groups were reacting to the rigidities of an earlier Calvinism. He finds they had many experiences and theological viewpoints in common. "In the Beginning Was Finney . . . Or Was It Bushnell? The Holy Spirit and the Spirit of the Age in American Protestantism, 1880–1910," an unpublished paper discussed at the Notre Dame Seminar in American Religion, March 12, 1983.

23. See, e.g., William R. Hutchison, *The Modernist Impulse in American Protestantism* (Cambridge: Harvard University Press, 1976).

24. A. B. Simpson, "Our Trust," *Alliance Weekly* 55 (August 6, 1921): 322.

25. E.g., "The claims which things make are corrupters of manhood, mortgages on the soul, and a drag anchor on our program towards the empyrean." William James, *The Varieties of Religious Experience: A Study in Human Nature* (New York: Collier Books, 1961), p. 255.

26. Norris Magnuson in *Salvation in the Slums: Evangelical Social Work, 1865–1920* (Metuchen, N.J.: The Scarecrow Press and The American Theological Library Association, 1977).

4. Beginnings: Some Founders

1. Albert B. Simpson, "My Own Story," manuscript in "Simpson Scrapbook," Nyack College Library, p. 5.
2. Simpson, "My Own Story," p. 6.
3. Simpson, "My Own Story," pp. 9–11.
4. Simpson, "My Own Story," p. 11.
5. Simpson, "My Own Story," pp. 11–12. Note that Christ is said to have died at three o'clock.
6. Simpson, "My Own Story," p. 7.
7. Simpson, "My Own Story," p. 7.
8. Simpson, "My Own Story," p. 13.
9. Simpson, "My Own Story," p. 12.
10. Simpson, "My Own Story," p. 12.
11. Simpson, "My Own Story," p. 17.
12. Simpson, "My Own Story," p. 17.
13. Simpson, "My Own Story," p. 20.
14. A. W. Tozer, *Wingspread: Albert B. Simpson—A Study in Spiritual Attitude* (Harrisburg, Pa.: Christian Publications, Centenary Edition, 1943), p. 40.
15. Simpson, "My Own Story," p. 20.
16. A. B. Simpson to Margaret Simpson, June 8, 1871, from "Letters from Abroad," in "Simpson Scrapbook," p. 104.
17. Kenneth Mackenzie, "My Memories of Dr. Simpson" (VIII), *Alliance Weekly* 72 (August 21, 1937): 535.
18. Albert B. Simpson, "A Surviving Diary," transcribed in "Simpson Scrapbook," p. 152 (November 22, 1879), Nyack College Library.
19. Simpson diary, November 25, 1879, p. 153.
20. Simpson diary, December 16, 1879, p. 161.
21. Simpson diary, November 24, 1879, p. 153.
22. Simpson diary, February 18, 1880, p. 177.
23. Simpson diary, December 21, 1879, p. 161.
24. Simpson diary, December 23, 1879, p. 161.
25. Simpson diary, p. 152. As this and other diary entries show, Simpson was obviously deeply affected by the doctrine of sanctification, but it is not clear exactly when he was "sanctified."
26. Simpson diary, February 11, 1880, p. 173.
27. A. E. Thompson, *A. B. Simpson: His Life and Work* (Harrisburg, Pa.: Christian Publications, 1960), p. 120.
28. "Simpson Scrapbook," p. 248.
29. Simpson diary, November 24, 1879, p. 153.
30. Simpson diary, February 22, 1880, p. 177.
31. Thompson, *A. B. Simpson*, p. 85.
32. Newspaper account of Simpson's sermon (n.d.), in "Simpson Scrapbook," p. 188. The suggestions about simple attire and social style recall those of the Plymouth Brethren. Certainly Simpson was familiar with Brethren ideas.
33. Thompson, *A. B. Simpson*, p. 120.
34. "Simpson Scrapbook," p. 191.
35. "Simpson Scrapbook," p. 195.
36. John H. Cable, *A History of the Missionary Training Institute: The Pioneer Bible School of America* (Harrisburg, Pa.: Christian Publications, 1933), p. 17.
37. *Christian Alliance* 1 (January 1887): 11.
38. *After Fifty Years: A Record of God's Working Through the Christian and Missionary Alliance* (Harrisburg, Pa.: Christian Publications, 1939), p. 18.

39. Thompson, *A. B. Simpson*, p. 126.

40. There are also references to a "Midland Bible Institute," with no location given.

41. For Gordon's life and activities see Ernest B. Gordon, *Adoniram Judson Gordon: A Biography* (New York: Fleming H. Revell Co., 1896); George Houghton, "The Contributions of Adoniram Judson Gordon to American Christianity" (Th.D. dissertation, Dallas Theological Seminary, 1970).

42. Gordon, *A. J. Gordon*, p. 108.

43. *Catalogue and Prospectus of the Boston Missionary Training School, 1892*.

44. *Christian and Missionary Alliance* 24 (March 3, 1900): 1.

45. For accounts of the genesis of the school see Nathan R. Wood, *A School of Christ* (Boston, 1953); Houghton, "The Contributions of Adoniram Judson Gordon"; F. L. Chapell, "Dr. Gordon and the Training School," *The Watchword* 17 (February and March, 1895): 61–62.

46. *Christian and Missionary Alliance* 24 (March 10, 1900): 147.

47. *Christian and Missionary Alliance* 24 (March 24, 1900): 180.

48. *Christian and Missionary Alliance* 24 (March 24, 1900): 180.

49. For Moody's life, see especially James F. Findlay Jr., *Dwight L. Moody: American Evangelist, 1837–1899* (Chicago: University of Chicago Press, 1969).

50. Findlay, *Moody*, p. 61.

51. Findlay, *Moody*, p. 106.

52. Findlay, *Moody*, p. 78.

53. Findlay, *Moody*, p. 132.

54. For early Institute history see Gene A. Getz, *MBI: The Story of Moody Bible Institute* (Chicago: Moody Press, 1969), pp. 26–69.

55. Getz, *MBI*, p. 36.

56. The Institute took Moody's name after his death in 1899.

57. Getz, *MBI*, pp. 40–41.

5. Beginnings: The Religious Training Schools

1. "Missionary Training Colleges," *Christian Alliance* 1 (May 1888): 76. At this time the word "college" could be and was applied to just about any educational institution above the common school level. Simpson did not sign this article but it is almost certainly from his pen.

2. E.g., A. J. Gordon said of Johanneum, the training school started by Theodor Christlieb in Germany, "The feeling raised against this movement in Germany was such that Christlieb was obliged to appeal to America and England for help in training and sending out these lay evangelists. I had the honor to serve as one of the American committee for receiving and transmitting funds. . . ." Quoted in Ernest Gordon, *Adoniram Judson Gordon: A Biography* (New York: Fleming H. Revell, 1896), pp. 271–72.

3. "Missionary Training Colleges," p. 76. The Guinness school also received mention in J. N. Murdock's contribution to "Missionary Training Schools—Do Baptists Need Them? A Discussion," *Baptist Quarterly Review* 12 (January 1890): 77.

4. See W. Y. Fullerton, *C. H. Spurgeon: A Biography* (London: Williams and Norgate, 1920); Charles Ray, *The Life of Charles Haddon Spurgeon* (London: Passmore and Alabaster, Isbister and Co. Ltd., 1902); Ernest W. Bacon, *Spurgeon: Heir of the Puritans* (London: Allen and Unwin, 1967).

5. A. T. Pierson, *The Crisis of Missions: Or, the Voice Out of the Cloud* (New York: Robert Carter and Bros., 1886), p. 333. The praise for Spurgeon's school contin-

ued: "How far would the evangelical testimony in the Baptist churches of Great Britain be heard today, were it not for the hundreds of ministers and missionaries who were trained in Spurgeon's Pastors' College?" *Moody Bible Institute Monthly* 32 (June 1932): 472.

6. Quoted in Gordon, *A. J. Gordon,* pp. 246–47.

7. Gordon, *A. J. Gordon,* p. 247.

8. Gordon, *A. J. Gordon,* p. 271.

9. Gene A. Getz, *MBI: the Story of Moody Bible Institute* (Chicago: Moody Press, 1969), p. 32; letter from Maria Hale Gordon to her family, Paris, July 8, 1888 (in Gordon College Archives); "Missionary Training Colleges," p. 76; Getz, *MBI,* p. 34.

10. "Missionary Training Colleges," p. 76.

11. C. F. Schlienz, *The Pilgrim Institution of St. Chrischona, near Basle, in Switzerland* (London: John Farquhar Shaw, 1850), p. xxx.

12. Schlienz, *Pilgrim Institution,* pp. 149–50.

13. Schlienz, *Pilgrim Institution,* pp. 111–13.

14. Pierson, *Crisis of Missions,* p. 327.

15. "Mr. Moody's New Plan," cited in *An Annotated Bibliography of D. L. Moody,* compiled by Wilbur M. Smith (Chicago: Moody Press, 1948), p. 78.

16. Quoted in James F. Findlay Jr., *Dwight L. Moody: American Evangelist, 1837–1899* (Chicago: University of Chicago Press, 1969), p. 327.

17. Pierson, *Crisis of Missions,* p. 322.

18. Quoted in Samuel N. Slie, "A History of the Christian Religion in the Life of Springfield College: A Study Made in Conjunction with the Religion in Higher Education Course with Prof. C. P. Shedd, Yale Divinity School, 1950." Unpublished paper, Springfield College Archives, pp. 1–2.

19. Pierson, *Crisis of Missions,* pp. 331–32.

20. Henry C. Mabie, "Missionary Training Schools—Do Baptists Need Them? A Discussion," *Baptist Quarterly Review* 12 (January 1890): 100.

21. Quoted in Gordon, *A. J. Gordon,* p. 260.

22. Cited in Getz, *MBI,* p. 36. From the address at Farwell Hall, Chicago, January 2, 1886.

23. Murdock, "Missionary Training Schools," p. 81.

24. Quoted in Renald Showers, "A History of Philadelphia College of the Bible" (Th.M. thesis, Dallas Theological Seminary, 1962), p. 62.

25. Quoted in Gordon, *A. J. Gordon,* pp. 171–2.

26. A. B. Simpson, "The Training and Sending Forth of Workers," *Christian and Missionary Alliance* 18 (April 30, 1897): 419.

27. Lucy Rider Meyer, *Deaconesses, Biblical, Early Church, European, American* (Chicago: The Message Publishing Co. 1889), p. 90.

28. Charles A. Briggs, "Theological Education and Its Needs," *Forum* 12 (January 1892): 643.

29. Murdock, "Missionary Training Schools," pp. 77, 81.

30. It was not until the 1930s that a majority of American youngsters of high school age began even to attend high school, let alone graduate. Edward A. Krug, *The Shaping of the American High School* (Madison: University of Wisconsin Press, 1972), II: 41.

31. See Virginia Lieson Brereton and Christa Ressmeyer Klein, "American Women in Ministry: A History of Protestant Beginning Points," in *Women of Spirit,* eds. Rosemary Ruether and Eleanor McLaughlin (New York: Simon and Schuster, 1979), pp. 301–32.

32. Pierson, *Crisis of Missions,* p. 331.

33. Pierson, *Crisis of Missions,* pp. 340–41.

34. A. J. Gordon, "Short Cut Methods," *The Watchman* 70 (November 7, 1889): 1.

35. Clifton J. Phillips, "The Student Volunteer Movement," in *The Missionary Enterprise in China and America,* ed. John K. Fairbank (Cambridge: Harvard University Press, 1974), p. 103.

36. Pierson, *Crisis of Missions,* p. 327.

37. Simpson, "The Training and Sending Forth of Workers," p. 419.

38. Pierson, *Crisis of Missions,* pp. 337–38.

39. Getz, *MBI,* p. 37.

40. This emphasis on brevity conflicted with the trend of the time toward more schooling for everyone, and, indeed, as time went on most training schools strove to keep their students for longer and longer periods of time.

41. Gordon, "Short Cut Methods," p. 1.

42. Gordon, "Short Cut Methods," p. 1.

43. *The King's Business* (March 1927): n.p.

44. Quoted in Gordon, *A. J. Gordon,* pp. 171–72.

45. *The Gordon School of Newton Theological Institution, Catalog,* 1910–11, p. 3.

46. For a more extensive treatment of the fate of the training schools see Virginia Lieson Brereton, "Preparing Women for the Lord's Work; The Story of Three Methodist Training Schools, 1880–1940," in Hilah F. Thomas and Rosemary S. Keller, ed., *Women and New Worlds: Historical Perspectives on the Wesleyan Tradition* (Nashville, Tenn.: Abingdon Press, 1981).

47. Joel A. Carpenter, "Fundamentalist Institutions and the Rise of Conservative Protestantism, 1929–1942," *Church History* 49 (1980): 62–75.

48. Carpenter, "Fundamentalist Institutions," pp. 72–73.

6. A Typology of Bible School Development

1. "Bible Schools That Are True to the Faith," *The Sunday School Times* (February 1, 1930): 63.

2. Don O. Shelton, "Instrumentalities God Chooses *and* Uses," *Moody Bible Institute Monthly* 33 (June 1933): 449.

3. *Catalog for 1914–1915,* p. 72.

4. *World's Crisis* (January 3, 1913).

5. *Boston Bible School and Ransom Institute,* 1903 catalog, p. 7.

6. *Catalogue and Prospectus of the Boston Missionary Training School with Abstract of Third Annual Report,* 1892, n.p.

/f7. Boston Bible School catalog, 1903, p. 10.

8. Boston Bible School, *Catalogue, 1905–6,* p. 11.

9. Boston Bible School, *Catalogue, 1907–8,* p. 18.

10. *Catalogue,* 1892 (BMTS), n.p.

11. Quoted in Henry K. Shaw, *Buckeye Disciples* (St. Louis: Christian Board of Publication, 1952), p. 344.

12. *Gordon College of Theology and Missions, Catalog for 1923–24; Announcement for 1924–1925,* p. 104.

13. James O. Henry, manuscript history of Bible Institute of Los Angeles, chapter 10, p. 22. (This is Henry's description, not a direct quotation of the board.)

7. Inside the Bible School: Classroom Teaching

1. Guy Linwood Vannah, "The New England School of Theology," *World's Crisis,* probably 1924. Scrapbook in archives at Berkshire Christian College.

2. Quoted in Thomas F. Henstock, "A History and Interpretation of the Curriculum of Central Bible Institute" (M.A. thesis, Central Bible Institute, 1964), p. 52.

3. Bible Institute of Los Angeles *Bulletin* 5 (Catalogue Number) (October 1920): 23; 33.

4. *Scofield Reference Bible* (New York: Oxford University Press, 1909), p. v; James M. Gray, *Synthetic Bible Studies* (Cleveland: F. M. Barton, Publisher, 1900), title page.

5. Gray, *Synthetic Bible Studies*, pp. 10 and 11.

6. Gene A. Getz, *MBI: The Story of Moody Bible Institute* (Chicago: Moody Press, 1969), pp. 255–56. Torrey's biographer described his teaching technique: Torrey "asked the students to take Scripture passages for recitation. His procedure was rigidly inductive. Once the passage was read, Torrey endeavored to draw out from the student its meaning by asking him a series of pointed questions. It was vital that the student should see it for himself." Roger Martin, *R. A. Torrey: Apostle of Certainty* (Murfreesboro, Tenn.: Sword of the Lord Publishers, 1976), pp. 91–92.

7. Katherine Elizabeth Bowman, "Columbia Bible College: A Leader in a New Movement in Religious Education" (M.A. thesis, School of Education, University of South Carolina, 1941), p. 72.

8. Biola *Bulletin* 5 (Oct. 1920): 23.

9. American biblical scholars had been using the adjective "inductive" in connection with Bible study for several decades. It was an application to Scripture of the Baconian inductive method for studying nature which had been introduced to America in the early nineteenth century by Princeton professors who had been studying in Scotland. There, from the Scottish Commonsense Realists, they had learned to venerate the ideas of Francis Bacon, including the inductive approach to studying everything from nature to Scripture. See Theodore Dwight Bozeman, *Protestants in an Age of Science: The Baconian Ideal and Antebellum American Religious Thought* (Chapel Hill: The University of North Carolina Press, 1977), especially chapter 7.

10. "Examination Questions given by Dr. Simpson to one of his Nyack classes," Note No. 5 in "Simpson Scrapbook," Nyack College Library, p. 373.

11. For the source of these phrases see Acts 17:11, where the Bereans are described as "more noble than those in Thessalonica, in that they received the word with all readiness of mind, and searched the scriptures daily, whether those things were so."

12. "Summer Bible School at Nyack" *Alliance Weekly* 39 (March 1, 1913): 349.

13. For White's ideas about Bible study see author's study of the early history of New York Theological Seminary in manuscript form. On the subject of studying the Bible by books, C. I. Scofield said, "the Bible is a book of books . . . each of the sixty-six books is complete in itself and has its own theme and analysis" (*Scofield Reference Bible*, p. v.). I. M. Haldeman advised the student to know the "meaning and purport of each book of the Bible," because each book has some special characteristic, some particular purport. *How to Study the Bible: The Second Coming and Other Expositions* (Philadelphia: Philadelphia School of the Bible, 1904). G. Stanley Hall, not a member of the conservative camp, also claimed that "the study of the Bible by books is fundamental to all Bible study." Howard T. Kuist, "The Premises of a New Strategy for Education" (Typewritten manuscript, New York Theological Seminary Library, n.d.), p. 8. (Hall is quoted indirectly here.)

14. Gray, *Synthetic Bible Studies*, p. 9.

15. Gray's assumption was that God as the real author of Scriptures had caused the books of the Bible to appear in that order for specific reasons, which could be ascertained by careful study of the Bible as a whole.

16. Gray, *Synthetic Bible Studies,* p. 15.

17. Gray, *Synthetic Bible Studies,* pp. 15–18. A student notebook from one of Gray's Synthetic Bible Study classes is in the Gordon College Archives. In constructing the "outline facts" with their subheadings, the student used different colored inks and also underlinings to distinguish various sections and to emphasize certain ideas.

18. Gray, *Synthetic Bible Studies,* pp. 19–21.

19. Gray, *Synthetic Bible Studies,* p. 16.

20. Gray, *Synthetic Bible Studies,* p. 21.

21. Gray, *Synthetic Bible Studies,* p. 17.

22. Gray, *Synthetic Bible Studies,* p. 15. For Abraham material, see p. 20.

23. George M. Marsden, *Fundamentalism and American Culture: The Shaping of Twentieth Century Evangelicalism, 1870–1925* (New York: Oxford University Press, 1980), pp. 55–62; Marsden, "Understanding Fundamentalist Views of Science," Ashley Montagu, ed. *Science and Creationism* (New York: Oxford University Press, 1984), pp. 95–116. See also Gray, *Synthetic Bible Studies,* p. 17 and Bozeman, *Protestants in an Age of Science.*

24. Edith Metcalf, *Letters to Dorothy* (Chicago and New York: Fleming H. Revell Co., 1893), pp. 10–11. Metcalf was writing at a time when Gray taught at the Bible Institute only for two or three months—possibly even less—during the summer. His home base was still Boston. Ordinarily the coverage of the Old Testament took longer than the three weeks reported by Metcalf, but the particular timing in this case must have necessitated an accelerated or condensed course.

25. Bowman, "Columbia Bible College," p. 21.

26. Frank J. Davis, "After Seven Years," *World's Crisis,* n.d. Scrapbook, Berkshire Christian College Archives.

27. P. C. Headley, *George F. Pentecost: Life, Labors, and Bible Studies* (Boston: James H. Earle, Publisher, 1880), p. 191.

28. Metcalf, *Letters to Dorothy,* p. 11.

29. Charles Stelzle, *A Son of the Bowery* (New York: George H. Doran Co., 1926), p. 57.

30. See Haldeman, *How to Study the Bible,* pp. 51–52.

31. Metcalf, *Letters to Dorothy,* p. 11.

32. Charles H. Brackett, "The History of Azusa College and the Friends" (M.A. thesis, University of Southern California, 1967), p. 65.

33. "George Pardington," *Alliance Weekly* 43 (April 24, 1915): 59–60.

34. Carol Talbot, *For This I Was Born: the Captivating Story of Louis T. Talbot* (Chicago: Moody Press, 1977), p. 26.

35. *Catalogue of the Moody Bible Institute of Chicago,* 1911–12, p. 37.

36. Biola *Bulletin* 5 (Oct. 1920): 35.

37. H. W. Pope, "Daily Bible Reading," *The Christian Workers Magazine* 16 (December 1915): 278.

38. Metcalf, *Letters to Dorothy,* p. 16.

39. Metcalf, *Letters to Dorothy,* pp. 26–9.

40. Robert Harkness, *Reuben Archer Torrey: The Man, His Message* (Chicago: The Bible Institute Colportage Association, 1929), pp. 124–26. It is not clear from the narrative whether Harkness or Torrey was the worker in question.

41. H. W. Pope, "The Value of Memorizing Scripture," *The Christian Workers Magazine* 16 (September 1915): 92.

42. Quoted in William Cobb, "The West Point of Fundamentalism," *American Mercury* 16 (1929): 104.

43. For definitions of expository preaching see Rev. Ira M. Grey, "Expository Preaching," *The Christian Workers Magazine* 16 (June 1916): 762–64; Lew Wade

Gosnell, "The Value of Bible Institutes Shown by a Sample Product," *Moody Bible Institute Monthly* 33 (April 1933): 363; *Moody Bible Institute Monthly* 32 (November 1931): 213: "There are innumerable ways in which one may expound the Bible. One may take a book and go through it week after week. A line of thought may be traced from beginning to the end of the Bible and its various phases set forth. God's working in history as developed in Scripture will bring out the meaning of life in a remarkable way. We expound the Scripture when we take up the remarkable character delineations found in the record. There is no end to the ways in which we may carry on expository preaching. A very able preacher spent weeks placing the first two chapters of Genesis before his listeners. . . ." See also Thornton Whaling, "Some Failures of the Ministry," *Moody Bible Institute Monthly* 33 (September 1932): 5; Horton Davis, "Expository Preaching: Charles Haddon Spurgeon," *Foundations* 6 (January 1963): 14–25. Davis makes it clear that Spurgeon was widely hailed by American fundamentalists for his skill in expository preaching.

44. Beulah Edwards, "The Imperative Need of More Bible Study," *The Theologian* 6 (February 1927): 17–18.

45. Gray, *Synthetic Bible Studies*, p. 11.

46. Samuel H. Sutherland, teaching personal evangelism at the Bible Institute of Los Angeles in the thirties, for instance, had his students memorize—"word perfect"—130 Scripture verses, including Matt. 11:28; 1 Tim. 1:15 (aimed at the individual who claimed to be "too big a sinner to be saved"); Rom. 3:23; Psalm 14:1 (addressed to the complacent Christian); 2 Cor. 6:2 (to the procrastinator who wanted to wait to be saved). Conversation with Samuel H. Sutherland, July 25, 1982.

47. A good example of the technique of building bridges to potential converts is provided by the account of the superintendent of Jewish work at the Bible Institute of Los Angeles. She reported approaching a "sweet-faced Jewess": "I told her of my great love for and interest in her people and of the great debt I owed them that it was through the Jews I had any knowledge of God, that I owed my Bible to them for both Old and New Testaments were written by Jews and Jesus our Saviour was a Jew." *The King's Business* (1915): 78.

48. *Catalogue of MBI*, 1911–12, p. 36.

49. *Biola Bulletin* 5 (October 1920): 30.

50. In most Bible schools "classes" did not mean the same thing as "courses." The word class was used as most educators use it, but the word "course" was often reserved for a series of classes, a program of studies extending over time. A "course" could last a few weeks, a year, two years, or more. To avoid confusion, I have tried to follow the Bible school usage here.

51. E.g., said the 1920 *Bulletin* of the school's "Homiletics Department," "The object . . . is to qualify men and women to deliver sermons, Gospel addresses, Bible readings and expositions of God's Word wherever needed—for pulpit, street, jail, shop, or cottage. Practical demonstration in sermon outline and structure is given, and frequent use is made of the blackboard to illustrate same. From time to time, students are required to prepare for criticism outlines of sermons and addresses. The last term in Homiletics is wholly devoted to preaching by students in the classroom" (pp. 31–2).

52. *Boston Bible School and Ransom Institute Catalog*, 1913–14, p. 23.

53. The 1920 Biola *Bulletin* described the Personal Work course as "a course in real and practical psychology and not in mostly imaginary and theoretical psychology, so common today" (p. 30).

54. The Gordon catalogs for the teens, twenties, and thirties reveal that a large number of students at the time came from small towns in Maine, New Hampshire, and the eastern provinces of Canada.

55. "Every public speaker . . . should . . . be free from those mistakes in English speech which weaken the effect of his best work. It is vital that those students whose use of language is weak or defective should be brought to a higher standard, and that all should be taught to speak and write in clearness and beauty." (*The Gordon School of Newton Theological Institution, Catalog*, 1910–11, p. 10.)

8. Inside the Bible School: Beyond the Classroom

1. E.g., Moody Bible Institute of Chicago, *Fortieth Annual Catalogue*, 1927–28, p. 35: "No city in the world offers a better clinic for observation and experience than Chicago."

2. *The King's Business* 7 (1916): 74.

3. *The Christian Workers Magazine* 13 (July 1913): 691.

4. "The Training and Sending Forth of Workers," *Christian and Missionary Alliance* 18 (April 30, 1897): 419. Simpson's reference to plucking brands is probably from Zechariah 3:2.

5. G. Jennings, "Students' Evangelistic Work," *Alliance Weekly* 38 (June 29, 1912): 204.

6. *The Christian Workers Magazine* 11 (October 1910): 87.

7. Carol Talbot, *For This I Was Born: The Captivating Story of Louis T. Talbot* (Chicago: Moody Press, 1977), p. 27.

8. "Notes from Nyack Institute," *Alliance Weekly* 38 (June 29, 1912): 203.

9. "The Nyack Corner," *Alliance Weekly* 38 (August 24, 1912): 381.

10. "The Nyack Corner," August 24, 1912, p. 381.

11. "The Nyack Corner," *Alliance Weekly* 38 (August 17, 1912): 317.

12. Christina E. Lang, "My Call to India," *World's Crisis* (October 18, 1922). Scrapbook, Berkshire Christian College Library. For the source of Lang's quote see Matt. 28:20.

13. *The Christian Workers Magazine* 11 (February 1911): 87.

14. *The King's Business* (1927): 106.

15. John H. Cable, *A History of the Missionary Training Institute: The Pioneer Bible School of America* (Harrisburg, Pa.: Christian Publications, 1933), p. 12. The alumnus's reference to the "third Heaven" comes from 2 Cor. 12:2. The phrase "things unlawful to utter" seems a slight variation of 2 Cor. 12:4. Even allowing for the glow supplied by memory and for the somewhat formulaic quality of this description, the alumnus gives us some feel for the relationship between students and a teacher like Simpson.

16. *Chritian Alliance and Missionary Weekly* 6 (April 17, 1891): 249. For a biographical sketch of Whittemore see David J. Fant, "Early Associates of A. B. Simpson" ("Mother" E. M. Whittemore), *The Southeastern District Report of the Christian and Missionary Alliance* (January–February 1977): 4.

17. W. C. Stevens, "Notes from Nyack Institute," *Alliance Weekly* 38 (April 27, 1912): 55.

18. *Christian Alliance and Missionary Weekly* 6 (January 16, 1891): 50; "Missionary Training College," *Christian Alliance and Missionary Weekly* 6 (February 6, 1891): 81.

19. Charles C. Washburn, "The Ministry of Music," *Alliance Weekly* 55 (August 6, 1921): 330.

20. Washburn, "Ministry of Music," p. 330.

21. Florence L. Bartlett, "The Spiritual Life of the New England School of Theology," *World's Crisis* (September 16, 1923). Scrapbook, Berkshire Christian College Library.

22. Charles H. Brackett, "The History of Azusa College and the Friends" (M.A. thesis, University of Southern California, 1967), p. 55.

23. 1920 Catalog, Bible Institute of Los Angeles, p. 13.

24. *Moody Bible Institute Monthly* 22 (March 1922): 844.

25. Ellen C. Coburn, "How I Came to the New England School of Theology," *World's Crisis*, August 1, 1923. Scrapbook, Berkshire Christian College Library. See also the testimonies in Shirley Nelson, *The Last Year of the War* (New York: Harper and Row, 1978); although fictional, they are authentic in tone. Also, "Student Testimonies," *Alliance Weekly* 55 (August 6, 1921): 329. E.g.,

> When wandering for years in sin and darkness Jesus found me and brought me home; now how can I help but love Him when He first loved me.
>
> I can say to the glory of God that Jesus satisfies the longing desire of my soul and He is far more precious than any outward object seen. Jesus is real to me. He leads me daily in the paths of righteousness and Glory to God! 'Tis far better to follow Jesus than to follow him who led me in darkness. Never a trial confronts me but my Lord is always there to meet the need. Jesus is mighty to save and mighty to heal for He saved and healed even me. He healed all that came unto Him in those early days and Praise God "He is just the same today."

26. Lang, "My Call to India."

27. *Tenth Annual Report of the Christian and Missionary Alliance* (1907), p. 77.

28. Yearbook from Central Bible Institute, n.d., p. 39.

29. Robert Williams and Marilyn Miller, *Chartered for His Glory: Biola University, 1908–1983* (La Mirada, California: Associated Students of Biola University, 1983), p. 71.

30. *Tenth Annual Report of the Christian Missionary Alliance* (1907), p. 76.

31. MBI Catalog, 1927–1928, p. 15.

32. Interview with Ella M. Brettell, May 4, 1978. In Brettell's case the maternal hopes bore fruit, for she was converted: a Nyack friend "led me to the Lord," she reported.

33. *Boston Bible School and Ransom Institute*, 1905–06, p. 22.

34. Catalog of New England School of Theology, 1931–32, p. 35.

35. Catalog of New England School of Theology, 1931–32, p. 35.

36. "New England School of Theology," *World's Crisis*, November 8, 1939.

37. "New England School of Theology," *World's Crisis*, April 15, 1936.

38. "The Nyack Corner," *Alliance Weekly* 39 (November 9, 1912): 93.

39. Christian and Missionary Alliance, *Annual Report* (1911), p. 57.

40. Interview with Samuel H. Sutherland, July 25, 1982.

41. David J. Fant, "Early Associates of A. B. Simpson" (Cora Rudy Turnbull), *Southeastern District Report of the Christian and Missionary Alliance* (Special Edition), May 1977, p. 14.

42. Interview with Ella M. Brettell.

43. Interview with Samuel H. Sutherland, July 25, 1982.

44. David J. Fant, "Early Associates of A. B., Simpson" (W. C. Stevens), *Southeastern District Report of the Christian and Missionary Alliance*, January–February 1976. This is only a tantalizing glimpse; one wishes that Fant had furnished more details.

45. *The King's Business* (1927): 108.

46. Williams and Miller, *Chartered for His Glory*, pp. 40–41.

47. Fant, "Early Associates of A. B. Simpson" (W. C. Stevens). Biola administrators had to deal with at least one student who engaged repeatedly in homosexual activities off campus. Interview with Samuel H. Sutherland, July 25, 1982.

9. Worlds within the Bible School

1. "Student Volunteers," *Hypernikon* 1 (1923): 71.
2. *Hypernikon* 9 (1931): 74–77.
3. "Student Volunteers," p. 71.
4. Biola catalog, 1949, p. 41.
5. Biola catalog, 1949, p. 41.
6. W. C. Stevens, "Notes from Nyack," *Alliance Weekly* 37 (April 13, 1912): 27. A. Mrs. Graham, a missionary to the Sudan, who spoke on two occasions, described how she was "led" to the Sudan despite her initial conviction that "Africa, the Sudan, was not the place for a fleshy person like her. And it cost her a very death itself to say 'Yes' to the forcible call. But, the result has proved that the Lord made no mistake in calling her and that she had made none in following." She spared the students none of the grim details of missionary life in her chosen field. And she ended with an exhortation:

> She expressed the conviction that every station ever opened in the Sudan would still be manned if every Nyack student had been faithful to God's purpose. Special watch needs to be exercised against Satan's wiles through the tender affections. Married couples are especially needed in Africa, and yet every care needs to be exercised lest sexual affections frustrate God's purpose. So many, she said, had told her of their missing God's best through this snare.

7. *The King's Business* (March 1927): n.p.; Moody Bible Institute *Bulletin* 8 (December 1928): 5.
8. S. A. Witmer, *The Bible College Story: Education with a Dimension* (Channel Publishers, 1962), p. 111.
9. *World's Crisis* (October 19, 1924). Scrapbook, Berkshire Christian College archives.
10. William V. Trollinger, Jr., "One Response to Modernity: Northwestern Bible School and the Fundamentalist Empire of William Bell Riley" (Ph.D. dissertation, University of Wisconsin, 1984), p. 134.
11. Nathan R. Wood, *A School of Christ* (Boston, 1953), p. 192.
12. *Christian Alliance* 1 (June 1888): 96.
13. A. J. Gordon, "The Ministry of Women," p. 4. Typed, duplicated document, Goddard Library, Gordon-Conwell.
14. MBI catalog, 1927–1928, pp. 28–29.
15. Nathan R. Wood to Emmet Russell, June 28, 1919, in Gordon College archives.
16. Wood, *School of Christ*, p. 155.
17. Biographical file on William Whiting Borden, Moodyana Room, Moody Bible Institute library.
18. P. E. Osborne, "Self-Denial Week," *World's Crisis*, about 1911. Scrapbook in archives at Berkshire Christian College.
19. *World's Crisis*, October 11, 1911.
20. Undated item from *World's Crisis*, probably 1911, in scrapbook, archives at Berkshire Christian College.
21. *World's Crisis*, October 1917. Scrapbook in archives of Berkshire Christian College.
22. James O. Henry, "Black Oil and Souls to Save," *BIOLA Broadcaster* 3 (December 1973): 15.
23. Gene A. Getz, *MBI: the Story of Moody Bible Institute* (Chicago: Moody Press, 1969), p. 91. In 1927 David R. Breed of Western Theological Seminary, who sent

a questionnaire to fifty Bible schools and received twenty-six replies, reported that four schools each had more than a million dollars in endowment. But since he did not identify the schools or define what he meant by "endowment," it is difficult to make very much of his information. Presumably Moody was one of the institutions he was thinking of. "Bible Institutes of the United States," *The Biblical Review* 12 (1927): 374.

24. Timothy Weber, *Living in the Shadow of the Second Coming: American Premillennialism, 1875–1925* (New York: Oxford University Press, 1979), pp. 8–9.

25. Robert Williams and Marilyn Miller, *Chartered for His Glory: Biola University, 1908–1983* (La Mirada, California: Associated Students of Biola University, 1983), p. 51. Certainly it was difficult to buck the tide forever. The general educational wisdom of the time, especially as preached by the accrediting associations, state education departments, and some of the philanthropic foundations, decreed that effective education demanded financial security. By 1912, for instance, the North Central Association required colleges seeking membership to have endowments of at least $200,000. John P. Nevins, *A Study of the Organization and Operation of Voluntary Accrediting Agencies* (Washington, D.C.: The Catholic University of America Press, 1959), pp. 213–14.

26. "The Nyack Corner," *Alliance Weekly* 38 (August 10, 1912): 301.

27. Trollinger, "The Empire of William Bell Riley," p. 8.

28. *World's Crisis*, October 19, 1927.

29. Carol Talbot, *For This I Was Born: The Captivating Story of Louis T. Talbot* (Chicago: Moody Press, 1977), p. 23.

30. Biola catalog, 1920, p. 52.

31. *The King's Business* (March 1922), n.p.

32. Dorothy Martin, *Moody Bible Institute: God's Power in Action* (Chicago: Moody Press, 1977), p. 69.

33. Martin, *God's Power*, p. 77.

34. William M. Runyan, *Dr. Gray at Moody Bible Institute* (New York: Oxford University Press, 1935), p. 153.

35. *Moody Bible Institute Monthly* 28 (April 1928): 395.

10. The Bible School and the Fundamentalist Movement

1. Those Bible schools that served as regional bases initiated a variety of evangelistic and educational activities in a given geographical area, staffed evangelical institutions in that territory with their students, faculty, and graduates, and often wielded a good deal of influence over the shape that Protestantism took in that region. Most Bible schools did this to a degree, but some achieved more success than others; for one of the most effective regional schools, see William V. Trollinger, Jr., "One Response to Modernity: Northwestern Bible School and the Fundamentalist Empire of William Bell Riley" (Ph.D. dissertation, University of Wisconsin, 1984).

2. Joel Carpenter has examined this split with care and acuity in his study, "The Renewal of American Fundamentalism, 1930–1945" (unpublished Ph.D. dissertation, Johns Hopkins University, 1984).

3. Carpenter, "The Renewal of American Fundamentalism," p. 60.

4. *Christian Alliance and Missionary Weekly* 6 (February 27, 1891): 146.

5. My impression of this basic division in the Alliance was confirmed in conversation with a friend who grew up in the Alliance and attended Nyack College.

6. I would go further, in fact; I would argue that, as soon as we define our focus as Bible schools we automatically end up dealing with the less extreme forms

of fundamentalism. Even if one were concentrating upon pentecostal educational institutions, the same would hold true; the study would necessarily deal with the more organized, less flamboyant streams of pentecostalism. Leaders in the Assemblies of God, those who were concerned with setting up at least a minimal denominational order and apparatus, were instrumental in establishing the first Assemblies of God Bible school. Moderation might not be a dominant theme, on the other hand, in an exploration of the largely uninstitutionalized (until recently) "fundamentalism and politics." One needs only to recall the extremism of the fundamentalist groups that Richard Hofstadter described in *The Paranoid Style in American Politics and Other Essays*. Apparently the more moderate fundamentalists turned to education, using institutional forms to work toward their goals. (Or perhaps, alternatively, their educative activity made moderates of them.)

7. *Moody Bible Institute Monthly* 22 (February 1922): 808.

8. *Moody Bible Institute Monthly* 22 (January 1922): 763.

9. *Moody Bible Institute Monthly* 22 (December 1921): 695.

10. "Dispensationalism Running Wild," *Moody Bible Institute Monthly* 33 (December 1932): 253; "What About Mrs. Aimee Semple McPherson?" *Moody Bible Institute Monthly* 22 (November 1921): 648; *Moody Bible Institute Monthly* 22 (November 1921): 647; A. C. Gaebelein, "Christianity vs. Modern Cults," *Moody Bible Institute Monthly* 22 (March 1922): 859; *Moody Bible Institute Monthly* 22 (February 1922): 807–809.

11. William M. Runyan, *Dr. Gray at Moody Bible Institute* (New York: Oxford University Press, 1935), p. 15.

12. Robert Harkness, *Reuben Archer Torrey: The Man, His Message* (Chicago: The Bible Institute Colportage Association, 1929), p. 108.

13. Quoted in Gene A. Getz, *MBI: The Story of Moody Bible Institute* (Chicago: Moody Press, 1969), p. 142.

14. Runyan, *Dr. Gray*, p. 122.

15. None of his biographers states where Gray went to school, but it is clear that either he had attended a college (or seminary) or had studied extensively on his own.

16. Dorothy Martin, *Moody Bible Institute: God's Power in Action* (Chicago: Moody Press, 1977), p. 70.

17. Getz, *MBI*, p. 99.

18. Getz, *MBI*, pp. 212–19.

19. Roger Martin, *R. A. Torrey: Apostle of Certainty* (Murfreesboro, Tenn.: Sword of the Lord Publishers, 1976), p. 91.

20. Harkness, *Torrey*, pp. 105; 106.

21. Harkness, *Torrey*, p. 10.

22. Runyan, *Dr. Gray*, p. 111.

23. D. Martin, *Moody Bible Institute*, p. 86.

24. James M. Gray "To the Members of the Faculty," July 29, 1908, in Moodyana Collection, Moody Bible Institute Library.

25. R. Martin, *Torrey*, p. 94.

26. James M. Gray, "To Whom It Concerns," March 19, 1926, in Moodyana Collection, Moody Bible Institute Library.

27. "What About Mrs. Aimee Semple McPherson?" p. 647.

28. *Moody Bible Institute Monthly* 22 (April 1922): 956.

29. *Moody Bible Institute Monthly* 22 (May 1922): 1004.

30. Henry Ostrom, "Why Disagreement on Holiness" *Moody Bible Institute Monthly* 22 (August 1922): 1142.

31. Wilbur M. Smith, "The Conflict of the Latter Days—the Strategic Position of the Bible Institute," *Moody Bible Institute Monthly* 33 (May 1933): 397.

32. R. Martin, *Torrey*, p. 214.

33. R. Martin, *Torrey,* p. 214.

34. Carpenter in "The Renewal of American Fundamentalism" quotes a reader who actually assumed Moody Bible Institute *was* a denomination and admonished the *Moody Monthly* editors, "Why don't you publish something on the other denominations once in a while?" (p. 22).

35. "Miss Rader and the Crerar Memorial Church," *The Christian Workers Magazine* 16 (August 1916): 960.

36. Wilbur M Smith, *Will H. Houghton: A Watchman on the Wall* (Grand Rapids, Mich.: Eerdmans Publishing Co. 1951), pp. 111–12.

37. Faculty minutes, May 6, 1930, p. 19. Biola College library.

38. "The New Dean of the Los Angeles Bible Institute," *Christian Fundamentals in School and Church* 7 (July–September 1925): 25–26; "Breaking the Bible School Defense Line," *Christian Fundamentalist* 1 (April 1928): 5–9, 25; "Biola Boiling," *Christian Fundamentalist* 1 (May 1928): 5–10; "The MacInnis Controversy," *Christian Fundamentalist* 1 (June 1928): 12–14; "Dr. Campbell Morgan and the Los Angeles Bible Institute," "Dr. Riley Replies to Dr. Campbell Morgan," "The MacInnis Book Again," *The Christian Fundamentalist* 2 (August 1928): 12–17; "The MacInnis Controversy," *The Christian Fundamentalist* 2 (December 1928): 13; "Biola and the Bible, or Dr. MacInnis Resigned," *Christian Fundamentalist* 2 (June 1929): 9–10. It is probable that all these editorials were penned by W. B. Riley himself, though they are unsigned. I am grateful to William Trollinger for bringing these articles to my attention.

39. A. E. Thompson, *A. B. Simpson: His Life and Work* (Harrisburg, Pa.: Christian Publications, 1960), p. 9; "A Long and Faithful Ministry," *Alliance Weekly* 63 (January 7, 1928): 4–5; David J. Fant, "Early Associates of A. B. Simpson" (George F. Pardington), *Southeastern District Report of the Christian and Missionary Alliance,* Special Edition, March 1977.

40. Runyan, *Dr. Gray,* pp. 137–39; John David Hannah, "James Martin Gray: His Life and Work" (Th.D. dissertation, Dallas Theological Seminary, 1974), pp. 125–33.

41. E. Schuyler English, *H. A. Ironside: Ordained of the Lord* (Grand Rapids, Mich.: Zondervan Publishing House, 1946). See, e.g., p. 170: after refusing an invitation to join the faculty of Dallas Theological Seminary in 1926, Ironside reflected, "I keep wondering if I would ever be satisfied to be tied down after having had so wide and varied an itinerant ministry for so many years."

42. R. Martin, *Torrey,* p. 223.

43. For early Advent Christian history see Albert C. Johnson, *Advent Christian History: A Concise Narrative of the Origin and Progress, Doctrine and Work of this Body of Believers* (Boston: Advent Christian Publishing Society, 1918); Frank Burr, "Early and Later Conventions of Adventists," *World's Crisis* 47 (January 16, 1910): 1–2; United States Department of Commerce, Bureau of the Census, *Religious Bodies: 1936,* Vol. 2 (Washington, D.C.: Government Printing Office, 1941), p. 15; David A. Dean, "The Origin in Millerism of Conditionalism," *Henceforth* 3 (Spring 1975): 75–80.

44. *Catalogue of the Boston Bible School and Ransom Institute, 1913–14,* p. 20.

45. *World's Crisis,* ca. 1910. Scrapbook in archives at Berkshire Christian College.

46. About the turn of the century a denominational leader sounded a warning to the youth of his church; his words are almost indistinguishable from those of other conservative evangelicals:

> I exhort you, young people, rally round this great standard of truth, the Bible, the inspired Word of God. Skepticism and infidelity are rife on every hand. 'Higher criticism' is rapidly gaining ground. The popular churches have joined affinity with the world. The Spirit of God is being withdrawn

from them. Nothing but the literal Word of God, and strict adherence to its precepts, will stand the final test. Uphold it, propagate it, . . .

George J. French, "A Timely Plea for Our Young People," pamphlet in archives at Berkshire Christian College. Another denominational author wrote apocalyptically of the "great battle for the future, not only for Adventism, but for all those who hold to a return of Christ, and to an actual period of judgment of the world, and renovation of the earth, . . ." "The Advent Hope," *World's Crisis,* February 8, 1911.

47. E. O. Sellers, "Work for Men," *The Christian Workers Magazine* 11 (February 1911): 507.

48. *Catalogue of the Moody Bible Institute of Chicago,* 1911–12, p. 40. A short review of a book, *Building up Business by Mail,* by William E. Clifford, appeared in a 1916 issue of *The Christian Workers Magazine:* "This is not a religious book, but contains suggestions about building up secular business by the proper use of the mails, that would be very properly studied by the church in these days, when advertising has taken a place in its activities that cannot be displaced." "Book Notices," *The Christian Workers Magazine* (May 1916): 708.

49. "For Sermon and Scrapbook," *Moody Bible Institute Monthly* 22 (January 1922): 773.

50. *Moody Bible Institute Monthly* 22 (March 1922).

51. William Cobb, "The West Point of Fundamentalism," *American Mercury* 16 (1929): 104.

52. James M. Gray to A. F. Gaylord, September 12, 1908.

53. "Young Baptists Visit the Institute," *The Christian Workers Magazine* 16 (August 1916): 960.

54. E.g., "Life at Moody Institute," *Moody Bible Institute Monthly* 27 (November 1926): 148.

55. *Moody Bible Institute Monthly* 32 (November 1931): 216.

56. Chase A. Sawtell, "What Grew from a Coupon," *Moody Bible Institute Monthly* 32 (June 1932): 534.

57. James M. Gray to A. P. Fitt, October 30, 1906.

58. Carol Talbot, *For This I Was Born: The Captivating Story of Louis T. Talbot* (Chicago: Moody Press, 1977), p. 99.

11. The Bible Schools and American Education

1. John Dewey, *Democracy and Education* (New York: Macmillan Co., 1916), pp. 89–90.

2. Johns Hopkins Medical School, an exemplum for many that followed it, was founded in 1893. Harvard Medical School underwent extensive reforms in 1871: "The autopsies and clinical work which ambitious students had earlier undertaken quite apart from the medical school course became a standard part of the work toward the degree." Hugh Hawkins, *Between Harvard and America: The Educational Leadership of Charles W. Eliot* (New York: Oxford University Press, 1972), p. 61.

3. Dorothy Rogers, *Oswego: Fountainhead of Teacher Education, A Century in the Sheldon Tradition* (New York: Appleton-Century-Crofts Inc., 1961), p. 67; Charles A. Harper, *Development of the Teachers College in the United States with special reference to the Illinois State Normal University* (Bloomington, Ill.: McKnight and McKnight Publishers, 1935), p. 116.

4. Rogers, *Oswego,* p. 50; Harper, *Development of the Teachers College,* p. 194.

5. For normal schools in general see Jessie M. Pangburn, *The Evolution of the*

American Teachers College (New York: Teachers College Press, 1932); Paul H. Mattingly, *The Classless Profession: American Schoolmen in the Nineteenth Century* (New York: New York University Press, 1975); and Jurgen Herbst, "Nineteenth-Century Normal Schools in the United States: A Fresh Look," *History of Education* 9 (1980): 219–27.

6. Correspondence study was a recent innovation. The formal beginning of study by mail dates from the early 1880s, when William R. Harper and others organized a system of correspondence teaching at the Chautauqua College of Liberal Arts; the highly successful International Correspondence Schools date from 1891. Extension study, summer schools and institutes, evening classes, and of course university presses were widely used by universities, which were just coming into being in the post Civil War period, in their attempt to reach large numbers of would-be students.

7. Robert Clark, "Bible Institutes and Theological Seminaries," *Moody Bible Institute Monthly* 22 (March 1922): 853.

8. "Decay of Evangelism," *Moody Bible Institute Monthly* 28 (February 1928): 259.

9. "Pedantic Snobbishness," *Moody Bible Institute Monthly* 32 (May 1932): 423.

10. Joseph Taylor, "Is Prohibition to Blame?" *Moody Bible Institute Monthly* 33 (September 1932): 14.

11. Quoted in Richard J. Storr, *Harper's University: The Beginnings* (Chicago: The University of Chicago Press, 1966), p. 59.

12. Timothy P. Weber, in "The Two-Edged Sword: The Fundamentalist Use of the Bible," in Nathan O. Hatch and Mark A. Noll, eds. *The Bible in America: Essays in Cultural History* (New York: Oxford, 1982), pp. 101–120, argues that, though fundamentalists claimed to be saving the Bible for the common people, who, using their methods, could study it for themselves, in fact the system of dispensationalism made independent Bible study impossible. "Fundamentalist lay people were only slightly less reliant on their Bible teachers than liberal lay people were on the higher critics," he claims (p. 116). And again, "The ultimate irony of the fundamentalist approach to the Scriptures is that it had produced so little really independent Bible study." Weber is right if by "independent study" he means the sort of effort, not overly inhibited by prior assumptions, that issues in original and imaginative conclusions about Scripture. If, however, one thinks of "independent study" as what people do when they study the Bible on their own, with the help, for instance, of Scofield's Notes, then I think Weber overstates the case. As a result of the tutelage of Bible schools and other institutions, many people formed the habits of self-study and gained the self confidence to proceed on their own, with the aid of resources they had learned about in Bible schools or Bible classes. Weber, I think, also overestimates the complexity of dispensationalism—at least the amount of complexity a lay person would have to master in order to accomplish a dispensationalist reading of Scripture. Perhaps, too, he exaggerates the degree to which dispensationalism belonged to an old paradigm and was therefore dysfunctional for the followers of dispensationalist Bible teachers (see my discussion of dispensationalism in chapter 2 for a different view of the matter).

13. It should be noted that *most* schools showed more tolerance for underprepared students than the same schools would nowadays; several decades ago requirements were less rigid and of course students had not received as much schooling as their presentday counterparts. Many colleges found it necessary to maintain preparatory departments, though they usually dropped them as soon as possible. Bible schools simply carried this tendency further and for a longer time.

14. Renald Showers, "A History of Philadelphia College of the Bible" (Th.M. thesis, Dallas Theological Seminary and Graduate School, 1962), p. 50.

15. E.g., Bible Institute of Los Angeles's *The King's Business*, Philadelphia School of the Bible's *Serving-and-Waiting*, and of course Moody Bible Institute's *Monthly*. The Northwestern Schools, founded by W. B. Riley, had a publication which went by a variety of names, among them *Christian Fundamentalist* and *Northwestern Pilot*. Most schools produced at least a bulletin.

16. *Moody Bible Institute Monthly* 33 (September 1932): 25.

17. Johnson Bible College began as a correspondence school, the Correspondence Bible College, which eventually became a residential school; the American Home Bible Institute, founded in the teens in Washington, D.C., focused exclusively on study by mail (it was later merged with two other Washington Bible schools to form Washington Bible College). See Alva Ross Brown, *Standing on the Promises* (1928); Robert E. Black, *The Story of Johnson Bible College* (Kimberlin Heights, Tenn.: Tennessee Valley Printing Co., 1951); and a pamphlet entitled "Washington Bible College," n.d.

18. See the gospel song, "I'm Using My Bible for a Roadmap" (Reno—Schroder).

Appendix: Defining Fundamentalism

1. H. Richard Niebuhr, "Fundamentalism," *Encyclopedia of the Social Sciences*, 15 vols. (New York: Macmillan Co., 1931), VI; 526–27.

2. Stewart G. Cole, *The History of Fundamentalism* (New York: Harper and Row, 1931), pp. 34; 98 ff.; 103; 106; 108; 129; 223; Norman F. Furniss, *The Fundamentalist Controversy, 1918–1931* (New Haven: Yale University Press, 1954), pp. 13; 16; 50; 72; 119; 129–22; 130–33.

3. Ernest R. Sandeen, *The Roots of Fundamentalism: British and American Millenarianism, 1800–1930* (Chicago: University of Chicago Press, 1970); *The Origins of Fundamentalism: Toward an Historical Interpretation* (Philadelphia: Fortress Press, 1968); "The Princeton Theology, One Source of Biblical Literalism in American Protestantism," *Church History* 31 (1962): 307–21.

4. George M. Marsden, "Defining Fundamentalism," *Christian Scholar's Review* 1 (Winter 1971): 141–51.

5. LeRoy Moore, Jr. "Another Look at Fundamentalism: A Response to Ernest R. Sandeen," *Church History* 37 (June 1968): 195–202.

6. Ernest R. Sandeen, "Defining Fundamentalism: A Reply to Professor Marsden," *Christian Scholar's Review* 1 (Spring 1971): 227–32.

7. George M. Marsden, *Fundamentalism and American Culture: The Shaping of Twentieth Century Evangelicalism, 1870–1925* (New York: Oxford University Press, 1980).

8. Bruce Shelley has also recognized the holiness dimensions of fundamentalism. See, e.g., "Sources of Pietistic Fundamentalism," *Fides et Historia* 5 (Spring 1973): 68–78. Shelley generally accepted Sandeen's definition, but concentrated upon what he called "fundamentalist life styles." He identified three such styles: rationalistic (the eminent Princeton Seminary conservative, J. Gresham Machen, would be an example), militant (describing those individuals who became involved in right-wing politics), and pietistic. As his title indicated, he addressed himself primarily to the third category, and went on to offer some insights into the holiness origins of fundamentalism, which had been largely overlooked by most of the other historians of the movement.

9. Marsden, *Fundamentalism and American Culture*, p. 4.

10. Richard Hofstadter, "Pseudo-Conservatism Revisited—1965," in *The Paranoid Style in American Politics and Other Essays* (New York: Alfred A. Knopf, 1965), pp. 66–92.

11. The term "fundamentalist" appears to have first been used by Curtis Lee Laws, editor of the Baptist journal, *The Watchman-Examiner,* in 1920. He said, "We here and now move that a new word be adopted to describe the men among us who insist that the landmarks shall not be removed. 'Conservatives' is too closely allied with reactionary forces in all walks of life. 'Premillennialists' is too closely allied with a single doctrine and not sufficiently inclusive. 'Landmarkers' has a historical disadvantage and connotes a particular group of radical conservatives [Baptists]. We suggest that those who still cling to the great fundamentals and who mean to do battle royal for the fundamentals shall be called 'Fundamentalists.' By that name the editor of *The Watchman-Examiner* is willing to be called. It will be understood therefore when he uses the word it will be in compliment and not in disparagement." Cited in Robert L. Wenger, "Social Thought in American Fundamentalism, 1918–1933" (Ph.D. dissertation, University of Nebraska-Lincoln, 1974), p. 46.

BIBLIOGRAPHIC ESSAY

Students of the Bible school movement and of fundamentalism in general face formidable bibliographic problems. Most studies in these subjects are highly partisan; a few betray the bias of opponents of conservative evangelicalism, but more often the sources are laudatory and celebratory, especially those dealing with schools and individuals. Few biographies or institutional histories have been written with even a pretension to objectivity or neutrality. This is true even of many of the scholarly works; the bulk of doctoral dissertations and masters' theses come out of evangelical schools or are written by historians whose ties to fundamentalist traditions are all too obvious.

The inaccessibility of original materials on fundamentalism poses the greatest difficulty of all. They exist, but for the most part they are widely scattered and largely unorganized and uncatalogued. Many valuable papers reside in attics and storage rooms in unlabeled boxes; frequently, crucial information about dates and authorship has been lost. Many important items exist only in single copies. If historians are to gain greater access to fundamentalist sources, particularly those on Bible schools, there is great necessity for microfilming and other kinds of duplication, for archives in individual institutions, and for a central depository. Fortunately, in the past few years conservative evangelicals have turned to their history with increasing interest and sense of its importance; likewise, scholars and historians have started to take the study of twentieth century evangelicalism more seriously. These two developments ought to result in more attention to the collection and preservation of the historical sources. Indeed, the recent establishment of the Billy Graham Archives at Wheaton College in Illinois has been an encouraging sign.

The starting place for any bibliography on Bible schools is a survey of the general sources on fundamentalism. Until recently the literature of fundamentalism was distressingly short of self-consciously interpretive attempts. Now two fine general works stand out: Ernest R. Sandeen, *The Roots of Fundamentalism: British and American Millenarianism, 1800–1930* (Chicago: University of Chicago Press, 1970), and George M. Marsden, *Fundamentalism and American Culture: The Shaping of Twentieth Century Evangelicalism, 1870–1925* (New York: Oxford University Press, 1980). Sandeen's major theses were first broached in a brief work, *The Origins of Fundamentalism: Toward an Historical Interpretation* (Philadelphia: Fortress Press, 1968). More recently, Martin E. Marty in *Modern American Religion: The Irony of It All, 1893–1919* (Chicago: University of Chicago Press, 1986), offers a general interpretation of fundamentalism and also a metaphor for fundamentalism's stance toward the rest of the world: he refers to the "carapace" fundamentalists built around themselves. Of interest in arriving at a general notion of the liberalized, post-1940 conservative evangelicalism—often referred to as neoevangelicalism—is Marsden's history of Fuller Seminary, *Reforming Fundamentalism: Fuller Seminary and the New Evangelicalism* (Grand Rapids, Mich: Eerdmans, 1987). Though institutional histories are often too narrow in scope, Marsden's is not; he offers an abundance and richness of theological, educational, and cultural context that deepens our understanding of the recent past.

The best dissertations I know of are Joel A. Carpenter, "The Renewal of American Fundamentalism, 1930–1945" (Ph.D. dissertation, Johns Hopkins University,

1984), shortly to be brought out by Oxford University Press, and Donald George Tinder, "Fundamentalist Baptists in the Northern and Western United States" (unpublished Ph.D. dissertation, Yale University, 1972). Carpenter's study provides a convincing and rich picture of the vitality of fundamentalism during its supposedly "dead" period, and is therefore an important work of revision. Though Tinder's study concentrates upon the Baptists, his observations often are more generally applicable. Donald Tinder, "Why the Evangelical Upswing?" *Christianity Today* 22 (October 21, 1977): 10–12, focuses on the present but makes use of his insights into the history of the movement.

The most important general articles on the subject of fundamentalism are Ernest R. Sandeen, "The Princeton Theology: One Source of Biblical Literalism in American Protestantism," *Church History* 31 (1962): 307–21; George M. Marsden, "The New School Heritage and Presbyterian Fundamentalism," *Westminster Theological Journal* 32 (May 1970): 129–47; and George M. Marsden, "Fundamentalism as an American Phenomenon, A Comparison with English Evangelicalism," *Church History* 46 (June 1977): 215–32. A spate of significant articles emerged in response to the appearance of Sandeen's works on fundamentalism: LeRoy Moore Jr., "Another Look at Fundamentalism: A Response to Ernest R. Sandeen," *Church History* 37 (June 1968): 195–202; George M. Marsden, "Defining Fundamentalism," *Christian Scholar's Review* 1 (Spring 1971): 227–32; Ernest R. Sandeen, "Defining Fundamentalism: a Reply to Professor Marsden," *Christian Scholar's Review* 1 (Winter 1971): 141–51; and Bruce Shelley, "Sources of Pietistic Fundamentalism," *Fides et Historia* 5 (Spring 1973): 68–78. In a valuable essay, "Fundamentalist Institutions and the Rise of Conservative Protestantism, 1929–42," *Church History* 49 (March 1980): 62–75, Carpenter summarized some of the themes that subsequently he developed further in his dissertation.

As background for debates about definitions of fundamentalism, the following works are critical: H. Richard Niebuhr, "Fundamentalism," *Encyclopedia of the Social Sciences*, Vol. VI (New York: Macmillan Co., 1931), pp. 526–27; H. Richard Niebuhr, *The Social Sources of Denominationalism* (New York: Meridian Books, 1957); Richard Hofstadter, *Anti-Intellectualism in American Life* (New York: Alfred A. Knopf, 1963); Stewart G. Cole, *The History of Fundamentalism* (New York: Harper and Row, 1931); and Norman F. Furniss, *The Fundamentalist Controversy, 1918–1931* (New Haven: Yale University Press, 1954). These writers have contributed to many current assumptions, both examined and unexamined, about the nature of fundamentalism and fundamentalists.

Several studies provide necessary context for the phenomenon of fundamentalism. William R. Hutchison, *The Modernist Impulse in American Protestantism* (Cambridge: Harvard University Press, 1976), illumines the religious movement against which fundamentalists were reacting. Robert T. Handy, "Fundamentalism and Modernism in Perspective," *Religion in Life* 24 (1955): 381–94, places fundamentalism and modernism in the context of the centuries-old tensions between faith and reason. Paul A. Carter, *The Spiritual Crisis of the Gilded Age* (DeKalb: Northern Illinois University Press, 1971), sketches the general religious conditions that gave rise to fundamentalism, among other movements, in the last half of the nineteenth century. One contribution of William G. McLoughlin, *Modern Revivalism: Charles Grandison Finney to Billy Graham* (New York: Ronald Press Co., 1959), is to position fundamentalism within the larger American revivalist tradition. Finally, one cannot ignore that preeminent journalist, Walter Lippmann, *A Preface to Morals* (New York: Macmillan Co., 1929), in seeking to understand the intellectual and cultural situation of the 1920s.

Biographies and autobiographies of fundamentalists aid greatly in understanding the movement. Fortunately, they exist in relative abundance, since they were thought to be useful in inspiring others. One of the few critical studies, C. Allyn

Russell, *Voices of American Fundamentalism* (Philadelphia: Westminster Press, 1976), is a collection of biographical sketches. Among the biographies and autobiographies of exemplary Christians are Mary Ella Bowie, *Alabaster and Spikenard: The Life of Dr. Iva Durham Vennard* (Chicago: Chicago Evangelistic Institute, 1947); James Oliver Buswell, "Reflections on My Liberal Education" (Part I), *The Bible To-Day* (February 1924): 485–90; E. Schuyler English, *H. A. Ironside: Ordained of the Lord* (Grand Rapids, Mich.: Zondervan Publishing House, 1946); Arno Clemens Gaebelein, *Half A Century: the Autobiography of a Servant* (New York: Publication House of "Our Hope," 1930); Gordon P. Gardiner, *Champion of the Kingdom: The Story of Philip Mauro* (Brooklyn: Bread of Life, 1961); P. C. Headley, *George F. Pentecost, Life, Labors, and Bible Studies* (Boston: James H. Earle, Publishers, 1880); James and Marti Hefley, *Uncle Cam: The Story of William Cameron Townsend, Founder of the Wycliffe Bible Translators and the Summer Institute of Linguistics* (Waco, Texas: Word Books, 1974); Charles Gallaudet Trumbull, *The Life of C. I. Scofield* (New York: Oxford University Press, 1920); Philip E. Howard, *Charles Gallaudet Trumbull: Apostle of the Victorious Life* (Philadelphia: The Sunday School Times, 1944); R. G. LeTourneau, *Mover of Men and Mountains* (Chicago: Moody Press, 1960); A. T. Pierson, *George Muller of Bristol and His Witness to a Prayer-Hearing God* (New York: Baker and Taylor Co., 1899); Ned B. Stonehouse, *J. Gresham Machen: A Biographical Memoir* (Grand Rapids, Mich.: Eerdmans Publishing Co., 1954); Delavan Leonard Pierson, *A. T. Pierson: A Spiritual Warrior, Mighty in the Scriptures: A Leader in the Modern Missionary Crusade* (New York: Fleming H. Revell Co., 1912); Oral Roberts, *The Call: An Autobiography* (Garden City, N.Y.: Doubleday and Co., 1972); Mr. and Mrs. Howard Taylor, *J. Hudson Taylor: A Biography* (Chicago: Moody Press, 1965); and "The Stewarts as Christian Stewards, the Story of Milton and Lyman Stewart," *Missionary Review of the World* 47 (August 1924): 595–602. Among the more disinterested studies are Edmund Gosse, *Father and Son: Biographical Recollections* (New York: Charles Scribner's Sons, 1908); David Edwin Harrell, Jr. *Oral Roberts: An American Life* (Bloomington: Indiana University Press, 1985); Lawrence W. Levine, *Defender of the Faith: William Jennings Bryan: The Last Decade, 1915–1925* (London, New York, Oxford: Oxford University Press, 1965); Brenda M. Meehan, "A. C. Dixon: An Early Fundamentalist," *Foundations* 10 (January–March 1967): 50–63; and William G. McLoughlin, *Billy Sunday Was His Real Name* (Chicago: University of Chicago Press, 1955). Gosse, particularly, provides a moving and perceptive insight into the thought and attitudes of evangelicals, in his case, the English Plymouth Brethren.

Among the noteworthy studies of fundamentalist denominations and agencies are Timothy L. Smith, *Called Unto Holiness: The Story of the Nazarenes: The Formative Years* (Kansas City, Mo.: Nazarene Publishing House, 1962); John W. V. Smith, *The Quest for Holiness and Unity: A Centennial History of the Church of God (Anderson, Indiana),* (Anderson, Ind.: Warner Press, 1980); and Robert George Delnay, "A History of the Baptist Bible Union" (Th.D. dissertation, Dallas Theological Seminary, 1963). The sources on pentecostalism are Walter J. Hollenweger, *The Pentecostals: The Charismatic Movement in the Churches* (Minneapolis: Augsburg Publishing House, 1972); and Vinson Synan, *The Holiness Pentecostal Movement in the United States* (Grand Rapids, Mich.: Eerdmans Publishing Co., 1971). See also David W. Faupel, "A Brief Bibliography of Pentecostal Literature" (Typed manuscript, Union Theological Seminary Library, New York, n.d.).

In understanding the phenomenon of holiness in Methodism , George E. Failing, "Developments in Holiness Theology after Wesley," in *Insights into Holiness: Discussions of Holiness by Fifteen Leading Scholars of the Wesleyan Persuasion,* edited by Kenneth Geiger (Kansas City, Mo.: Beacon Hill Press, 1962), pp. 11–31; John L. Peters, *Christian Perfection and American Methodism* ((Nashville, Tenn.: Abingdon Press, 1956); Charles Edwin Jones, *Perfectionist Persuasion: The Holiness Movement and American Methodism, 1867–1936* (Metuchen, N.J.: Scarecrow Press, 1974); and Timothy L. Smith, *Called Unto Holiness*, are valuable. The Keswick holiness movement has its chroniclers: J. C. Pollock, *The Keswick Story: The Authorized History of the Keswick Convention: Its Message, Its Method, and Its Men* (London: Marshall Bros.; Keswick House, 1907); and A. T. Pierson, *The Story of Keswick and Its Beginnings* (London: Hodder and Stoughton, 1964). Everett L. Cattell, "An Appraisal of the Keswick and Wesleyan Contemporary Positions," in Geiger, *Insights into Holiness*, pp. 263–80, clarifies some of the differences and similarities between Keswick and Wesleyan traditions of holiness. Such a great number of leading fundamentalists claimed the experience of holiness that biographies provide valuable sources for understanding how the phenomenon affected individual lives.

The subject of divine or faith healing has not attracted the efforts of very many historians. Donald Meyer, *The Positive Thinkers: A Study of the American Quest for Health, Wealth and Personal Power from Mary Baker Eddy to Norman Vincent Peale* (New York: Doubleday and Co., 1965), and Stephen Gottschalk, *The Emergence of Christian Science in American Religious Life* (Berkeley: University of California Press, 1973), both fine volumes, contribute to the understanding of this subject, though neither deals with fundamentalism itself. Though he concentrates on the past few decades, David Edwin Harrell, *All Things Are Possible: the Healing and Charismatic Revivals in Modern America* (Bloomington: Indiana University Press, 1975), offers insights into the phenomenon. Of related interest are Dennis Voskuil's thoughtful volume on the Reformed Church of America's Robert Schuller: *Mountains into Goldmines: Robert Schuller and the Gospel of Success* (Grand Rapids, Mich.: Eerdmans, 1983) and Raymond J. Cunningham, "From Holiness to Healing: The Faith Cure in America, 1872–1892," *Church History* 43 (December, 1974): 499–513. Again, the testimonies of those who declared themselves cured by extra-medical means, in biographies and periodicals, offer some of the best insights into divine healing.

The subject of premillennialism has attracted a substantial amount of scholarship. The classic work on the European movements is Norman R. C. Cohn, *The Pursuit of the Millennium: Revolutionary Messianism in Medieval and Reformation Europe and Its Bearing on Modern Totalitarian Movements* (London: Secker and Warburg, 1957). Besides the much-cited Sandeen, *Roots of Fundamentalism*, Timothy P. Weber, *Living in the Shadow of the Second Coming: American Premillennialism, 1875–1925* (New York: Oxford University Press, 1979), constitutes a major contribution to understanding the American movement. Adventism, a particular stream of American premillennialism, is well covered in Edwin Gaustad, ed., *The Rise of Adventism: Religion and Society in Mid-Nineteenth-Century America* (New York: Harper and Row, 1974). Ernest R. Sandeen, "The Baptists and Millenarianism: Suggestions for Further Research," *Foundations* 13 (January–March 1974), is, like Sandeen's other efforts in this field, useful and capable of wider application.

Dispensationalism, that particular form of premillennialism embraced by large numbers of fundamentalists, has two historians: Clarence R. Bass, *Backgrounds of Dispensationalism: Its Historical Genesis and Ecclesiastical Implications* (Grand Rapids, Mich.: Eerdmans, 1960), and C. Norman Kraus, *Dispensationalism in America: Its Rise and Development* (Richmond, Va.: John Knox Press, 1958). Neither writer sufficiently explains the popularity of an apparently complex system or explores its wider theological context. In understanding dispensationalism I have benefited greatly from discussions with my colleague on the Auburn Seminary history project, Glenn T. Miller. His unpublished paper, "'The Only True Guide to Faith and Practice': Perspectives on the Bible, 1870–1900," is full of insight. Among primary sources on dispensationalism, William E. Blackstone, *Jesus Is Coming* (Chicago: Fleming H. Revell, 1908); C. I. Scofield, *Rightly Dividing the Word of Truth* (New York, Chicago, Toronto: Fleming H. Revell, n.d.); and C. I. Scofield's *Refer-*

ence Bible (New York: Oxford University Press, 1909) most repay study. Frank E. Gaebelein's pamphlet, "The Story of the Scofield Reference Bible, 1909–1959" (New York: Oxford University Press, 1959), outlines the circumstances of the Bible's publication and subsequent editions. Cornelius Woelfkin, "The Religious Appeal of Premillennialism," *Journal of Religion* 1 (1921): 255–63, is particularly revealing because Woelfkin had abandoned the doctrine by the time of the article but still understood its attractions.

Willis B. Glover, *Evangelical Nonconformists and Higher Criticism in the Nineteenth Century* (London: Independent Press Ltd., 1954); Norman H. Maring, "Baptists and Changing Views of the Bible, 1865–1918" (Parts I and II), *Foundations* I (July and October 1958): 52–75; 30–61; and Glenn T. Miller, "Trying the Spirit: Conflicts over Biblical Interpretation in Late-Nineteenth-Century America" (unpublished paper, 1980), write in a particularly illuminating fashion about the reactions of Protestant conservatives to the biblical higher criticism. The fascinating subject of "changing views of the Bible" merits far more attention than it has received to date and, as a paradigmatic study, could contribute greatly to the understanding of American intellectual history (and indeed Western intellectual history) in the nineteenth and twentieth centuries.

For the political, social, and educational views and activities of fundamentalists I have drawn upon many of the works cited in the preceding pages. Robert Elwood Wenger, "Social Thought in American Fundamentalism, 1918–1933" (Ph.D. dissertation, University of Nebraska, 1973), offers much helpful information in these areas; so also does Carroll Edwin Harrington, "The Fundamentalist Movement in America, 1870–1920" (Ph.D. dissertation, University of California, Berkeley, 1959). Another useful source is Louis Gasper, *The Fundamentalist Movement* (The Hague: Mouton and Co., 1963). Timothy Thoresen, "Anti-Intellectualism among the Protestant Fundamentalists in the 1920's" (Ph.D. dissertation, Purdue University, 1967), did not ask hard enough questions to fulfill the promise in his title. Granville Hicks, "A Spokesman for the Fundamentalists, An Interview with Hilyer Hawthorne Straton," *The Baptist* 8 (April 2, 1927): 440, enhances understanding of fundamentalist attitudes. Probably one of the best sources of all is the *Moody Bible Institute Monthly.*

In dealing with the politics of the religious far right, Richard Hofstadter, *The Paranoid Style in American Politics and Other Essays* (New York: Alfred A. Knopf, 1965), is unsurpassed. Though Hofstadter's right-wing fundamentalists were probably not the same people as made up the constituency for Bible schools, his work is useful when one tries to apply a relative term such as "moderation" to a part of the fundamentalist camp. Cole, *History of Fundamentalism,* and Furniss, *Fundamentalist Controversy,* both cited above, provide detailed descriptions of the ecclesiastical conflicts within the major denominations; Robert Hastings Nichols, "Fundamentalism in the Presbyterian Church," *Journal of Religion* 5 (January 1925): 14–36, is another source on this subject.

In thinking about the cultural, social, religious, and psychological dimensions of fundamentalism, I have not found sociological categories particularly helpful, including the church-sect distinctions found in the work of Ernest Troelsch, H. Richard Niebuhr, and others. Often sociologists concentrate upon the most exotic forms of fundamentalist thought and behavior. Robert P. Monaghan, "Three Faces of the True Believer: Motivations for Attending a Fundamentalist Church," *Journal for the Scientific Study of Religion* 6 (1967): 236–45; and Martha L. Rogers, "A Fundamentalist Church as an Autonomous Community and Its Relationship to the Larger Community," *Journal of Psychology and Theology* 3 (1975): 210–15, are of limited usefulness. H. Richard Niebuhr, *Social Sources of Denominationalism,* cited earlier, is more fruitful, though one must take care not to get ensnared in his categories. Very valuable is James Davison Hunter's sociological study, *American*

Evangelicalism: Conservative Religion and the Quandary of Modernity (New Brunswick, N.J.: Rutgers University Press, 1983); though Hunter focuses on the present, his insights can often be applied to the past; indeed, his study takes account of evangelical history. Finally, anyone attempting to comprehend intense religious experience must peruse William James, *Varieties of Religious Experience* (New York: Collier Books, 1961).

Fundamentalist attitudes toward science have received increased attention in recent years, as have Baconian ideas about science popular in the nineteenth century that have influenced fundamentalist thinking. It is difficult fully to understand fundamentalist approaches to the Bible without knowing their views of science. As background see Theodore Dwight Bozeman, *Protestants in an Age of Science: The Baconian Ideal and Antebellum American Religious Thought* (Chapel Hill: The University of North Carolina Press, 1977), and Douglas Sloan, *The Scottish Enlightenment and the American College Ideal* (New York: Teachers College Press, 1971). For a picture of fundamentalist science Marsden's *Fundamentalism and American Culture* and his "Understanding Fundamentalist Views of Science," Ashley Montagu, ed. *Science and Creationism* (New York: Oxford University Press, 1984), are valuable. One of the best primary sources for understanding fundamentalist reactions to the theory of evolution is William Jennings Bryan, *In His Image* (New York: Fleming H. Revell Co., 1922). Fundamentalist attitudes toward scientific thought are also reflected in Clarence H. Benson, *The Earth, the Theater of the Universe: A Scientific and Scriptural Study of the Earth's Place and Purpose in the Divine Program* (Chicago: The Bible Institute Colportage Association, 1929).

No studies of fundamentalist rhetoric have come to light, even as parts of larger works on the movement. As background, H. L. Mencken, *The American Language: An Inquiry into the Development of English in the United States* (New York: Knopf, 1963), and Kenneth Burke, *The Rhetoric of Religion: Studies in Logology* (Boston: Beacon Press, 1961), are useful. Though she does not deal with twentieth century fundamentalism, Sandra S. Sizer, *Gospel Hymns and Social Religion: The Rhetoric of Nineteenth-Century Revivalism* (Philadelphia: Temple University Press, 1978), suggests some fruitful ways of thinking about the rhetoric of American evangelical Protestants.

When we leave the general subject of fundamentalism—the context for Bible school education—and turn to the schools themselves, the material becomes sparser. Most of the founders are unknown to American historians, and often their literary remains have not been systematically collected. Fortunately there is some very rich material on A. B. Simpson. At the Nyack College Library, Nyack, New York, the "Simpson Scrapbook," which contains a diary, a short autobiographical account of his early life, letters to his wife, and personal recollections of those close to him, provides some illuminating insights into his personality and into the movement he led. Of the two biographies, A. E. Thompson, *A. B. Simpson: His Life and Work* (Harrisburg, Pa.: Christian Publications, 1960), and A. W. Tozer, *Wingspread: A. B. Simpson—A Study in Spiritual Attitude* (Harrisburg, Pa.: Christian Publications, 1943), Thompson is the more valuable for a historian's purposes, though neither is a critical study of the man. Kenneth Mackenzie, an associate of Simpson, wrote a series of reminiscences that contain revealing anecdotes about Simpson and the Christian and Missionary Alliance: "My Memories of Dr. Simpson" (Parts I–X), *Alliance Weekly* 72 (May 22, June 5, July 17, July 24, July 31, August 7, August 14, August 21, September 4, September 11, 1937): 324–25; 357–59; 452–53; 470-71; 485–86; 500–01; 516–17; 535, 538, 542; 564–66; 580–81. Katherine Alberta Brennan, "Mrs. A. B. Simpson, The Wife or Love Stands" (pamphlet available at Nyack College Library), recalls some of the personal and family life of Simpson.

For Adoniram Judson Gordon, the primary sources are the biography by his son, Ernest B. Gordon, *Adoniram Judson Gordon: A Biography* (New York: Fleming H. Revell Co., 1896); and an account of his spiritual pilgrimage by Gordon himself, *How Christ Came to Church: The Pastor's Dream: A Spiritual Autobiography* (Philadelphia: American Baptist Publication Society, 1895). George G. Houghton, "The Contributions of A J. Gordon to American Christianity" (Th.D. dissertation, Dallas Theological Seminary, 1970), contains useful information, but does not attempt to explore Gordon's character or motivations in any depth.

The life of Dwight L. Moody has of course elicited much hagiography; fortunately, Moody is also the subject for a critical study, James F. Findlay, Jr., *Dwight L. Moody: American Evangelist, 1837–1899* (Chicago: University of Chicago Press, 1969). Gene A. Getz, *MBI: The Story of Moody Bible Institute* (Chicago: Moody Press, 1969), is another good source for the activities of the great revivalist. The biographies of other Bible school founders and prime movers were cited earlier: Bowie, *The Life of Dr. Iva Durham Vennard*, Trumbull, *Life of C. I. Scofield*, and "The Stewarts as Stewards."

Materials on the missionary training schools, European and American, are scarce. For Charles Haddon Spurgeon's schools one must turn to biographies: W. Y. Fullerton, *C. H. Spurgeon: A Biography* (London: Williams and Norgate, 1920); Charles Ray, *The Life of Charles Haddon Spurgeon* (London: Passmore and Alabaster, Isbister and Co. Ltd., 1902); and Ernest W. Bacon, *Spurgeon: Heir of the Puritans* (London: Allen and Unwin, 1967), none of which deals at any length with the Pastors' College. The Chrischona school in Switzerland, however, has a chronicler: C. F. Schlienz, *The Pilgrim Institution of St. Chrischona, near Basle, Switzerland* (London: John Farquhar Shaw, 1850). The sources on the American training schools have proven a little richer, since some bulletins and catalogs survive. A primary apology for the missionary training school is contained in A. T. Pierson, *The Crisis of Missions: Or, the Voice out of the Cloud* (New York: Robert Carter and Bros., 1886). Other defenses and discussions appeared in "Missionary Training College," *Christian Alliance* 1 (May 1888): 76; "Missionary Training Schools—Do Baptists Need them? A Discussion," *Baptist Quarterly Review* 12 (January 1890): 69–100; "Editorial Department: The New Schools," *Baptist Quarterly Review* 12 (January 1890): 101–108; "Mr. Moody's New Plan," in *An Annotated Bibliography of D. L. Moody*, edited by Wilbur M. Smith (Chicago: Moody Press, 1948), p. 78; A. B. Simpson, "The Training and Sending Forth of Workers," *Christian and Missionary Alliance* 18 (April 30, 1897): 419; Charles A. Briggs, "Theological Education and Its Needs," *Forum* 12 (January 1892): 643; A. J. Gordon, "Short Cut Methods," *The Watchman* 70 (November 7, 1889): 1; and Dwight L. Moody letter, quoted in Samuel N. Slie, "A History of Christian Religion in the Life of Springfield College: A Study made in conjunction with the Religion in Higher Education course with Prof. C. P. Shedd, Yale Divinity School, 1950" (typed manuscript, available at Springfield College, Springfield, Massachusetts), pp. 1–2. *The Training of Teachers* (Edinburgh and London: Oliphant, Anderson and Ferrier, and New York, Chicago and Toronto: Fleming H. Revell Co., n.d.), a report that issued from the 1910 missionary conference in Edinburgh, set forth the requirements of education for missionaries and greatly influenced the curricula of training schools, including Bible schools. Clifton J. Phillips, "The Student Volunteer Movement," in *The Missionary Enterprise in China and America*, edited by John K. Fairbank (Cambridge: Harvard University Press, 1974), describes the training recommended by the Student Volunteer Movement.

Many of the early training schools were intended for women, who were assuming more significant roles in Protestant endeavors. Some history of the training schools for women is included in Virginia Lieson Brereton and Christa Ressmeyer Klein, "American Women in Ministry: A History of Protestant Beginning Points," in *Women of Spirit* (New York: Simon and Schuster, 1979), pp. 302–332. [This essay was reprinted in Janet W. James, ed., *Women in American Religion* (Philadelphia: University of Pennsylvania Press, 1980)]. A more detailed discussion of these training schools appears in Virginia Lieson Brereton, "Preparing Women for the Lord's Work: The Story of Three Methodist Training Schools, 1880–1940," in *Women and New Worlds: Historical Perspectives on the Wesleyan Tradition*, edited by Hilah F. Thomas and Rosemary Keller (Nashville, Tenn.: Abingdon Press, 1981). Warren Palmer Behan, "An Introductory Survey of the Lay Training School Field," *Religious Education* 11 (1916): 47–52, offers a complete picture of the religious training schools in existence in 1916.

There are few general studies of the Bible schools. Safara Witmer, *The Bible College Story: Education with Dimension* (Manhasset, N.Y.: Channel Press, 1962), is best known and contains a small amount of historical material. For the origin of the Bible schools, Lenice F. Reed, "The Bible Institute in America" (M.A. thesis, Wheaton College, Wheaton, Illinois, 1947), is the best source among theses and dissertations. William Stuart McBirnie, "A Study of the Bible Institute Movement" (D.R.E. dissertation, Southwestern Baptist Theological Seminary, 1952), is valuable chiefly for its list of Bible schools then in existence. Hubert Reynhout, Jr. "A Comparative Study of Bible Institute Curriculums" (M.A. thesis, Department of Education, University of Michigan, 1947), and Harold W. Boon, "The Development of the Bible College or Institute in the United States" (Ph.D. dissertation, School of Education, New York University, 1960), are studies of curricula; like so many other books and essays mentioned in this essay, they suffer from the lack of wider reference points but contain useful factual information. The title of John S. Best, "The Bible College on the March" (M.A. thesis, Pacific College of Azusa, 1955), suggests its unabashedly biased orientation, but it too provides useful information. Though Frank E. Gaebelein, *Christian Education in a Democracy: The Report of the N.A.E. Committee* (New York: Oxford University Press, 1951), offers a chapter on Bible schools, its approach is not historical.

Many of the general conclusions about the Bible schools advanced in chapter 6 are derived from detailed knowledge of the five schools that figure especially prominently in this study: Berkshire Christian College, Biola College, Gordon College, Moody Bible Institute, and Nyack College. The only history of Berkshire Christian College, earlier known as the New England School of Theology and still earlier as the Boston Bible School, is a small booklet, Harold Wilson, "Seventy-Five Years: Berkshire Christian College, 1897–1973." A primary source for the denomination's history is Albert C. Johnson, *Advent Christian History: A Concise Narrative of the Origin and Progress, Doctrine and Work of This Body of Believers* (Boston: Advent Christian Publishing Society, 1918). Other sources are Frank Burr, "Early and Later Conventions of Adventists," *World's Crisis* 47 (January 16, 1901): 1–2; United States Department of Commerce, Bureau of the Census: 1–2; United States Department of Commerce, Bureau of the Census, *Religious Bodies: 1936*, vol. 2 (Washington, D.C.: U.S. Government Printing Office, 1941); and David A. Dean, "The Origin in Millerism of Conditionalism," *Henceforth* 3 (Spring 1975): 75–80.

When I was researching Berkshire Christian College the archives were in the process of being ordered and catalogued. The librarian there had indexed items about the school's early years that appeared in the denominational journal, the *World's Crisis*. Later volumes of *World's Crisis* continued to be rich in news of the school, but were not similarly indexed. Several scrapbooks containing clippings about the school from the *World's Crisis* were available and useful, but often documentation of dates, volume, and pages numbers was missing. Among other documents from the historical collection is a pamphlet, George J. French, "A Timely Plea for Our Young People," n.d., and a handwritten manuscript, author and date unknown, which describes the educational situation in the denomination in the two or three decades preceding the founding of the Boston school.

As usual, catalogs proved invaluable, as did a student yearbook, *The Theologian.* Most biographical data on faculty members had to be gleaned from the pages of the *World's Crisis.* The Union Theological Seminary library, New York, is the source for a useful *Catalogue of Books, Tracts, Pamphlets and Periodicals, Published and For Sale by the Advent Christian Publishing Society* (Boston, n.d.).

Histories of Biola are Robert Williams and Marilyn Miller, *Chartered for His Glory: Biola University, 1908–1983* (La Mirada, California: Associated Students of Biola University, 1983); James O. Henry, "Black Oil and Souls to Save," *BIOLA Broadcaster* 3 (December 1973): 4–28; and James O. Henry's draft of a history of Biola (typed manuscript). All three are rich in details about the school's history. A biography of Louis T. Talbot, a leading figure in the school's history, is celebratory but useful: Carol Talbot, *For This I Was Born: The Captivating Story of Louis T. Talbot* (Chicago: Moody Press, 1977). Other valuable sources of school history are the catalogs and the *The King's Business,* a publication issued by the school that was meant to be of general interest to conservative evangelicals.

An important source for Gordon College is Nathan R. Wood, *A School of Christ* (Boston, 1953). The archives at Gordon are partially organized. The letters of A. J. Gordon have been arranged, but the multitudinous correspondence of Nathan R. Wood has not. The archives contain several early student notebooks that reveal something of what students learned, or at least noted down in class. Ernest B. Gordon's biography of A. J. Gordon and George Houghton's dissertation on Gordon, both cited earlier, provide information on the early history of the school; so do articles such as F. L. Chapell, "Dr. Gordon and the Training School," *The Watchword* 17 (February and March 1895): 61–2; Mrs. A. J. Gordon, "Gordon Bible and Missionary Training School," *Watchword and Truth,* July–August 1907, pp. 234–36; Helen Harrell, "My Mother Mrs. A. J. Gordon," *Bread of Life* 12 (May 1963): 3–4, 7–8; A. J. Gordon, "Short Cut Methods," *The Watchman* 70 (November 7, 1889): 1; Nathan R. Wood, "Gordon College of Theology and Missions: A Brief Record of a Supernatural Work," *Hypernikon* 9 (1931): 7; Nathan R. Wood, "A Brief History of Gordon College of Theology and Missions," *Hypernikon* 6 (1928): 47; "Gordon Training School," *Christian and Missionary Alliance* 24 (January 13, 1900): 28; and Nathan R. Wood, "The Gordon School—A Great Opportunity," *Newton Theological Institution Bulletin* 4 (1912): 9–13. A pamphlet, "Gordon College Seventy-Fifth Anniversary" (1964), deals as well with the later history of the school. George W. Dollar, "The Reverend F. L. Chapell, Early American Dispensationalist," *Bibliotheca Sacra* 120 (April–June 1963): 126–36, discusses the theological thought of one of the school's important early leaders. Catalogs are crucial in understanding the history of the school, as is the student yearbook *Hypernikon,* which began publication in 1923.

In writing on Moody Bible Institute one has advantages not available in the study of other Bible schools. First, Gene A. Getz, *MBI,* cited earlier, is a full length study of the Institute. While not critical in the fullest sense, it supplies a great deal of information in orderly and convenient fashion and provides an extensive bibliography. Second, the archives of the Institute are ordered and catalogued. Biographical files have been collected on many of the faculty members; the James M. Gray File contains valuable letters. Third, many of the principal actors in the Institute's history are the subjects of biographies: Robert Harkness, *Reuben Archer Torrey: The Man, His Message* (Chicago: The Bible Institute Colportage Association, 1929); Roger Martin, *R. A. Torrey: Apostle of Certainty* (Murfreesboro, Tenn.: Sword of the Lord Publishers, 1976); William M. Runyan, *Dr. Gray at Moody Bible Institute* (New York: Oxford University Press, 1935); and John David Hannah, "James Martin Gray: His Life and Work" (Th.D. dissertation, Dallas Theological Seminary, 1974); Richard Ellsworth Day, *Breakfast Table Autocrat* (Chicago: Moody Press, 1946)—on H. C. Crowell; Wilbur M. Smith, *Will H. Houghton: A Watchman* on the Wall (Grand Rapids, Mich.: Eerdmans Publishing Co., 1951); Warren W. Wiersbe, William Culbertson, a Man of God (Chicago: Moody Press, 1974); Jerry B. Jenkins, Generous Impulse: The Story of George Sweeting (Chicago: Moody Press, 1987); and Robert G. Flood and Jerry B. Jenkins, The Men Behind Moody (Chicago: Moody Press, 1984). Again, these biographies are hardly critical, but with the exception of the Day and Harkness volumes, they are relatively straightforward.

Supplementing the information in the Getz study are three other Institute histories: Dorothy Martin, Moody Bible Institute: God's Power in Action (Chicago: Moody Press, 1977); Bernard De Remer, Moody Bible Institute: A Pictorial History (Chicago: Moody Press, 1960); and Robert G. Flood and Jerry B. Jenkins, Teaching the Word, Reaching the World: Moody Bible Institute, the First 100 Years (Chicago: Moody Press, 1985). James Albert Mathisen, "The Moody Bible Institute: A Case Study in the Dilemmas of Institutionalization" (Ph.D. dissertation, Northwestern University, 1979), is a study of MBI's organizational difficulties. Edith E. Metcalf, Letters to Dorothy (Chicago and New York: Fleming H. Revell Co., 1893); and Margaret Blake Robinson, A Reporter at Moody's (Chicago: The Bible Institute Colportage Association, 1900), give early views of the Institute from the point of view of students. William Cobb, "The West Point of Fundamentalism," American Mercury 16 (1919): 104–12, is a hostile but impressed observer of the twenties. Charles Stelzle, A Son of the Bowery (New York: George H. Doran Co., 1926), provides a brief but valuable view of MBI in the 1890s. "Rock of Ages at the Edge of Old Town," Midwest, January 27, 1974, pp. 4–5, 8, is a recent survey of MBI activities and accomplishments. Gerald S. Strober, "My Life as a Christian," Commentary 73 (June 1982): 34–39, is the account of a Jewish convert to Christianity who attended Moody Bible Institute in the late 1950s.

As in the case of the other Bible schools, catalogs and prospectuses are invaluable sources of information about the curriculum, student life, and administrative aspirations. Despite its wider focus, the Moody Bible Institute Monthly (earlier called the Institute Tie and The Christian Workers Magazine) has contained continuous news of the school and its graduates. A Moody Bible Institute Bulletin, which concentrates more exclusively on school matters, dates from 1920.

On Nyack College, John H. Cable, A History of the Missionary Training Institute: The Pioneer Bible School of America (Harrisburg, Pa.: Christian Publications, 1933), is celebratory but useful. A history of the Christian and Missionary Alliance is contained in After Fifty Years: A Record of God's Working Through the Christian and Missionary Alliance (Harrisburg, Pa.: Christian Publications, 1939). The Annual Reports of the Alliance are more useful for Alliance history, however, and also contain a substantial amount of material on the school. C. Donald McKaig, "The Educational Philosophy of A. B. Simpson, Founder of the Christian and Missionary Alliance" (Ph.D. dissertation, New York University, School of Education, 1948), is something of an apology for Simpson's educational ideas, but contains information on the early curriculum and student bodies of the school.

The denominational journal, the Alliance Weekly (earlier called the Christian Alliance, The Christian Alliance and Foreign Missionary Weekly, and the Christian and Missionary Alliance) is an abundant source for the history of the Missionary Training Institute. Often a special column or page was devoted to news of the school. This periodical also contains rich biographical data that greatly aid an understanding of those Christians who joined the Christian and Missionary Alliance. The Nyack College archives furnish a typed index of biographies, mostly obituaries, that appeared in the Alliance Weekly between 1928 and 1939. Biographical sketches also appeared at intervals in a series entitled "Associates of A. B. Simpson," in the Southeastern District Report of the Christian and Missionary Alliance in 1976–1977.

Pamphlets are available in the archives of Nyack College: "Forty-Ninth Year, September 10, 1931–May 10, 1932"; "The Romance of the Missionary Institute at Nyack-on-Hudson, New York," n.d.; and Gilbert H. Johnson, "The Pilgrimage of Joseph Douglas Williams: A Brief Portrayal of His Life" (Harrisburg, Pa.: Christian Publications, 1955); Williams was a teacher at the Missionary Training Institute.

In addition to the sources on the five schools above, there exist materials on some of the other Bible schools. William V. Trollinger, "One Response to Modernity: Northwestern Bible School and the Fundamentalist Empire of William Bell Riley" (Ph.D. dissertation, University of Wisconsin, 1984), will, I hope, furnish a model for other studies in the future. Thomas F. Henstock, "A History and Interpretation of the Curriculum of Central Bible Institute" (M.A. thesis, Central Bible Institute, 1963); and Renald Showers, "A History of Philadelphia College of the Bible" (Th.M. thesis, Dallas Theological Seminary, 1962), have proven particularly useful. Neither deals very much with the wider context in which each school developed, but both provide abundant factual information. Also worth looking at despite their severe limitations are Robert E. Black, *The Story of Johnson Bible College* (Kimberlin Heights: Tennessee Valley Printing Co., 1951); Alva Ross Brown, *Standing on the Promises*, 1928 (on Johnson Bible College); David Eubanks, "An Historical Account of the Development of Johnson Bible College" (Th.M. thesis, Johnson Bible College, 1958); Katherine Elizabeth Bowman, "Columbia Bible College: A Leader in a New Movement in Religious Education" (M.A. thesis, School of Education, University of South Carolina, 1941); "Washington Bible College" (a recent pamphlet, n.d.); Charles H. Brackett, "The History of Azusa College and the Friends" (M.A. thesis, University of Southern California, 1967); Alva Don Sizemore, "The History of Christian Normal Institute, Grayson, Kentucky" (B.D. thesis, Butler University, 1944); John Hehl and Alleene Spivey Hehl, *This Is the Victory* (West Columbia, S.C.: Wentworth Publishing Corp. 1973); R. Arthur Mathews, *Towers Pointing Upward* (Columbia, S.C.: Columbia Bible College, 1973); and G. H. Spence, "History of the Northwest Bible College" (B.S. thesis, Minot State College, 1974). Shirley Nelson, *The Last Year of the War* (New York: Harper and Row, 1978), although a fictional work, conveys a sense of what it was like to be a Bible school student in the late 1940s, at an institution that sounds very much like Moody Bible Institute.

For knowledge of the educational setting out of which Bible schools developed, I have relied on a number of standard studies and upon my work with the Auburn Seminary history of Protestant theological education in the United States. Edward A. Krug, *The Shaping of the American High School* (Madison: University of Wisconsin Press, 1972), and James McLachlan, *American Boarding Schools: A Historical Study* (New York: Scribner's, 1970), furnished some of the secondary school background. In considering the reformist educational thought of the time, I profited from Lawrence A. Cremin, *The Transformation of the School: Progressivism in American Education, 1876–1957* (New York: Vintage Books, 1964), pp. 1–176, and from a reading of John Dewey, *Democracy and Education* (New York: Macmillan Co., 1916). The sources on the changes affecting professional and semi-professional education in the late nineteenth and early twentieth centuries are abundant: Nathan Glazer, "The Schools of the Minor Professions," *Minerva* 12 (July 1974): 346–63; Ernest V. Hollis and Alice L. Taylor, *Social Work Education in the United States* (New York: Columbia University Press, 1951); Donald H. Fleming, *William H. Welch and the Rise of Modern Medicine* (Boston: Little, Brown, 1954); Alfred Z. Reed, *Present-Day Law Schools in the United States and Canada* (New York, 1928); Arthur E. Sutherland, *The Law at Harvard: A History of Ideas and Men, 1817–1967* (Cambridge: The Belknap Press of Harvard University, 1967); Hugh Hawkins, *Between Harvard and America: The Educational Leadership of Charles W. Eliot* (New York: Oxford University Press, 1972); Robert Stevens, "Two Cheers for 1870: The American Law School," *Perspectives in American History* 5 (1971):

405–550; and Everett C. Hughes et al., *Education for the Professions of Medicine, Law, Theology, and Social Welfare* (New York: McGraw-Hill, 1973). A comparison between normal and Bible schools is aided by Paul H. Mattingly, *The Classless Profession: American Schoolmen in the Nineteenth Century* (New York: New York University Press, 1975); Jessie H. Pangburn, *The Evolution of the American Teachers College* (New York: Teachers College Press, 1932); Merle Borrowman, ed., *Teacher Education in America: A Documentary History* (New York: Teachers College Press, 1965); and Jurgen Herbst, "Nineteenth-Century Normal Schools in the United States: A Fresh Look," *History of Education* 9 (1980): 219–27. For the activities of William Rainey Harper, Richard J. Storr, *Harper's University: The Beginning* (Chicago: University of Chicago Press, 1966), is a source. However, no biography or history of the University of Chicago deals adequately with Harper's complex role as both popularizer and biblical scholar.

In recent decades a relatively new institution, the Christian day school created by conservative evangelicals, has emerged on the education scene. It shares many characteristics with the Bible schools, including common religious parentage, a powerful biblicism, and a strong sense of responsibility for student morals. A detailed sociological study of one of these Christian schools, Alan Peshkin, *God's Choice: The Total World of a Fundamentalist Christian School* (Chicago: University of Chicago Press, 1986), gives a feel for what it might have been like to be at the strictest Bible schools, especially in the twenties and thirties.

INDEX

Addams, Jane: 64
Advent Christians: 150–51, 167
American Home Bible Institute: 73
Assemblies of God: 13
Azusa College. See Training School for Christian Workers

Baptist Missionary Training School, Chicago: 55, 61
Barnhouse, Donald Grey: 22
Benson, Clarence H.: 143
Berkshire Christian College. See Boston Bible School
Bible: The Living Bible, xiii, 24; conferences, xv–xvi, 1; Scofield Reference Bible, xvi; biblicism, 3–4; influence of King James Version, 24; higher criticism, 88, 89, 90, 160–61; expository preaching, 99, 185–86; Princeton Seminary inerrancy, 165
—study: methods, 22–23; in English, 88; inductive, 89–90, 184n9; as literature, 91; Berean (at Missionary Training Institute), 91; analysis, 96; memorization, 96; geography, 96; introduction, 96; blackboard drawing, 97; by books, 184n13
Bible Institute of Los Angeles (Biola): curriculum, 21, 87, 101; early history, 39, 66, 80, 132; foreign missions, 70, 128; locations, 79, 82, 85; practical work, 107, 108, 109, 110; prayer, 119–20; fundraising, 135; interdenominationalism, 140; Evangelical Teacher Training Association, 143; curbing dissent, 146, 147; "Jesus Saves" signs, 154; mentioned, 55, 72, 80
—students: first student, 80; entrance requirements, 82; morality, 114; ages, 122; highjinks, 125; jobs, 136, 137
Bible Institute of Pennsylvania: 22, 72, 161
Bible Institute of Washington (D.C.): 74
Bible schools: nomenclature, xvii; accreditation, xviii, 35, 144, 164; faculty, 80, 116; Great Depression, 84; evangelism, 98; practical work, 107, 110; cities, 112; foreign missions, 113–14, 118, 128, 128–29; alumni/ae, 117; prayer, 119–20; founded by denominations, 150; compared with normal schools, 156–58; statistics, 171n3
—curriculum: specialization, 83; foreign missions, 102; Christian education, 102; General Bible Course, 102; pastoral training, 102–103; social sciences, 103–104; science, 104; history, 104; literature, 104; music, 118–19
—students: conversion of, 2–3; upward mobility, 27; Christina Lang, 28, 121; early students, 80; testimony of Ellen Coburn, 120–21; student testimony, 188n25
Blackstone, William E.: xvi, 16–17, 20, 29, 78
Boardman, William E.: 4
Bob Jones University: xiii
Borden, William Whiting: 118, 133
Boston Bible School: founding, 39, 151; early enrollments, 79; students, 80, 81, 82; move to Lenox, Mass, 85; degrees, 85; Bible, 87, 95, 99–100, 104; prayer, 119; discipline, 123–24; foreign missions, 129; women preachers, 130; fundraising, 133–34; jobs, 136; conditionalism, 150–51; fundamentalist connections, 151–52; mentioned, 71
Boston Missionary Training School. See Gordon College
Brainerd, David: 118
Briggs, Charles A.: 33, 60
Brookes, James: 41, 45
Bryan, William Jennings: xiv, 29, 31, 38, 166
Bushnell, Horace: 2

Central Bible Institute, Springfield, Mo.: premillennialism, 12; pentecostalism, 13; Bible, 87; preparatory department, 103; revival, 121–22; mentioned, 73
Chapell, F. L.: 10, 51
Chapman, J. Wilbur: xvii
Chicago Evangelistic Institute: 72. See also Vennard, Iva
China Inland Mission: 70, 167, 173n15. See also Taylor, J. Hudson
Christian and Missionary Alliance: holiness, 7–8, 29; emotional excesses, 15; socioeconomic status, 28; tensions within, 141; mentioned, 167. See also Missionary Training Institute; Simpson, A. B.
Christian Science: 10. See also Eddy, Mary Baker
Christlieb, Theodor: 57, 181n2
Cole, Stewart G.: 165
Columbia Bible College: 89, 95
correspondence study: 194n6
Cullis, Charles: 47

Dallas Theological Seminary: 34
Darby, John: 16
Dewey, John: 155
dispensationalism: Hal Lindsay, xiii; Scofield, Rightly Dividing the Word of Truth, xvi; Scofield Reference Bible, 17; the Rapture, 17,

VIRGINIA LIESON BRERETON teaches history and writing at Harvard. In her essays and articles she has explored the themes of Protestant fundamentalism, religious rhetoric, and the role of women in American religious history. Indiana University Press will soon be publishing her book on Protestant American women's conversion narratives.